FROM CLIENTS to **CROOKS**

FROM CLIENTS to CROOKS

An Insider Reveals
THE **REAL** WASHINGTON D.C.

LESLIE SORRELL

NEW YORK

NASHVILLE • MELBOURNE • VANCOUVER

FROM CLIENTS to CROOKS
An Insider Reveals THE REAL WASHINGTON D.C.

© 2017 LESLIE SORRELL

Published in New York, New York, by Morgan James Publishing. Morgan James and The Entrepreneurial Publisher are trademarks of Morgan James, LLC. www.MorganJamesPublishing.com

The Morgan James Speakers Group can bring authors to your live event. For more information or to book an event visit The Morgan James Speakers Group at www.TheMorganJamesSpeakersGroup.com.

Shelfie

A **free** eBook edition is available with the purchase of this print book.

CLEARLY PRINT YOUR NAME ABOVE IN UPPER CASE

Instructions to claim your free eBook edition:
1. Download the Shelfie app for Android or iOS
2. Write your name in **UPPER CASE** above
3. Use the Shelfie app to submit a photo
4. Download your eBook to any device

ISBN 978-1-68350-313-2 paperback
ISBN 978-1-68350-314-9 eBook
ISBN 978-1-68350-315-6 hardcover
Library of Congress Control Number: 2016917188

Cover Design by:
Rachel Lopez
www.r2cdesign.com

Photo courtesy of:
Steve Shipley Photograph

In an effort to support local communities, raise awareness and funds, Morgan James Publishing donates a percentage of all book sales for the life of each book to Habitat for Humanity Peninsula and Greater Williamsburg.

Get involved today! Visit
www.MorganJamesBuilds.com

Dedicated to all those crooks out there that
provide anecdotes for voters' entertainment.

CONTENTS

Foreword   *ix*

Preface   *xiii*

1   Remember the Alamo   1

2   Granny Takes Down the Establishment   9

3   Kentucky Girl Goes to D.C.   13

4   Rules—What Rules?   28

5   Ways Washington Works   40

6   The Congresswoman   51

7   The Faith, Family, and Freedom Candidate   64

8   A Doctor in the House   76

9   The Attorney Versus the Establishment   81

10   The Builder   91

11   The Conspiracy Theorists   96

12   The Billionaire   105

13   The CPA   121

14   The Incumbent   135

15   The Challenger   148

16	The Beginning of the End	155
17	The Campaign That Never Ends	177
18	Dirty Tricks	193
19	Everything has an End, Except a Sausage has Two	205
20	Red, Blue, It's All the Same	213
	About the Author	*231*
	Acknowledgements	*232*

FOREWORD

2011 turned out to be the best, and worst, year of my life. It was the year I put my wild plan of running for Congress into action. I knew the system was rigged but I thought I could beat it. So did Leslie Sorrell. We were wrong.

I was honored when Leslie agreed to take a meeting with me to talk about my future campaign. She was well known in political circles as a quiet warrior, one of the best in the business when it comes to fundraising and strategizing. It's why she was my first and last call when it came to picking the person to lead my campaign. You see Leslie isn't brash or pompous like strategists you see on the cable networks each night. She's prefers to operate behind the scenes. It's a tribute to her as leader.

When Leslie agreed to take me on as a client I knew I would change her life, I had no idea I would destroy it, at least the life she knew.

I will be forever grateful to this woman who also happened to change my life, for the better.

She forced me to think before I react. She forced me to listen more than speak. But most of all she forced me to never accept mediocrity from myself.

Leslie never ever held back when she disagreed. A rare quality in an industry filled with weasels whose sole job is to appease the Congressman they are paid to suck up to. She didn't want to make me someone I wasn't, she just wanted to pull out the best in me.

With my first town hall just days away, Leslie insisted I practice. I always felt I was "a gamer," a player who peaked during the game, someone who didn't need practice. I was so confident in my abilities as a communicator and my grasp of the issues I laughed at the thought of practicing. I did live TV for 20 years, how hard could a town hall be? Leslie refused to take no for an answer.

The next day, during a mock town hall, I flopped. I was awful. She had the campaign staff come up with questions I had no idea how to answer. I looked foolish in front of Leslie and a dozen other campaign staffers who had dedicated their immediate lives to my success. I was embarrassed and ashamed. Leslie wasn't angry, even though I let her down. She looked me in the eye and said, "good thing that wasn't the real deal." We both started laughing and immediately went to work insuring that would never happen again. It's what Leslie does. She identifies a weakness and finds a solution. For nearly a year, Leslie Sorrell was my Guardian Angel. She cared. She was committed and she did her best to protect me from the negative attacks that the establishment launched from all directions.

Leslie was a blessing. My supporters were too. I was humbled by the sheer number of people who put so much faith in me. There would never have been that many people if it wasn't for Leslie.

America is the greatest nation in the world. And Leslie Sorrell is a great American. Sadly, many of the leaders of this country turned against her simply for having faith in me and her quest for a better nation. It's disgusting how corrupt and conniving our elected leaders can be when you threaten their gravy train life as a member of the ruling class. They will stop at nothing to crush anyone who gets in their way. Even a kind, optimistic, principled young lady who supported someone she believed in.

I am forever apologetic, for the damage I brought to Leslie's political career. But really, it's Congressmen like Kenny Marchant and Eric Cantor that owe her a sincere apology.

I will also be forever grateful for Leslie. Because of her I am a better man today. She's a thought pioneer and sees angles to issues most people fail to consider. My success today is due in large part to Leslie. My campaign loss set up my victories as a conservative commentator.

I believe this book is Leslie's way of bringing her quest for a better, more principled nation to the masses. There are lessons in this book you will learn from. It will make you think and ask hard questions of your elected officials. It will also make you realize how far we, as a nation, have fallen. But because of people like Leslie Sorrell and her willingness to take on the Washington elite, America can be saved. It starts with next page.

—**Grant Stinchfield**, Conservative T.V./radio host

PREFACE

A few of the names have been changed for various reasons, but mostly to protect good guys from crooked vengeance. Other times I simply left out a name all together because I didn't want them to have the satisfaction of being mentioned. But most of the names have remained the same because I believe you want to know. The description of places and events is as close to reality as I can get.

1 REMEMBER THE ALAMO

I didn't exactly raise my hand and shout "I want to work for the devil!" but I ended up doing his bidding anyway. Ironically, more than a few people told me I was doing the Lord's work. I knew better than that. I wasn't saving anyone's soul or leading them to Jesus. But, I did believe I was saving the country.

Saving the country was a goal that I thought I could achieve by putting good people in office. So, I started a political consulting firm in Texas called the Magnolia Group, a "special forces team" for political campaigns and causes. We rooted for the underdog. We made the impossible happen. I could do all of these things because I believed that politics represented the greatest ideals of our society.

Most of my efforts were with people running for the United States Congress. But I also worked with those vying for judge, sheriff, senator, governor, and even those trying to be president of the United States.

One of the best ways to get someone elected is to raise a bunch of money. So, that's what I did. President Bill Clinton's finance director wrestled an alligator for a $15,000 contribution, a stunt that made him famous overnight and he is now the Governor of Virginia. But my climb as a fundraiser was not as death defying as his. Instead of wrestling gators, I could be found doing less sexy tasks like sitting in front of a computer, studying contributor data into the early morning hours.

How did I raise millions of dollars? I became the girl who believed there wasn't enough money in the system. Seriously. It's common to hear people say "I hate asking for money." But, I didn't hate asking for money. I loved it. I would say "Not enough people participate. There's too little money. There needs to more money. More investors—not less." I believed every word that I was saying. No one doubted my sincerity. People gave me obscene amounts of money. My talk. Their money. Together we were saving our country.

At one meeting of potential donors, I not only defended Governor Mitt Romney's remarks about "corporations are people," I defended him because I thought he was right. By the time I was done elaborating everyone in the room agreed and concluded their business couldn't afford not to get involved—which meant they gave me large sums of both personal and corporate money.

My clients almost always had large campaign chests because of our efforts. And if they didn't have the ability to raise money, we didn't want them. An underperforming client simply consumed too much time without benefiting our bottom line - or theirs. Our hard work paid off. In the first six months of my firm's operations, our bonus checks were larger than my previous year's salary when I'd been a congressional campaign staffer.

Here's the fatal paradox: it was my success in growing the Magnolia Group from a start-up to a successful and influential national political consulting firm that transformed my understanding of the real world of politics. I'd been in that world for years, making one little compromise after another before I realized that I was in a world that no one tells you about and that the media fails to cover. It's a world none of us want to want to believe in – me least of all.

Magnolia Group's typical client was successful in business and wanted to serve the country through elected office. They dreamed of giving back and making a difference…this was our honeymoon phase. Over the years, I watched my clients slowly transform from those awkward candidates I fervently believed in to slick politicians. I envisioned them becoming great statesmen, but not one of them went that direction. Instead as time passed, they moved closer and closer to the line between right and wrong, until working on the edge became routine and the line itself began to fade.

As I began to question whether any of my work made a difference, I was filled with an unexplained restless energy. Maybe this true-believer was worn out with her do-gooder ways and I began to strongly consider converting to cynicism. If it hadn't been for Congressman Kenny Marchant, a Republican from Texas, I might have buried my energy underneath a couple of piles of cash and become just another hack socking away the dough.

But Kenny Marchant, a man I helped put into office, saved me. Sort of. Marchant was so arrogant, so self-serving and so greedy that even my hyped-up idealism couldn't stand up against him. He doubled his net worth to $50 million during the economic collapse. He did plenty of other things I didn't approve of, but hadn't every congressman? I'm not convinced that Marchant deserves the credit. Maybe it was Grant Stinchfield, a brash young newscaster who thought he could defeat an incumbent.

The first time I met Grant Stinchfield was over a cup of coffee in a noisy café in Dallas. He was running late and came dressed in a grey North Face pullover. Most of my clients hadn't ventured past dark suits and ties. "Hey, sorry for being late. If we work together, I'll value your time. Promise," Grant said before sitting down. Apologizing for making me wait was a new line that hadn't been used on me before.

Grant dove right in as he was eager to talk about his plans of taking his investigative skills to Washington to uncover waste, fraud, and abuse. Never quick to encourage someone to run for office, I spent the next couple of hours quizzing Grant as I usually try to talk them out of it.

I wasn't the only one with questions though. Grant sounded just like the reporter he was—grilling me too. We were interviewing each other for several hours. We agreed more than we disagreed, both believing Washington is broken and in the need of fundamental changes in the way our elected officials thought about the way they worked.

I came at Grant like a typical insider and shot down just about everything he had to say. "How would you get things done? Legislation passed? Secure good committee assignments? Get other Members of Congress on your side?"

Grant said he wanted to be accountable to his constituents and not worry about his colleagues. He would like to be on a good committee but thought that should take a back seat to "exposing Washington" and "informing and motivating the public to take action." I thought he was naive and maybe a bit crazy but I continued our meeting because I was intrigued.

"Exposing Washington, particularly as a Congressman, is not going to be popular," I told Grant. "In fact, they may hate you." And as I listened to Grant, I realized he would be true to his mission given that he wasn't going into this to be "liked" by those in Washington.

I wanted to learn more about Grant. "So, how did you get into the news business?" I asked, testing his bio to see if I could sell it to voters. He told me that after college he returned home to New York to join his father in working for the family construction business. After a physically and mentally draining work day, Grant came home and crashed on the couch. "All I could think is I can't keep doing this. I turned on the TV, the news was on, and thought 'but I could do that'!"

"A news anchor?" I asked him, thinking his younger self must have been a bit arrogant—but bold too. I liked it.

"Investigative reporter" he said with a bit of a laugh, reading my thoughts as I summed up his ego.

The thing that especially impressed me about the story was that Grant didn't listen to the outsiders and detractors who doubted the possibility that he could be a TV reporter. He made a video and sent it out to over 300 new stations across the country, and the folks in Missoula, Montana believed in him and offered him his dream job. He packed his bags and never looked back.

Over the years, Grant climbed the ladder. "I was proud to be a part of the news business," he told me. And I didn't doubt him when he said "Investigative reporting made me feel like I was making a difference."

Before Grant knew it, he had made it to the number four media market in the country working for NBC5 in Dallas. I learned he became a four-time Emmy award-winning journalist for his investigative pieces. Because of his work, Texas laws were changed regarding the protection of people from identity theft, long before it became a "hot" topic. I was impressed and thought voters would be too.

Grant shared the infectious enthusiasm of a fellow true-believer. We imagined transforming the political world. And boy, did we imagine big. We dreamed and spoke of a world where republicans no longer lost the PR battle; they would lead it. It would be a world where republicans could make their point without being angry... a world where republicans would focus more on an energy and immigration plans that on abortion and birth control. No doubt, we were getting carried away.

"I'd go straight to the American public. Empower them and demand meaningful change," Grant said enthusiastically. We were excited and ideas kept flowing.

"I'll go on Rachel Maddow and light her up!" he declared, embracing the opportunity to share his conservative message instead of running from reporters. Drawing on his experience as a reporter, he believed that as a politician he would be able to tell his story to so many people that meaningful reform and legislative accomplishments would follow.

Taking Grant Stinchfield as a client would not only mean professionally pitting my firm against a former client Congressman Kenny Marchant, but worse, challenging a Republican congressman in a Republican primary. Ronald Reagan declared "thou shall not talk ill of a fellow Republican" and somewhere along the way this became known as "the 11th commandment." Yet, here I was, possibly about to commit the very sin that would result in ex-communication from the Church of the Republican Party and its members.

As I painstakingly premeditated going against the old guard, I reached the same conclusion each and every time: if I believed in our political system, I had to protect it. If I believed the person in office was not doing a good job, I should work to elect someone better.

They tried to keep me a part of their faithful flock. Congressman Marchant's Chief of Staff, Brian, called. I knew him well from my days on the hill and worked with him years afterward. Although we had a long conversation, the message was simple and concise. He warned me in no uncertain terms that we insiders don't go against each other. Period.

Wanting to make sure I understood his counsel, Brian, who in addition to being a chief of staff, owned a high-end beauty salon, reiterated his advice in an email:

"You have worked very hard to build your firm the Magnolia Group. You have come a long way and I have always been shocked and impressed with you. You have built a good, solid business. You have a great reputation. You know national politics, local politics, and state politics.

It's different going against a well-liked incumbent- you know that. Right or wrong, that's the way it is. It's a very risky venture. Could he or anyone beat Kenny in the primary? The honest and truthful answer is no.

I know you well. If I didn't care about you, I promise I would have slept better last night.

If you want to talk, I will keep my Kenny hat off and talk to you as a makeup store owner who does have a little knowledge of politics left in him. If you choose to help him, you still have my respect and friendship. Brian"

Re-reading the email, quite a bit was missing. Brian didn't once say "Kenny Marchant is the best darn Congressman! We need to keep him up here!" Brian didn't give me a laundry list of the Congressman's accomplishments. He didn't argue with me about the Congressman losing his way. None of that was in his email or our phone conversations. Instead, Brian put his energy into telling me how the deck was stacked against me for daring to take on "one of our own" in a primary. What we believed was best for our country was never brought into the conversation.

Excited about someone wanting to do things differently, Grant wooed me into wanting to be a part of his campaign for Congress. Brian was right. I really did know better. But Marchant's sleaze and Stinchfield's fresh-faced idealism somehow tipped me over. So, when Stinchfield came to the Magnolia Group and asked us to manage his campaign against Marchant, I did the unthinkable and committed the sin. I said yes. I said I'd break the 11th commandment and take on an incumbent United States congressman. I knew I was violating the political insider code. I knew my political friends would be horrified. I knew I was in for a rough ride. But I didn't know the half of how bad it was going to get. Before that campaign ended, I'd find myself stripped of every ideal I'd ever had about politics. I'd be forced to realize that the real losers in American politics are the American people.

As a courtesy, I called Brian and got voice mail. He simply responded with another email.

"I was disappointed in your decision. After a discussion with my wife, I informed Kenny that I was returning to work full-time and putting my personal goals and plans aside. I have the greatest respect for him as a Christian, a friend, and as a Congressman. It's a small sacrifice on my part to help him win this campaign. Brian"

When politicians and their groupies begin sharing how Christian someone is and how God is on their side, ironically, that's the moment when I know they've begun operating on the wrong side of things. Hopefully, God is too busy to hear about all these good Christian politicians ripping off His people. On Election Day, the tax-payers may not be as forgiving, I hoped.

What did the taxpayers think about Congressman Marchant paying his Chief of Staff a big fat salary when Brian owned and focused his time on his beauty business? By keeping Brian on the payroll, even though he worked part time, the congressman allowed his top aide to continue to earn tenure for his federal pension plan. Ultimately, Brian will retire with an annual pension providing him more than six figures for the rest of his life. Even more, what kind of logic was at work that allowed Brian to suggest that by doing his job, one that the Congressman hired him for was a small sacrifice?

Congressman Marchant and his team pulled back the curtain and revealed to me that being a bully pays off and that there's not much elected officials aren't willing to do to hold on to their power. I am sharing my story to expose what's behind the politicians' curtains from an insider's perspective. Let me clear though, Congressman Marchant is not unique among Congressmen. This could have easily been any race where a fresh, energetic challenger took on an incumbent.

It's becoming more common and accepted that incumbents prioritize seniority over merit, and secrecy over transparency and their paychecks over ours. And the biggest lie tells us that there is nothing we can do about the way our elected officials operate. I am here to tell you otherwise. My goal is to arm Americans with insider knowledge and to shed light on the political world in Washington D.C that isn't talked about—-the one where congressmen quietly increase their power while decreasing the peoples' power.

The media told me they can't cover such a story because they weren't willing to go against a Congressman—Kenny Marchant—a Congressman that they thought would end up winning anyway. They thought it was too much to risk. I didn't. But then again, I lost that bet.

Who would the voters choose if they had the full story on those representing them? Grant? Only 60,000 people voted in that election. If more Americans thought they could change the ways things are going, would they decide to go vote instead of stay home? I am telling my story to hear what you think.

2 GRANNY TAKES DOWN THE ESTABLISHMENT

I didn't major in political science and I didn't dream of a career in politics. And while I wouldn't describe my family as political, there are some who would say otherwise. My first memory of any type of politics is my Grandmother's campaign for Edmonton Kentucky's County Property Valuation Administrator. My Grandmother, Lucy Bowles, was taking on the incumbent, Woodrow Wilson. He and the Wilson family had been in office for as long as anyone can remember.

It was an exciting time for our family. Grandmother and Granddaddy recruited many people in the community to help her win, and people wanted to help. A local girl created hand-painted signs reading "I Love Lucy." Someone else ordered straw hats with the same slogan. People went door-to-door talking to their neighbors about my grandmother.

When we arrived in Edmonton, the campaign role assigned to me and my sister Laurie was to play "charming grandchildren." At age five, this was not easy for me as it required wearing a dress, tights, and my long hair down in the exceptionally hot and humid weather. Usually, I could be found in shorts and flip flops and my hair in doggy ears. I was confident I could secure the much-needed votes while talking to people dressed in my typical attire. My family thought otherwise. From Grandmother's campaign, I learned that politics meant doing and wearing things you didn't like for the sake of votes.

While Mom joined Granddaddy in his pick-up truck to work the farmers' votes, I remained at the courthouse passing out sample ballots and asking people to vote for Lucy Bowles. Although not a shy person, I was intimidated by the idea of going up to strangers and asking them to vote for Grandmother. Without much choice or sympathy from anyone, I took a big breath, headed toward a group of men in overalls and belted out "Today is Election Day and I hope you'll vote for my Grandmother—Lucy Bowles!"

"No, we won't!" the largest of the men shouted back and laughed—at me.

The other men broke out in laughter. I didn't expect that type of response. Securing votes was going to be hard and make for a longer day than I had anticipated. Still shocked, I just stood there on the sidewalk embarrassed, already feeling my cheeks turning pink. I moped back to my family where Grandmother announced "Leslie just asked Woodrow Wilson (her opponent) for his vote!"

How did I know who Woodrow Wilson was? And why didn't my family point him out. I took note: Know your opponent. So, Mr. Woodrow Wilson gave me more motivation than I had come to town with. Now, determined to approach every person I saw and to ask them to vote for my Grandmother, I would do whatever was in my power. He had embarrassed me in front of a big crowd and I didn't much appreciate it.

My strategy included sharing with people how Grandmother played old maids and hearts with me for hours on end and how we took long walks and worked in her rose garden together. I made sure not to share with them that Grandmother put spaghetti and beans in her chili or wore funny aqua-marine house shoes — or surely they would not vote for her. I didn't see much point in telling them about her generous use of Jergens lotion, perfume, and bright red lipstick as I figured they could see and smell it for themselves.

I embraced my role by drawing red hearts around Grandmother's name on the ballot. Much to my delight, people smiled as they looked at the sample ballot I handed them. I concluded they liked my work. As the day wore on, the large over-all wearing men seemed more and more mean to me with each passing hour. I found a different colored pencil and began "X-ing" out Woodrow Wilson's name. My Daddy scolded me: "Those X's are not necessary. Just stick to your hearts." Reluctantly, I agreed. Even then, I knew the effectiveness of negative campaigning.

Everyone predicted a close election and long day. While passing time, many people shared stories about Granddaddy rather than worrying out loud about the results. Granddaddy worked as a tobacco farmer and this was considered a good and proud profession in Kentucky. I hadn't remembered Granddaddy falling from the rafters of a tobacco barn, breaking every bone in his body, and spending months in the hospital before returning home. I did remember that Granddaddy and his back were never the same. No one told me how important it was to my family that Grandmother win the election and secure this job.

What I did know is that every time I came to town, Granddaddy would take me to the grill on the square. Granddaddy didn't talk much but we shared a love of grilled cheese and chocolate shakes made with vanilla ice cream. He was the only grown up I knew who thought it was perfectly fine to eat the same thing every day. We both preferred to sit at the counter—something I didn't get to do with my Mom.

We waited for the election results in the crowded courthouse with no air-conditioning and a poorly functioning water fountain, with me securing a seat on a narrow stairway. The Coca-Cola machine had been emptied out earlier in the day and still sat with no drinks even now. Being hot and thirsty seemed to make the time go by even slower. I suspect all the discomfort was worth it because I was awakened from my nap to the news that Grandmother won the election! From this, the seed was planted early in me: I knew that with good signs, a group of committed people, and the right outfit, a long-time office holder can be beat.

Pleased with my Grandmother's victory, I was ready to move up the political ladder and announced, "I want to be president of the United States!"

Questioning my bold proclamation and motives, Daddy frowned. "Why?"

Without hesitating, a big smile formed and "I wanna ride around in a limo!" came shouting out. "Go into business, make some money; get your own limo. Don't be a politician!" he advised. At only five years old, it was the first and last time I thought about running for public office.

3 KENTUCKY GIRL GOES TO D.C.

AND LEARNS THE BEEF INDUSTRY AND REPUBLICAN POLITICS ARE A LOT ALIKE

Once I realized that I wasn't going to save the world by holding political office, I had to find something to do with my life. Daddy had a great idea. I should go to Washington, D.C. and save the beef industry.

The beef industry needed me for sure. Our family and everybody in the beef business had the bad feeling in those days that beef was losing out to the well-marketed boneless, skinless chicken breast. At our house, we ate chicken – but only on Sundays. And we ate it fried, which Daddy said was the only way to eat chicken. Every other day of the week, we ate beef. That's how my parents grew up. That's how their parents grew up.

But times were changing. And the boneless, skinless chicken breast was to blame. Our family had spent some time thinking about this issue. Women used to buy whole chickens and cut them up. That was a messy but necessary job if you wanted chicken. Then people started buying boneless, skinless breasts. It was easy, and it was being called healthy. Beef was being called unhealthy. Beef was still big and clunky. It had fat on it. It had bones in it. It couldn't compete with that sleek new chicken breast.

I knew all this from my own girlfriends. They said meat "looks gross." They complained that they didn't know what to do with it. Many didn't know about the crucial 21 amino acids that only red meat contains, or how it's a fallacy that chicken is less fattening. They thought making penne pasta was quicker than cooking a filet.

There was so much misinformation out there! I wanted consumers to know the facts and make informed decisions. My passion for cattle and steaks is evident to everyone! The beef industry had so much unrealized potential, and nobody saw the menace and the solutions any better than I did. I knew I was just the person to connect with consumers, grow beef's market share, and tell the world how delicious, healthy, and easy beef is to prepare

Beef is a business I knew all about. My parents are both gifted, eccentric people who married at 19 as seniors in college and had a baby at 20. They spent their "honeymoon" traveling to West Texas searching for and securing clients. Their first piece of furniture was a desk. Together they built our family business, beginning with one cow and eventually came to own the largest cattle barn in the Southeast. Mom was fond of saying, "We had a million-dollar barn before we had a house." My parents were quite clear with my sisters and me that their early-marriage path was not a plan for success, despite it working for them. Otherwise; however, their lives served as good lessons in what to do. We learned early that it was better to spend money on things that generated income than on things calculated to impress.

I spent a great part of my childhood chasing cows who had escaped from that barn, which Daddy named Fox Creek. I grew up in a Kentucky town so safe that we not only didn't lock our house but everyone left keys in the cars' ignition, so as not to lose them. That was our parents' idea. But our parents were also cautious people. Even though Mom and Daddy didn't consider themselves gun people, Mom had a loaded pistol in the pantry by the flour and Daddy had a loaded shotgun by the front door.

My parents were modest people. Daddy grew up in a three-room cabin. He'd always say, "Don't be impressed that Abe Lincoln was born in a cabin. Be impressed that he got out of it." One time when a lady we knew well came to the barn to sell a handful of her cattle, she greeted my Mom by asking, "Oh, you still work here?" Since Mom owned the place, and this lady knew it, I started to set her straight. Shooting me a look that told me to close my mouth immediately, Mom merely smiled and said nothing. Later when I asked Mom for an explanation, she still said nothing. Daddy answered instead, "Your Mom knows business and plans on selling those cattle for a higher price and making money. Your Mom knows who she is." Lesson? It was better to be quiet and make money than prove a point.

A lady on an airplane once asked me how many cows we had. I answered, "I don't know. Hundreds. Thousands, maybe." Daddy heard me and later said, "Never say that. People will think you're bragging. Always say fifty. Anything more than that, they won't believe you." It was better to lie than to brag in our family.

We were taught to show the world a modest face. But inside the walls of our home, we got a very different lesson, one that would serve us equally well. We learned that we were brilliant; we could do whatever we wanted to do so long as we were willing to work hard.

It was Daddy's idea that I should save the beef industry, which he never doubted I could do. It was Mom's idea that I should be on TV along the way, which she never doubted I could do. But Mom wasn't so sure about my going to Washington, D.C., which is where the Cattlemen's Association was located and where I'd need to be if I was going to save the industry. We already knew we couldn't take guns to D.C., and we also knew it was the kind of place where I might want them. I hadn't been to D.C. but I had been to New York

City where we saw homeless people sleeping on the street. We suspected there were also homeless people in D.C., and we never doubted that they would be a menace. So yes, we were scared of the city, but we all knew I'd love that job. Beef needed me. And after the failure of my plans for political office, I needed beef. It was a perfect fit.

Our plan did have one flaw. The beef industry was not actually looking for a spokesperson. In fact, the beef industry didn't actually know that it needed rescuing from chicken. There was no actual evidence that the industry realized it needed a woman of my deep understanding to communicate with other women. It might even be said that the beef industry was completely clueless about its peril.

These were factors my family completely overlooked. The need was so great in my mind and the minds of my family that we were sure the kings of cow country would jump at the chance to be rescued by a girl of my long experience and great ideas. Not being entirely ignorant of the way the big world works, I made calls to folks in the industry who had bought cattle from my family or had a good relationship over the years, asking for their help and telling them of my plans to be in Washington D.C. Most of them shared their disgust for the place, but seemed genuinely happy that someone like me was willing to take on that town. They did seem disappointed I wouldn't be working alongside my family at Fox Creek, but I assured them I would return home after my service in the Nation's Capital.

Daddy was the kind of man who made a practice of not asking anybody for anything, but he wanted to make sure this happened for me. Leaving nothing to chance, he too called his fellow cattlemen and asked them to put in a good word for his daughter. And it worked. The Cattlemen's Association bought me a ticket to come up, interview, and tell them my idea.

For job interviews, my Mom always said "wear a navy suit." Mom thought black was too grown-up for her daughters, whom she called "young ladies." When my taxi pulled up to the office of the Cattlemen's Association on Pennsylvania Avenue, the same street as the White House, I was pretty much gob smacked.

All the D.C. cattlemen wore expensive suits with cuff links, cowboy boots, and hats. Back home, the cattlemen weren't so fancy. Most wore jeans. Some had big belt buckles, which was about as fancy as they got. My Daddy wasn't even that showy. He stuck to khakis, blue shirts, and a plain Fennell's leather belt. It was the same color as his boots, which was about as far into fashion as my Daddy went. I had just seen the association president on the cover of the cattlemen's magazine in an article that dubbed him the "Urban Cowboy," and being a big fan of John Travolta, that made me want even more to be part of it all. Fresh and well rested, wearing my navy suit and sensible pumps, my message firm and practiced, I was ready for anything they could throw at me. Or so I thought.

What they actually threw at me was a woman, and not a polite one either. She used abrupt sentences, hardly seemed at all happy to see me, and acted like she didn't much want me wasting her time. No boots. No cowboy hat. No spokesperson job.

It turned out the cattlemen's association was willing to interview me for an entry level communications job of sorts, but they weren't at all interested in my being their spokesperson. I told the lady about how the women grocery shoppers were the decision makers, and how they'd been seduced into wrongful meal planning by the insidious nature of the boneless chicken breast. I was pretty sure I could woo her with that. It had worked with everyone else. But she didn't look the least bit alarmed. In fact, she didn't look the least bit anything, just stone-faced cold.

Oddly, she did ask me my salary requirements, which gave me a ray of hope. It shouldn't have. We were repeatedly told in college that starting salaries were $36k. So, that's the amount I told her. She balked. Apparently, that is not a starting salary in Washington D.C. But I didn't budge off my number. No big-city cattlewoman was going to take advantage of me.

I was so shocked by the awful way our meeting was going that most of it was a blur. I do remember it ended with her saying, "To make it in this town, you need Hill experience." I didn't know what the Hill was. The only way I knew Hill deserved a capital letter was that when she said it her voice deepened like she was evoking some holy relic. By that time my pride was so hurt that I didn't even ask what the Hill was.

Daddy, thank the Lord, was not so easily put off. When I called him that night to tell him what she'd said, he listened without comment until I finished. Then without even a pause, he simply said, "Okay, we'll get you some Hill experience." Mom, on the extension, chimed in by saying that our congressman, Ed Whitfield, "lived down the street" in Hopkinsville, our hometown, usually referred to by locals as Hoptown. My parents didn't build one of the biggest cattle barns in the country by dwelling on the negative or letting their kids dwell on it either. I couldn't exactly remember the congressman, but I knew his Daddy. Everybody knew his daddy. We called him Mr. E.O.

Mr. E.O. always had a big smile on his face, and he greeted almost everybody with a bear hug. He'd been married to Mrs. Whitfield for what we always called practically forever, but the real number was closer to 70 years. Some said Mr. E.O. would have made a great congressman himself but he would have had to leave his beloved Hoptown, and Mr. E.O. would never do that. Like my parents, Mr. E.O. knew who he was and didn't want to be anyone else. Mr. E.O. lived in Hoptown's historic district downtown and always insisted that his son's staff from the D.C. office stay with him and Mrs. Whitfield in their home rather than in one of the few hotels in town. They did. No one could say no to Mr. E.O.

So Daddy called Mr. E.O.'s boy Ed, who was quite delighted to hear from him. Congressman Whitfield didn't have a position in his office, but he told Daddy that I could have an internship, while I was looking for a job on the Hill. The congressman explained to Daddy that you had to be on the Hill to get a job on the Hill. Even though the job as intern didn't pay anything, it put you ahead of all those people off the Hill.

So, we got ready for me to make the big move. Daddy thought I should fill the car with just a few clothes. Mom was more understanding of my desire to take dishes, vases, photos, and such. I'd need them to comfort me if I were to make his new city my home. Mom and I did spend a week worrying about my new D.C. wardrobe, which required pulling lots of clothes out of the closets and a shopping trip to add even more conservative clothes to my already conservative closet of navy, oatmeal, and khaki. I made sure to pack my Hartmann leather briefcase that Daddy had given me the Christmas before.

Mom decided Washington was too dangerous for me to drive my LeBaron convertible. Daddy backed her decision, even giving me his hunter green Jimmy instead. Disappointed at no longer being able to drive around with the top down, I at least had a sunroof and lots of extra space. After days of cramming the Jimmy full of stuff, there was no longer room for anything more. I'd concluded I must have everything one would need for D.C. when for the first time, it dawned on me that I didn't even know how to get there. Not sure exactly where I was going, or what to expect, I waved goodbye and followed the atlas route my parents had highlighted in yellow. I was so excited to start conquering my new town that I got a speeding ticket on the way.

Washington D.C. is like Vegas in that just being there creates an adrenaline rush. It's hard to explain, but the air and feel of the town are different. The moment I walked into Congressman Ed Whitfield's office with its prime location near the metro stop in the Cannon House Office Building; I knew I was at the epicenter of power.

New experiences and happenings around town were everywhere in D.C. In those early days, I was constantly learning and discovering. I saw two girls walking arm in arm and realized I hadn't seen that before. I had no idea that so many political conversations are spent debating gay and lesbian issues. I discovered Vietnamese food, which was very different than the "meat and three" from back home. I learned Ethiopian food is consumed with fingers, not utensils. That guys and girls could live together but not be dating— just saving money. I also learned that some guys and girls lived together, weren't married, but were dating. Really, before that moment, I didn't realize men and women shared a home unless they were married or just "those people." (I would later become one of "those people.") I learned some people didn't own cars and others didn't ever plan to own them, and I wanted to be like them. I always thought driving was over-rated and cars too expensive. Living in the "big city," picking up fresh baguettes, falling in love with pesto, going to Eastern Market and enjoying the "brick" breakfast sandwich were all adventures to me.

Growing up, I had listened to stories of my Mom taking the bus for a nickel, or something like that, so I figured it would be about a quarter in the modern world. It was more like a dollar ten and apparently exact change was required. . . It was obvious to all the riders that I was new to this system. I had not adjusted to the cold weather and had on an unusual amount of clothes and was struggling to find where my change was buried. The bus driver was yelling that I was holding up his schedule. Frustrated and frazzled, I told the driver to keep the five-dollar bill I'd found and please let me go sit down. That evening, instead of riding the bus back, I splurged on a cab.

After the bus fiasco, I was apprehensive about taking the metro. I read up, asked questions, and took all precautions to fully understand the color-coded routes, learned how to purchase a metro card, and studied the schedules before even considering approaching to ride. I also had a friend shadow me for back-up. Quickly though, I had my own system down and riding the metro made me feel quite grown up.

I lived in a few short-term, furnished apartments and houses all over the D.C./Northern Virginia area, which helped me to learn my new city even better. But a row house at 716 Maryland Avenue that I shared with three other twenty-something girls was my favorite place to call home. To make the rent payments manageable—or at least manageable for D.C.—my roommates Rebekah and Dawn and I decided to call the dining room a bedroom and rent it out to interns or short-term rentals. An intern named Megan made that room hers and by doing this, we each paid about $500 a month.

Seventh Street was the last "safe stretch" at the time. My roommate Rebekah, who has dark and curly hair like me and the kind of optimistic nature my parents would have liked, used to say, "The police car by the 7-11 always makes me feel safe." The rest of us didn't want to point out that the police were over there because a robbery, shooting, or murder was always happening close to our house. Despite these minor annoyances, I was infatuated with this amazing city and all it had to offer.

Every day I jumped out of bed eager to explore on my morning walks to work. To be one of a few people in the early morning, having the streets and parks to myself was magical. To my surprise, the people and the city were friendly. I felt like they were welcoming me each and every day. I often walked toward the Supreme Court or the Capitol and Senate office buildings, making my way toward the Washington monument while the grounds were untouched, still covered with the morning dew or snow. Almost all of the many Capitol Hill police waived and spoke to me as I passed them on the grounds during my morning walks. The homeless people claiming park benches for living quarters gave me a "hello nod" each day as well.

Security greeted me enthusiastically each morning as I made my way through the metal detectors at work. And I greeted them enthusiastically back, amazed at how polite they were each and every time I entered and re-entered the building. I never tired of the Washington D.C. experience. I felt blessed. My consolation prize for not getting a job with the Cattlemen was that all my preparation hadn't been in vain. It turned out the beef industry and Republican politics are a whole lot alike. Both the beef industry and the Republican Party produce images of "Bubba" in people's minds. Republicans market to older white males (who usually are already on their side). Republicans tend to forget that victory almost always comes down to women voters. Known as "swing voters", its women who generally decide elections.

In today's 24-hour news cycle, information over-load is common. As a result, voters don't always make informed decisions. They make emotional ones instead. And just like emotional eating, the outcome is not good for individuals – or in this instance, our country.

What all this added up to is that I quickly began to think that I was needed just as much working with Republicans as I'd been needed by the beef industry. It was up to me to save Republicans from themselves and secure women supporters. But, of course, the parallel didn't stop there. Just as with the Cattlemen, no Republican actually asked me to take on this mission. Still, I was up for it and my chances of getting a job on the Hill were looking better all the time.

Rich and famous people were everywhere in D.C., and making the rounds of the various parties and fundraisers improved one's chance of getting to catch a glimpse of them. It took a little work to get invited, but I was good at doing what it took. Just about every night I attended various receptions with lobbyists and Congressmen in order to meet new friends and network. As an added bonus, there were free food and drinks, which worked well for my bare-bones budget.

Some of the first people I met worked for the senator I most admired in Washington – Senator Phil Gramm of Texas, who ran unsuccessfully for president of the United States. I couldn't believe my luck. I shared with the Senator's staff that I was the only one in my political rhetoric class in college who chose Phil Gramm to support as president and that I received an "A" on my presentation. Since most Republicans supported Senator Bob Dole, I thought I might impress them with such news. I didn't.

I had never met Senator Gramm, but I admired him for putting principle before politics. He was a lone democrat who supported President Reagan's budget -a move that cost Gramm his chairmanship. (Senator Gramm was a democrat who later switched to a republican.) And I respected his budget-hawk ways. I'd long been saying "there needs to be more Phil Gramms," and I was happy to say it again to his staff. Years later, I was even more excited when Senator Phil Gramm's campaign manager for his presidential campaign, Jeb Hensarling, was running for Congress, and I got to be a part of that team. Senator Gramm campaigned hard for Jeb, and I got to spend a little time with my hero on the campaign trail. But that was far in the future. In the meantime, I had to eat.

While there were lots of receptions, I couldn't rely on them alone to provide my meals. I am not sure anyone could be self-sufficient on Hill entry-level salaries. Most other entry-level staffers I knew got a little something from back home and I was no different. But I hated doing that, so I asked for too little and made things harder on myself than I had to. And while everyone called the internships unpaid, in reality there was some type of small stipend but it didn't stretch out enough to cover the basics of rent and food.

So during my early days in D.C., I had to put my budget skills through tough tests. Things cost more here than in Hoptown. One way I did this was to learn about daily specials and happy hours around town. For example, Ireland's Four Courts in Arlington, on the Clarendon orange metro stop, served hamburgers, fries, and beer for $4 on Mondays. If you wanted cheese, they would charge another dollar, so I ate hamburgers. I didn't really like beer, but for $4, I spent every Monday enjoying a beer with my supper.

At the grill in the basement of the Longworth building, I could eat a cup of soup for lunch and a half a sandwich or a whole grill cheese for under $5. And when I was really in a penny-pinching mood, I would go to one of the many hot dog stands within blocks of the House office buildings and have their special—a hot dog, chips, and a coke for $1.25. This felt like a sacrifice because I wasn't a big fan of such food but I wanted to prove to myself and my family I could survive and that I was fiscally responsible.

When my parents worried that I was perhaps making too many sacrifices for my life on Capitol Hill, Mom sent care packages and "happys" with little encouraging notes saying how proud she was of me and "Here's an outfit I found. Hope it fits" (as if she wasn't shopping — just discovering items, so I wouldn't feel guilty about all the clothes she was sending). When she sent suits, knowing I would never go out and buy such nice things for myself, she included notes acknowledging such but assuring me "this was so cheap, I couldn't resist."

Mom complimented my money management skills, telling me she was proud and giving me advice. She always said, "When your Daddy and I wanted more money, we just worked harder and sold more cattle." Because raises and results don't quite work the same way on Capitol Hill, when I needed more money, I simply got another job to increase my income stream. I spent brief stints in the evenings working in retail and as a youth church coordinator. I also took a fundraising job with the National Republican Party from 7 to 11 at night. We called people over the phone, asked them for money, and received a commission on the amount we raised. We got bonuses for credit cards.

When callers said things like "If Congress would give us some tax relief, I would give, but I can't," I would say, "Good news. Just today in the Ways & Means committee they voted to lower the effective tax rate. It should go to the floor soon."

"What are you talking about?" one man shouted back. "Out here in Madison there's no relief." Frustrated, I moved to sit by the top fundraiser, who was a tall, thin, gay, African American man. I wanted to hear what he was saying.

"You bet. We're gonna impeach the president!" He was saying into the phone. "You betcha, I hear yah. Times are hard, but with your money I'll march up to Capitol Hill myself and give 'em hell."

When he hung up, I said, "There's no bill in Congress about impeaching the president. What congressman are you meeting with?"

He laughed, smacked his hand on his ripped jeans, and said, "Oh sweetie, I just tell them whatever they wanna hear. You know too much. They don't wanna hear all that mumbo jumbo you're spouting. Listen to the master!"

I practiced my new lines and sure enough it worked. My last call, an elderly woman, said she would like to give, but her children took away her check book. She went on, saying she really appreciated all the hard work her congressman was doing and sure wished she could help.

"They didn't leave you a credit card in case of emergencies?" I asked.

"Well, yes, they did. I hadn't thought about that. Oh, but they put a $1,000 limit on it."

"$1,000 is fine," I said, and she proceeded to read off the numbers. I hit my mark that night.

My exhilaration wore off about a block into the walk home. Had I been Catholic, I would have headed straight to confession. Being that I am not, I whispered "God, forgive me. Please, forgive me."

Even with these jobs, I couldn't have made it in Washington without my parents' help and I was grateful. But I very much wanted to be independent. "Keep smiling," Daddy would say, "and eat beef at least ten times a week." When I would tell him I couldn't always eat out, much less to enjoy red meat at a steak house, he insisted I go right away—that very night—to an upscale steak house like the Palm or Capital Grille and order a large steak. "Leslie, I am proud," he said, "and I like it that you're proud, but the cameras are rolling. Make sure you're enjoying it too." So sometimes, when I got tired of ramen noodles and reception food, I dined at the expensive steak houses D.C. is known for – on the family.

It was no secret I enjoyed the Washington social scene. Even after I got my first real job, my grandparents would ask "other than attending parties and having a good time, what else is it you do to earn your salary?" I was so good at making friends and influencing people that it didn't take long for me to be invited to play on a softball team– a major coup in D.C. where who you know can be far more important than what you know. Almost every Thursday after work, I played softball on the mall with a team of fellow Hill staffers. (The mall I learned is the area around the Washington monument, not a place to go shopping, which was a relief as I detest shopping). The importance of the softball team is so well recognized that sometimes, we would get to leave a little early for our games. Afterwards, we would go for drinks, discuss bills and legislation, and share all the exciting things we were working on, including stories about our bosses and offices dynamics. Carrie was one of the first new friends I made on the softball field as her boyfriend played on the team while she cheered him on.

On the day I was meeting her for drinks I had spent the day getting a "Dear Colleague" letter signed for Congressman Whitfield's office. The letter had something to do with the country Turkey. I was dressed that day in a Kentucky blue suit with matching heels that were much too tall. After a day spent trekking to House members' offices for signatures that were actually just stamps their staff applied to the letter, I was painfully aware that impractical shoes were not for Washington. My feet hurt so bad, I took a cab just a few blocks to Tortilla Coast, the restaurant where we were meeting, rather than walking. The cab driver thought my shoe story was hilarious and made fun of me the whole ride, after which he got an extra laugh by saying he had to charge a flat rate even for those handicapped by bad feet.

I got out of the cab to meet my friend at the restaurant and she looked like she should be working for a fashion magazine rather than on Capitol Hill. She had long blonde blown out hair before there were blow out bars and lots of make-up that looked good on her. Her toes matched her French manicured nails. Many of my girlfriends' closets had the same muted colored suits as mine, but hers was filled with brightly colored dresses and skirts instead.

When I arrived, she already had a margarita in hand, had secured a table with chips and salsa, and was laughing with an older man. Not sure I should join; I made eye contact but hesitated before approaching the table. She quickly waved me over. Without asking, her table companion ordered a margarita for me. I'd met some friendly people in D.C. but this was the best. All my worries about not being able to meet friendly people in the big city were clearly silly. When the man left us to finish our happy hour, he even paid our tab with the server!

As soon as he was out the door, my friend leaned in and whispered, "That's my boss," which confused me. She'd been an intern and I'd heard that with the help of her boyfriend, she had just gotten some great job opportunity on the Hill.

I looked at her stupidly for a minute and then I got it. The guy who just bought us drinks was her boss and a member of congress. A member of congress buying drinks for us? Big stuff. I turned, flagged the waiter, ordered a second margarita, and listened to her explain that he liked pretty girls and liked to flirt but was pretty much harmless, or so she thought and hoped. The congressman was so impressed with her, she told me that he said she didn't have to go back and finish her degree if she wanted a full-time job.

"So what exactly do you do?" I asked. Instead of answering "scheduler," which was her job, she answered, "I am his butt wiper." At that moment, I made a mental note — don't apply for any scheduling jobs. Once when I'd entered a D.C. restaurant alone to order a meal, the waiter took one look at me and said, "Welcome to the big city, country mouse." I never knew what tipped him off. I didn't feel like a country mouse. Not then, but my girlfriend's sophisticated attitude made me wonder. Maybe I was a country mouse in the big city, with a lot to learn. I hoped everyone who looked at me couldn't see it.

That night when my parents called to ask about my day, I left out the bit about having drinks with a friend and her boss. While nothing bad happened, my gut didn't feel good about a congressman flirting with young women. I couldn't understand why a congressman would advise anyone not to finish college, especially since my friend just had one semester left. I didn't know a bunch of congressman yet, but I was under the impression that's not how a congressman should be. Certainly, my Mom would have raised an eyebrow for me having drinks with someone who acted anything less than a gentleman- especially if they had the title of "Honorable" before their name. Later, when my grandparents said the "Republican people you are meeting can help further your career," I just agreed with them and didn't share the real Washington D.C. I was discovering. But that congressman? He went on to become a very powerful man, but that didn't stop his wife from filing for divorce twenty years later when she finally figured out he was having a whole bunch of affairs.

4 RULES—
WHAT RULES?

From my first days in D.C. I'd been told, "Everyone wants to be us — working and living here." My first thought was, "So this is what they mean by "Beltway Bubble."

I replied, "I thought everyone wanted to work in New York?"

They laughed. "No, D.C. is the most powerful city in the world, not New York."

"Everyone here is from a good family and good schools, practically reeking of money. They're all good people," I was told. I didn't particularly feel special or smell like money, but from my first months in D.C., I was constantly reassured otherwise because if I was not special, they were not special either.

In between making copies, filing, getting "dear colleague" letters signed and other boring but necessary duties that are an intern's life, I dedicated my time to passing out resumes, meeting people, and learning what my next move would be. My first ally was Congressman Whitfield's staff assistant, Jason, a good-looking William and Mary School of Law alum that towered above most people with his six foot-something frame. Jason lived just across the river in Arlington, on the orange line, like me. Sympathy can be in short supply in the shark tank of a political city. But Jason had been in the place I was not so long ago. He hadn't yet forgotten what it felt like to be the guy who did the worst jobs for no money. He tried to clue me in. Our commuting conversations were filled with his insights on how D.C. works. It was Jason who taught me Capitol Hill lingo.

It was like kindergarten. First he taught me my letters and my numbers. Before coming to D.C., I thought L.A. stood for Los Angeles, but in D.C. it means Legislative Aid. L.D. is code for Legislative Director, L.C., Legislative Correspondent. And then there is the House Office Buildings (HOB) numbering system. Three digits in an office number means it's located in the Cannon building. Four digits mean it's in the Longworth or Russell buildings.

But the most important thing Jason taught me was that I was lucky to be on the Hill even if I wasn't getting paid. He had a law degree from William and Mary. I didn't have a law degree. He wanted to be a healthcare LA, but when his internship ended, Congressman Whitfield offered him the staff assistant job. He took it because the Hill is a club people want to join. There were perks in being a member of this club. Jason partied in Virginia Beach at a "group house" while his law buddies pulled hellacious hours most weekends. A group house is a large house outside town that staffers pool their money to rent and party in on weekends. While Jason's law friends slaved through dinner, Jason usually got off early enough to take advantage of happy hour specials around town. All of these perks and then some, Jason shared with me over our neighborhood grills of Vietnamese and Greek—all standard fare for Jason, a city-boy from Northern Virginia, but exotic experiences to me. In exchange, I would share with him "insider information" about folks back home and such that the other staff may not share with him readily.

I wanted to join this club with its perks. So I continued to walk the halls of the House Office Buildings job hunting. I found pages of job openings in *The*

Hill and *Roll Call*; the two must read newspapers for Capitol Hill staff. But I couldn't land one. Job openings happened quickly and filling them happened just as quickly. If I were to have a chance, Jason told me I had to meet the people in the know. It's true everywhere but especially in D.C. who you know is what really counts.

Just as people predicted, I learned of an opening by word of mouth, from Congressman Whitfield himself. He told me a fellow member of the Kentucky delegation, Congressman Ron Lewis of the second district, was looking for a staff assistant.

The first step in the hiring process was an interview with Congressman Lewis' chief of staff, Greg Van Tatenhove, whose grey hair defied his youth and whose bow tie stood out in a world of ties. I was told that Lewis' staff was hesitant about hiring me because I was from the first district of Kentucky, not the second. This was my first lesson in what would be a long list of lessons in how small-minded D.C.'s insider rules can be.

Congressman Lewis made a brief appearance to introduce himself and shook my hand. What a surprise that was. I'd been expecting some bigger than life leader. That's not what I got – not then, not ever. His handshake was exactly the kind my daddy had warned me about, "like a dead fish." He spoke in a quiet tone with hunched over shoulders. This man had been a Baptist preacher before he came to D.C. I found myself struggling to imagine him shouting behind the pulpit with threats of Hell, like the other Baptist preachers I had known.

After the congressman left, Greg emphasized how important it was for me to be able to answer the phone and truthfully say I was from the district. I reminded Greg that my hometown was just an hour outside the district and went on to elaborated that I was born in Bowling Green, located in the second district, my entire extended family lived there, and that my parents owned farms there. When Greg said that none of that mattered, I was stunned. All of this should have been a big clue as to the level of dysfunction in this office.

Truthfully, most people don't know what cities are in their district, much less what number they live in. But to be fair, Greg was born in California, where there are 50 districts as opposed to Kentucky's six. And there's probably a big difference between California's urban beach-side cities and its centrally located towns. But to most of us in Kentucky, there isn't a whole heck of a lot of difference between Hopkinsville and Owensboro.

Second lesson of interview day: it's not what you are that matters in D.C. it's who you are and can pretend to be. But don't let me sound too cynical here. I didn't know how much I was learning about the inner workings of government. I was too in love with it all, too eager to be one of them to realize that I was already on the road to perdition and I didn't even have the job.

So, that was that. I wasn't from the district. I began the process of preparing my family for a word they didn't believe in—failure. "I may not get the job," I told them. You might think that by this time, my family would be accustomed to hearing that I'd failed. Not at all. Such shocking information took a while to digest. So while they choked it down, I continued. "Congressman Whitfield even called to put in a good word." I went on, "They're obsessed with me not being from the second district of Kentucky."

I was ready to give it up but the Kentucky Sorrells' don't fold so easily. Without my knowledge, Mom and Daddy began their own campaign to convince the Lewis office that I was the person to hire. All my kin were notified. And being that all my kin lived in the state of Kentucky, this was no small number. They began bombarding the Congressman's office with phone calls highlighting my ties to the district. Grandmother and Papa Herb (the man my Grandmother married after Granddaddy passed away) followed up their call with a letter gently reminding the Congressman that they held a successful fundraiser for his campaign in their home. Their crazy scheme worked. And this girl, from across the district lines, became staff assistant. But only because those that put pressure the Congressman come out ahead.

With a coveted Capitol Hill job and my head in the clouds, I realized my feet were only on the first rung of the ladder. But for a brief moment, I didn't care. That weekend I went home for champagne toasts with the family to celebrate our hard work paying off. "Here's to being on my way."

And then I met the congressman's wife.

A big part of my job was securing White House tickets and other tours for the folks back home visiting D.C. Tours were critical to the Congressman's wife, that everyone assured me I could call "Kayi" (pronounced Kay,) but I called "Mrs. Lewis," because I wanted to show her the utmost respect. Mrs. Lewis wore her bleached hair teased, was a bit on the chunky side, and made sure to never be seen without wearing her congressional spouse's pin so as not to be confused with a "nobody." Mrs. Lewis was driven by the strong belief that the key to her husband's re-election was playing tour guide to the entire second district of Kentucky. And since I was in charge of tours that meant Mrs. Lewis owned me. There were lots of rules around tours, and Mrs. Lewis never met a rule that she thought applied her. Capitol Hill offices could only request up to ten tickets for White House tours, and the White House was under no obligation to give us all ten requests. Worse still, ten didn't even come close to the many tickets Mrs. Lewis wanted for folks. Being green and eager to please, I set out to get more tickets. I learned how some staff assistants aggressively traded with other offices. States like the Dakotas, Oregon, Wyoming, Minnesota and others that were farther away than the two-hour flight from Kentucky made for good prospects. They didn't need their tickets. And I needed twice what I got. It was once again a matter of who you knew. So, I called on my friends from offices representing states far away. They gave me their tickets and I owed them a drink.

From day one I learned that keeping the congressman's wife happy was the game—a game I wanted to win. If you couldn't get all the tickets you needed, well, you were a loser. Was I breaking the rules? I didn't ask. It made the Congressman, his wife, and constituents happy

But that wasn't all Mrs. Lewis wanted. While most offices worked to secure tours for people visiting, tours don't dominate the work load of a staffer. But in our office, constituents would call me and say "Mrs. Lewis and I met in the grocery store and she told me to call you. She said you would get us booked up with tours for our trip." Other offices were comfortable telling people these tours are on first-come first serve basis. Not Mrs. Lewis. She wasn't okay with tickets running out. This is well before online forms, so the process was inefficient and required countless phone calls filled with strong persuasion skills. Mrs. Lewis had me calling up all kinds of places to make sure people not only got tickets that weren't available but to get them "VIP tours" while I was at it. My title was staff assistant but it should have been travel agent.

Mrs. Lewis didn't want me to direct anyone to the Capitol's tour guides. Nope. She wanted me to personally give everyone in our district a tour. During cherry blossom season, when tourists flocked to D.C. to see the trees beautiful pink blooms, it was not unusual for me to give five tours a day. I'd been hired to answer the phone and sort mail, but I had to come in early for that because almost all my time was taken up with tours. We weren't the only office offering private tours, but most offices reserved this perk for family and friends. Some offices didn't even give tours. Other offices gave one tour a day, if that. I was doing almost nothing else. She wanted so many tours that there weren't enough hours in the day for me to give them all. Sometimes the legislative staff had to pitch in.

Mrs. Lewis would call me on the weekend asking about tours. People on the Hill didn't take work home. People didn't call about work on the weekends and especially not the lowly staff assistant. But Mrs. Lewis did. I couldn't escape the woman. I dreamed about these tours in my sleep. I had come to Washington to make a difference, to see laws being made up close. I wanted to be a part of the action. But Mrs. Lewis wouldn't let go.

The tours never stopped. Mrs. Lewis thought securing constituents' tickets to the Holocaust Museum would be especially impressive. If a Congressman's office requests tickets, people can circumvent the long lines and proceed inside at the pre-assigned time. The catch to all this is that to be guaranteed tickets and go to the front of the line, a member of congress or their spouse must attend with the group. Escorting a Congressman or their spouse has special privileges regular people wouldn't get otherwise.

Mrs. Lewis had me request so many tours that the museum staff questioned her attendance. They suspected her for good reason. These were long somber visits. Nobody wanted to go to the Holocaust Museum several times a week, much less a day. I didn't. She didn't. I hadn't been on the job long before Mrs.

Lewis revealed her secret. She only escorted groups through the entrance and snuck out shortly afterwards.

But I couldn't admit that to the people giving us the tickets. I defended her aggressively. I had to. But I hated it. Good grief. This was the Holocaust Museum and God's chosen people. And I was lying.

To her credit, the day Mrs. Lewis invited me to the Holocaust Museum; she stayed the entire four hours with our group. She even shared a Snickers bar, offered some other snacks, and soft drinks she had brought in her purse. The problem was no food or drinks were allowed. The Congressman's wife thought the rules were for other people.

I don't think Congressman Ron Lewis agreed that his wife and office had to become the official tour guide for "everyone" she ran into. But since Mr. Lewis didn't stand up to Mrs. Lewis, she pressed on with her mission. Even offering their home, a row house conveniently located on Capitol Hill, to strangers. And while most the time it was the Congressman who would be left to entertain the masses in his home. (Mrs. Lewis was back in Kentucky.) At the end of Congressman Lewis's workday, he spent many nights sleeping on his office couch as opposed to walking the three blocks to be in his own bed. Congressman Lewis waited until his constituents headed out for their many tours I arranged to return home, to shower and shave.

I wanted to rebel, but if the Congressman was willing to make sacrifices, so was I.

But finally, I had enough the day Mrs. Lewis asked me to request a "Member's Only Dome Tour," I defied her for the first time. The rules say no one can go up without a member of congress escorting them. Such tours are not even allowed anymore because of dome deterioration. When Mrs. Lewis insisted, I request she be allowed to give a "Member's Only Tour," I was perplexed. "But Mrs. Lewis, you are not a member of congress." Stunned, Mrs. Lewis proceeded to inform me that she was like a member of congress.

I had finally stood up to this woman, a preacher's wife no less, who not only broke the rules herself but forced me to break them. She didn't deserve to win. But she did because the woman who made the decisions about the tours caved. She told me it would be all right for Mrs. Lewis to give the members-only tour for the congressman "this one time."

I was furious she was willing to break the rules for Mrs. Lewis. That woman didn't realize she had set a precedent and had no idea how many more of these "Member Tours" she would end up waiving the member requirement for Mrs. Lewis. The people who demanded the most in Washington were rewarded and the rules apply only to those who were willing to follow them.

Asking people to break the rules and constantly answering to the congressman's wife began to wear on me, so I went to the chief of staff, Greg Van Tatenhove, with carefully chosen words and asked "Do we work for the people of Kentucky or for Mrs. Lewis?" Without hesitating, he answered, "Appeasing Kayi is part of all of our jobs, particularly yours."

If that wasn't upsetting enough, when I read an article in *Roll Call* that documented a homeless man that netted more money than I by holding a can at the top of the escalators of the Capital South metro stop, I was devastated. I had probably passed that homeless man while getting off at that very stop. I called Daddy.

"The homeless guy begging at the metro makes more money than me!"

"So you want to be a homeless person?"

"Well, no."

"Then, go back to work." Daddy hung up.

All that did was make me madder. I wasn't ready to hear it. I turned to Mom. She was panicking. Four days later, care packages of soaps, toothpastes, paper towels, toilet paper and lotions arrived. Inside was a note letting me know that my Mom wanted to make sure I had more essentials than the homeless man. Mom didn't exactly see things Daddy's way. She agreed it was ridiculous the homeless man had more money than me and I was a Capitol Hill staff assistant.

But Daddy's words had hit their mark. I was still mad at him but he was right and I knew it. I had come to Washington because I wanted to work on the Hill. I got what I wanted. I was lucky to have it. Lots of people would be thrilled to have my job.

I thought of Jason, with his law degree, working two years as a staff assistant before there was an LA spot open for him in Whitfield's office. And just about every day job-seekers would come by unannounced to Congressman Lewis's office to drop off resumes. Almost all their resumes were impressive; a big list of Mr. and Mrs. Something's who did big things off the Hill.

Knowing all too well there was a real line of people who would gladly take my job and not wanting to be a homeless person, I vowed to give the best tours ever from that day forward. I decided whatever job or task I was assigned; I would do it with gusto. I would channel Ben Franklin "A job worth doing; is worth doing well." I secured lots of VIP tours for people—whether they wanted them or not. And I didn't care if I took all the White House ticket for our constituents. I gave personal tours of the Capitol with a new-found enthusiasm. A friend from back home, Paige, knew of my suffering as we had sizable long distance bills from our conversations. She'd heard from my family about my turnaround and shortly after a package arrived. Inside was a tasteful yet colorful patriotic scarf with instructions for me to "wave it enthusiastically" on my tours so people could find me. I couldn't quite bring myself to do that, but I did drape it around my neck.

And while I am not sure anyone in the office cared that I was leading the best tours of my life, the people receiving took notice. They thanked me profusely with handwritten notes following their trips to Washington D.C. A few families even sent me flowers. But the chief of staff, Greg, demanded that I throw them away because they violate the House gift ban. I wanted to let the flowers die then throw them away but he frowned upon that idea. Another family sent a $20 gift card thanking me. Greg insisted I return it.

The "gift ban's" intent was to stop people from influencing legislation. No one was trying to influence anything by sending me these small gestures of thanks. They knew I had no such influence. But Greg, whose job had all sorts of perks that our constituents might have frowned at, made sure to put that law degree of his to good use – especially when it was at my expense. I learned that the higher up you are, the more rules you are allowed to break.

Right or wrong, this is the way things worked. Greg had the final decision in all matters as the Congressman was usually nowhere to be found when these types of things happened. And it was Greg who set the tone in the office with there being two sets of rules—one for the chief of staff and one for the rest of us. Morale was low.

Most mornings Greg made his first appearance around 10 am or 11am announcing he had been golfing "for work." The rest of the office was required to start our days no later than 9am. With my day starting at 8:30am, to make sure the lights were on, the mail sorted, the temperature adjusted at a comfortable setting and the office was "ready" for the staff. Greg usually "headed out for lunch" shortly upon arriving for the day, while most of us ate at our desks.

You might think these small sacrifices would add up and be rewarded, but not so. Greg made sure to let me know it didn't pay off. Like the time he told me I was "so good at being staff assistant" he would not promote me. Or the time he said "While I am confident you could do the press work you're asking to do, it's more important for us to have you physically sitting out front." I wondered why I couldn't just sit out front and be given more responsibility.

Greg did pass along to me a Kentucky Derby poster he didn't want that had been given to him or the Congressman. My Mom had it framed beautifully and shipped back up to me at the office, instead of my house. "Had I known it would look that good, I might have kept it for myself." Greg told me.

During my six-month review, I asked "So, what you're saying is you have no complaints, you like my work, but that doesn't matter?" Greg didn't respond. We spent the next few minutes bantering back and forth with logic left out of the room. It didn't matter to him that constituents sent glowing thank you notes of my tours and work.

While some may have been surprised that Greg later received a federal appointment, I was not one of them. His days were filled with constant networking for himself, rounds of golf, meals with lobbyist, and raising money for those that counted. As his employee, I wished he'd been more concerned with doing his job well. But Greg understood how things worked. He spent his time doing what would get him ahead. And he was good at that.

Greg even toyed with a run for Congress. But the spot was not open because Congressman Lewis had decided to break his term-limit pledge in the "Contract with America." Had Greg stayed though, Congressman Lewis would have tried to anoint Greg as his successor, like Lewis unsuccessfully did for his then chief of staff when he retired.

Finding a chief of staff who doesn't want to be a member of congress is practically impossible. So instead of spending their time doing what they should be doing for the congressman and constituents, they do what will increase their own power on the Hill. Greg was no different than anyone else. He was just more blatant about it. And make no mistake, his hard work paid off. He was one of the youngest federal judges ever appointed. He's a very powerful person.

Meanwhile Mom was concerned. In one of her packages she enclosed a note with the words "I am worried about you. I hope you like what you're doing." Well, I wasn't sure I did like what I was doing. But what I was sure about, is that I had worked hard to get on this Hill and wasn't ready to get off. Not yet.

But to be truthful, Mom wasn't the only one panicking—so was I. I'd been there six months, but to me it felt like six years. Since my hard work had gone unnoticed, how would I ever be more than a staff assistant? I couldn't spend my life giving tours.

So, I decided to see a career counselor. What I really wanted was to see how I measured up. Was I a winner or a loser?

Gary, a milquetoast-looking counselor who wore jeans and an untucked shirt, took a while to make his point, asking me questions and going on for so long that I felt compelled to interrupt him. "When are you going to give me some tests?" I asked.

"In your case, we're not."

"But that's why I am here!" I said.

But Gary knew exactly who I was and he didn't need a test to confirm. "You're impatient, not confused."

What's wrong with being impatient? I thought to myself. As Gary continued talking, I tuned him out thinking; he doesn't get me at all. We knew we didn't agree with each other and since our time was just about up, decided to politely part ways. While I didn't verbally announce to Gary, "I think you're a loser," he knew I thought it.

D.C. is a town of winners and losers. I wanted to be a perfect fit for this town even if I wasn't yet sure I fit into this world— or even wanted to. But I darn-sure wanted to keep that option open.

And so, I did. Seven days after my review with Greg, I left for a better position with Congressman Larry Combest's office. When I gave my notice, Greg simply said, "During your interview your pro-life answer always seemed squishy to me."

5 WAYS WASHINGTON WORKS

Congressman Larry Combest represented the sprawling 19th District of Texas and had a well-earned reputation of running an efficient office that endeared staff to never leave. It was well-known that he had one of the largest offices on Capitol Hill, a sign that he was powerful and established. I heard about Larry Combest in the halls of Congress long before I ever met him as the buzz was akin to that of a mythical Greek god. A quick-witted and sharp man, he was known for being unusually nice to his staff and had dreams of being the Chairman of the Agriculture Committee. I hoped it was all true.

After meeting many congressmen, I should have known by now that most are not the John Wayne characters I made them out to be—living giants, big and powerful in size and life. Still, I was not prepared when I actually met Congressman Larry Combest and discovered he was a youthful man, small in stature. Everything else about Combest's office was different from my past experience.

When I came on board Rob Lehman, a tall, thin, dark-haired fella who was a basketball star in his college days was the chief of staff. Combest, impressed more by Rob's intellectual talent, did the unthinkable and made Rob his chief of staff at 26. This kind of thing was unheard of as most every chief I had known had been on the Hill for a couple of decades. So, this congressman hired people he thought could get the job done rather than on irrelevant details. Most important to me, that act of Combest gave me hope I too could move up the ladder.

One of the first stories told to me in the office was about the time Rob mixed up his supper order at a Texas diner. Shortly after Rob became chief, Combest had him fly out to Texas, see the district, and get to know the people. Being unusually young for an important position and from Maryland, it would have been understandable if Rob were nervous.

"Just order a chicken fried steak was some advice Rob decided to take" said one staffer.

"But when it came time to order, he forgot what it was called" said another staffer laughing. "Rob asked for a 'steak fried chicken'— instead of a chicken fried steak," hardly finishing their sentences from all the laughter. As the Combest crew shared the familiar story, it was Combest himself laughing the hardest.

Having plenty of chicken fried steaks in my life, I didn't have to worry about messing up an order. I took this interaction to mean this office was a real team that worked and joked together, the chief of staff was a part of the team too—not above them. And the Congressman wasn't so intense that he knew how to laugh. All kind of normal stuff. At last, I found my place on Capitol Hill.

Answering constituent mail in a timely manner took up much of my time—this was before automatic email responses, blackberries, and iPhones. In fact, there were times when the staff in our office would wait impatiently for our turn at the fax machine to communicate with constituents. Wanting to move up the ladder and impress, I strived for a "zero" mail report each week, meaning no piece of mail was left on my desk.

Writing the Congressman's press releases, floor speeches, or talking to reporters, took up what was left of my time. Most of what I wrote or discussed was whatever the news "of the moment" was—and during my time, there was more breaking stories than I cared to endure.

"There's a mad-man running through the halls!" a police officers warned us. He told us to lock the office door behind him and wait for the police to tell us when it was okay. That crazy man made his way through the Capitol tunnels to Congressman Tom DeLay's Whip office. While Congressman DeLay wasn't harmed, we heard that his staff hid under their desks terrified, while that man shot and killed two police officers.

The officers were honored by their caskets laying in state in the rotunda. We all wondered what if it were us? What if it were Congressman Combest? Congressman Combest never showed fear, assuring his young staff that we were safe. I believed him.

"Washington D.C. is the murder capital of the country," people back in Kentucky would warn me when they came up to visit the nation's Capital. Many others would warn Mom in the post office or when they would see her out too. I conceded some. "Mom, it's only certain areas, like Anacostia. I'm fine on the Hill." So when the Combest crew was once again locked in our office because of a bomb scare, I was relieved Mom never had to hear about such. Sure, it was a 24-hour news cycle, but it was a slower one then and certainly no social media. Sitting, waiting in the office, more than ready for lunch, we were anxious to get an update. The police dogs did their job and we were pleased to learn it had "just been a scare" and no real bomb. The police did keep the street closed for a few days where we entered our office building as a precaution.

So maybe we weren't safe, just lucky. Either way, there was no reason to let Mom worry or anyone else back in Kentucky know about these things. Congressman Combest received a death threat on the office answering machine late one night that I was not allowed to hear. When I arrived at work the following morning, I learned that threatening a United States congressman is a big deal. It meant the Capitol Hill police and the FBI piled in our office. By the time the work day ended, we were told the man who threatened the life of Congressman Combest—our boss—was arrested. I breathed for the first day that day. As far as I know no one on Capitol Hill, the media, or anyone back in Texas ever knew what had gone down that day.

Today, I can't imagine any scenario where a congressman in a similar situation would not have asked me to "just call and let the reporters know I am okay, I am with my wife, and we were not harmed. That I am proud of the job our hard-working men and women in uniform did and through this unfortunate incident saw first-hand the stellar work of the FBI." Seriously. Today's elected officials are media junkies and desperate for a hit. Those kinds of stories are almost a guarantee hit in the media. It raises more questions than answers and gives elected officials a human-quality and sympathy with voters. But Larry Combest did no such thing. Instead, he made sure it wasn't a story. Rather than telling the people thank you via the media, he personally thanked those investigating. He tried not to worry or bother anyone.

A small and symbolic gesture, demonstrating Combest's common sense style was the way in which he approached staff parking assignments. Parking spots were one of those measures of if you'd made it. I worked months with never receiving one on the Hill. When I finally did, it was about a mile away in a dark, secluded area that appeared abandoned. It looked so creepy, I preferred taking the metro than taking my chances out there. The few times I did, I made sure to have keys in hand, ready to poke out an eye or dart quickly in my car in case a bad guy lurked out there. Before Combest, my experience had been the best parking space went to the chief of staff and the worst parking space for the staff assistant.

Combest assigned the farthest away spaces to the men and the closest spaces to the women, which meant I walked about a dozen steps from my car to enter the front door of the Longworth House Office Building— where I now worked. That parking spot was so close to the front door that it is now forbidden to park there for safety reasons. Now, the street's been permanently closed off to cars as a precautionary measure of potential anthrax and bomb threats.

So never having a perk before, much less a prime parking spot, I was pretty excited— but knew better than to get my hopes us. I reluctantly brought it to Lynn's attention. Lynn had grey hair and wore it short and high, was the matriarch of the office, guardian of all things Combest. "The Congressman is not going to be responsible for you or anyone else not making it safely to their car," Lynn said matter of fact. At that moment, Combest came through the door heading toward his office, over-hearing the conversation, and piped in "You have the right space. Enjoy it." With that, Combest went into his office and closed the door.

I couldn't understand and Lynn read my confusion. She elaborated, explaining they were more comfortable with the fellas, most who had more muscles than the females in the office, being able to handle themselves going further away to get to their cars. No one considered this sexist. From what I could tell, there was no animosity about the parking spaces either; it just seemed like the practical thing to do. Larry Combest did what was best for his staff, throwing seniority out the door when it did not make sense. There's not a lot of "practical" in politics so these were big things going on.

Combest did a lot of things that would seem routine in the business world but on Capitol Hill they stood out and even seemed out of place. Like making sure each of us had some working knowledge of our co-workers' responsibilities, allowing the office to avoid crashing to halt in someone's absence. He also allowed for time off and closed his office during the holidays as he knew his staff would be traveling a long distance to see their families to the places they called home. Such kind gestures from congressmen were unique. Some members (of congress) severely discouraged taking a day off. My friend Helen, who was now a L.D. in another office, made sure I knew how lucky I was to be working with Larry Combest. "I had to work as a staff assistant for two years before Congressman Bunning let me take a day off." I didn't know if Helen was exaggerating or not—but the point was I was darn lucky to be in that office. Mom agreed.

When Mom called, it was around 3pm in the afternoon. Rain fell hard and the darkness outside contradicted the real time and the weather matched what was to come. Something was horribly wrong. Mom didn't call me at work. Eerily calm and maybe even rehearsed, and without taking a breath, she said in one big run-on sentence "Your Father wasn't feeling well when he got back from the Cattlemen's' meeting in Colorado so he went to the doctor. They put some fluid in him. He needs to have heart surgery tomorrow. We're at Baptist (a hospital in Nashville.) Don't worry. The doctors say it's routine. No need for you to come in. Don't worry. No one expects you to be here. We know you can't make it." She says all this the way you would say "I baked a cake and put chocolate icing on it."

I don't ever remember an incident when Mom thought it was a good time to worry, panic, or anything else. It's who she is and the calmer she is, the worse the situation. My mind speeds ahead to the worst because this is the calmest I've heard her in my life.

Daddy turned 50 three months ago. While not a poster child of health, the words "bypass surgery" took me aback. I didn't know anything Daddy couldn't do. But now, he was being prepped for major heart surgery. His Daddy died of a heart attack. Everyone said my father's father died young, but he was a lot older than Daddy. Wasn't he? I didn't know what age he was come to think of it. Was my Daddy going to die?

Like Mom, I figured I couldn't fly in. I hadn't built up enough days. Heck, I didn't even know how many days I got yet. After getting off the phone, I sat in my chair just long enough to swallow down the lump that had formed in my throat while Mom spoke to me. I was going to beg Rob to let me go see Daddy. I don't remember a word I said but it must have worked because I took off on the first flight I could catch. I arrived early enough to see Daddy before he went in to surgery that morning. I kissed his forehead and whispered in his ear "You didn't have to do this to get me home." He smiled "Glad your home, Bear." Occasionally, Daddy called my sisters and me "bear."

We were like any other family waiting in these situations. We sat for long hours in silence. Made small talk and runs for caffeine. We didn't say it but all of us waiting expected Dad to die. When the surgeon came toward us, we braced ourselves. "Gene's out and recovering. He did sustain some damage to part of his heart, but that was to be expected," the surgeon told us. So, we breathed.

I wanted to know what "damage to his heart" meant and looked toward Mom, hoping she would speak up. I knew she wouldn't though and I didn't dare because in our family, we believe it's impolite to talk about un-pleasantries or to ask questions about our health. For me to ask the doctor would have betrayed Mom. So, my mouth remained shut.

I learned soon enough. The morning Daddy was supposed to be checking-out, they called Mom and I into a small windowless grey room. It was there I got my answer. They told us rather matter of fact "Gene went into arrhythmia this morning. Because of the damage he sustained in part of his heart, we weren't able to pull him out of it. He's dead." I suppose they had a job to do but if I were writing that doctor's speech, I would have written it differently. More softly.

My Daddy was dead.

I don't remember what I said to Lynn, only that she told me not to worry about anything and take as much time as necessary. They insisted. Much to my relief, Combest's office allowed me to mourn without the additional burden of worrying about the responsibilities of my job. This worked out well because burying Daddy took a really long time.

Usually when someone dies, there is a visitation, followed by a funeral, and then a graveside burial. Ours was the same. Kind of. After the service in which I gave the eulogy, the mourners watched the hearse slowly drive off from the church with our family following in a black limo. We told them it was a "family-only graveside service." Only we didn't have one. Daddy's body went back to the funeral home and we went back to our home to wait. We only pretended to have a graveside service as outside forces were not cooperating with us. During this awkward time, it was Lynn I would call. I couldn't talk to anyone in Hoptown as they weren't supposed to know.

I was so comforted by her voice and words, that I began calling her each day. She shared what was appropriate to the Combest team as she was the ambassador between the staff, Congressman, and me. Lynn was kind enough to take time from her always heavy workload and listen to my babbling. I won't ever forget it. Finally, three long weeks later, we did have a family graveside service.

Back in D.C., nobody in the office wanted to go to the State of the Union so I lucked out and got the ticket. I was only sixteen seats away from the First Lady, Hilary Clinton dressed in a bright coral suit, when I heard President Clinton give his State of the Union address. (Yes, I counted.) Throughout the evening, Mrs. Clinton nodded a lot in response to what her husband was saying. I thought it was a bit much until I realized the T.V. cameras cut to her, close up, constantly for her reaction.

The audience stood up—a lot. And clapped—a lot. Sitting was not an option as I looked around on standing ovation number two thousand. There were times when Democrats were not pleased with their democrat president and clapped softly. Sometimes, Republican members of congress didn't join in standing. I was confused as when to stand and when not. But then, I discovered it was based on Party and not personal beliefs. Mrs. Clinton was not the only one performing for the television that night.

While I was an enthusiastic attendee, I felt like the night would never end. I was ready to go home. I later learned it was one of the longest State of the Union addresses ever delivered. Still, I couldn't help myself—I was mesmerized by President Clinton's speech. When he was done, I concluded our Union was in great shape. And realized maybe I got the Combest ticket because it's a long night preaching, energizing the base, ups and downs, much like a good ol'fashioned tent revival.

When the evening concluded, people were running out the doors to be at the front of the taxis and private cars lining the streets. I too wanted out and joined the masses in picking up my pace, managing to crash into Joe Kennedy, a Congressman from Massachusetts and part of the notorious Kennedy clan. I had seen him many times, but only on C-Span, always dressed impeccably and looking just what I thought a congressman should.

Tonight, was no different. Wearing a gray pin-striped suit, expensive cuff links, and a violet tie—a look he pulled off effortlessly—I realized I was checking him out. Not just for his good looks, but mostly trying to study a man who had been making headlines for paying off his Church. The papers reported he wanted an annulment so that he could marry his former scheduler. Embarrassing myself, I finally got out an "excuse me" and rushed on my way.

Those days a lot of issues were pushed aside to talk about sex. Sex dominated the conversations and I wasn't equipped. When a reporter first called me about some woman I never heard of—Linda Tripp and a blue dress, I was ill prepared. Harshly, I preached to the reporter "You may not like Bill Clinton and I know we (Combest) represent one of the most conservative districts in the country, but I respect the office of the presidency. It's inappropriate for you to call me and ask me or the Congressman to comment on such things." Perhaps my Mom's "we don't talk about sex" growing up was kicking in. Or maybe I was still too wide-eyed in this world. Unfortunately, minutes later, the story the reporter told me about had been confirmed. It was all over the world. You know the one.

I fled to Lynn. "I need a few minutes with the Congressman right now. Please," asking, demanding, and begging. To get such a meeting Lynn needed more details. Spilling my guts, she opened the door to Combest's office and waived me in. Wasting no time, I blurt out "I made a mistake. A big one." Then, I continued—awkwardly explaining how I knew President Clinton had made past mistakes, but now in the office of the presidency I didn't think he would...and somehow I fumbled my way through. Managing to apologize for being the only person in the world who thought President Clinton was not having sex with anyone other than Mrs. Clinton.

Clammy hands, red-faced and all, I struggled to discuss the situation—with a man no less, my boss, a United States Congressman! Why'd the President do this to me? Combest put me out of my misery didn't make me verbalize the situation. Looking back, I bet he might even laugh about it. I do, now. Oh, but at the time, I felt silly and unsophisticated. Combest simply told me, with no anger in his voice, "Call the reporter back. Tell him the truth" as he handed me a hand scratched statement to read on his behalf. It said something like "when a man's personal business interferes with his public life, that's a problem." Tell reporters the truth was a lesson the Congressman taught me when others told me the opposite.

These "situations" were everywhere in Washington and I found them shocking. "Family values" congressmen were having affairs! It dominated happy hour conversations. Waiting for my cocktail at the popular Capital Grille bar, I surveyed the crowded room. In one of the booths with curtains slightly open, the Speaker of the House, Newt Gingrich, dined with Callista—a staffer on the Ag committee—in what appeared to be a romantic meal. One of the guys in my group looked at my face and said with exasperation "Oh, grow up!" and went on to explain everyone knows of the affair. But I didn't. Why I am told to "grow up" when I mention Gingrich's affair, but to be disgusted about Clinton's?

A reporter called me to do a story on "interns and staff." He was vague but I visited with him about my internship anyway as well let him interview the Combest interns. The reporter couldn't hide his disappointment on the phone, hearing us describing attending committee hearings, taking notes for the legislative staff, getting "Dear Colleague" letters signed, making copies, opening and logging in the mail. In other words, no extra marital affairs with the Congressman came out of anyone's mouth. This was Larry Combest's office after all.

Why weren't there more like Larry Combest? The good guys? I wondered how all these other members got elected so I asked one of the Hill entrenched at yet another happy hour. "How did they get to be a congressman?" Their answer? "They had a good campaign manager, I guess."

My lesson? The best person didn't always win—but the best campaigner did. Intrigued, I wanted to see what campaigns looked like and get in on the ground level. Maybe I could find more Larry Combest's to put in congress. Maybe I could be a difference-maker. My bags were packed! I would go to the state that needed the most help, the one where a litter campaign also serves as the unofficial state motto. Texas.

"Everyone is going to be in awe of you because now you will be able to say you live in Texas," my roommate said envious of me leaving D.C. to go back to her native Texas. When I told her not all people would be in awe, she looked at me in disbelief and asked "Like who?"

6 THE CONGRESSWOMAN

Y ou got here as quick as you could!" Texans said, discovering my real non-Texas heritage. Texans thought I needed an excuse for not being born in Texas. Most expected me to chime in with a "that's right" or "sure did," but even after fifteen years of living in Texas, I couldn't ever bring myself to do it, much less adopt what other non-Texans did by using the frequently heard line "Got here as quick as I could!"

"Texas-ness" is important in Texas.

Texans are a proud lot. Being a foreigner, a few things took a while to grow on me. "Don't Mess with Texas" is a litter campaign as opposed to the state motto. It appears most people do not realize this and go around saying it frequently or putting it on their pick-up trucks. Even Texas's Attorney General, Greg Abbot, made mention of the phrase in his campaign announcement for Governor saying "I didn't invent the phrase 'don't mess with Texas,' but I have applied it more than anybody else," (referencing that he's sued the Obama administration 27 times.)

The words "Hill country" are always followed by "God's country" which brings to every non-Texan's mind the Garden of Eden only to be especially disappointed because the Hill country is not green, but brown. Texans love it anyway. Whenever Texans are in doubt as to how to decorate their offices or homes they simply sprinkle "Lone Stars" and Texas flags around.

Texans think something in the 1800's is old and I giggle to myself as my Grandmother's church in Kentucky began before the country in 1774. My friends from the UK laugh at me thinking I know old as one of them has a chair that is 400-years old. Texans sometimes get carried away and think "Remember the Alamo" means they won it. All this was important institutional knowledge that I needed to overcome to make connections not just to voters, but to people, to Texans. I indoctrinated myself to be successful in Texas politics.

The Mullendore name carried stature as "an old Texas name" but despite being divorced, Kay used her married name of "Granger" instead. She was a daughter of a police officer but followed in her Mom's steps and taught school children. That is until Kay realized the challenges of raising three children on a teacher's salary. So, Kay Granger started her own insurance business and quickly found financial success. Kay, wore her hair blond and short to her head for a sophisticated, no-nonsense look. She was the Mayor of Fort Worth and now represented the city in Congress. Such a feat made her the first Texas Republican woman to serve in the United States Congress. Texans know their mayors, and Kay had more name recognition than the average member of congress, making her more popular than most.

Working for Kay Granger was a big deal and I knew it. I got the job over others who had interviewed because a former Combest staffer, Barry Brown, became her chief of staff. In politics, it's always who you know. When I started with Kay's campaign I didn't know my way around Ft. Worth or the district, much less my way around political campaigns. But Barry thought I would find my way around the 12ᵗʰ District of Texas just like I did on The Hill. And he was right.

Kay Granger impressed most she met, including me. She had an uncanny ability to be perfectly dressed for each and every meeting and event she attended. I would struggle in future years to get other members to do the same as her. If they were on a long flight, they snapped at constituents or maybe their remarks would suffer, and sometimes even show up a wrinkly mess. But Kay, she never made excuses and looked as people expected. The political world was different than the Hill policy world. Appearances mattered more. Not just what we said, but how long or short we said something. We talked about people "liking us" and people "liked" Kay Granger.

Once again, I felt lucky that I landed in her campaign office because working for a member of Congress is helpful in learning about the inner workings of campaigns. People approached me all the time willing to help me, to get close the person in power. It's not the same when someone is unknown and running for office.

It was during this time, I learned all about the infrastructure of the political Parties and the technical aspects. Thankfully, the people in the Party shared with me all kinds of insider information, gossip, and background details. Without them, it would have taken me years to learn this stuff. There are all kinds of layers of people; donors, door openers, and do-ers as we call them. Some of the most challenging and interesting are the "precinct chairs" that I had not encountered before. I made sure to meet them all.

I started with the precinct chairs because I felt they may be less intimidating than the other more influential donors and door-openers. I wanted to practice first. One of my first task assigned by Kay was to meet party activist and seek out future sign locations. Precinct chairs work directly with the Party, helping candidates win elections. Precinct chairs do this by making sure their area—the precinct—-turns out for an election. Each chair has their own tactic and a few secrets how best to go about turning out voters. Some go door to door or host a coffee while others mail personal letters or make phone calls. Now days, these people may still do that, but more than likely they would send an email, post on Facebook, or something to that effect. Regardless, it's retail politics.

To be successful in my job I needed these people and the information they wanted to share. That's why I got up the nerve to cold-called precinct chairs, all strangers to me, and asked for their advice. Apparently, they were used to "young punks" trying to tell them how it is so they found my advice-seeking refreshing. That's how I found myself riding around the district with these Republican Party faithful's.

Carolyn, a retired teacher of 30 years, hair just like Kay's, was a shorter, friendly, less reserved woman than Kay. She was a huge asset. As a precinct chair, she did not take her responsibility lightly. Volunteering to show me the ropes in Parker County, the county next to Fort Worth's, Tarrant, she suggested I "come on over." She told me "I'll introduce you to everyone you need to know."

This meant me getting up well before the sun, much earlier than my 8:30am work day at the campaign office began as it was about 40 minutes to Carolyn's. Lots of extra work was involved but I did it because I wasn't trying to be average, I wanted to impress Kay. I wanted to make sure I understood the inner working of retail politics and I did this until Carolyn thought she had taught me what I needed to know. My kamikaze crash course lasted a couple of weeks.

Pulling into Carolyn's driveway, she would come flying out her front door, jumping in my car, eager to direct me for the day. Taking me to every little diner in rural Parker County, where breakfast crowds showed up at dawn, Carolyn not only told me where to go, but what to order. I followed like an excellent sheep.

Just like me, Carolyn knew the importance of me fitting in and winning over these influential people. "Now, just go over the train tracks here and pull in around back. We're gonna go in and act like we don't know what we want." There was no pretending on my part. I really didn't know what I wanted to eat—I had never been to this place, much less seen the menu. Carolyn continued "Jim and his group will already be there. You're new. He'll want to meet you and ask some questions about Kay. If it goes well—and it will— Jim will invite us to join his group for breakfast."

Some days we would leave the diner with Jim and his group only to turn around –after they left—-pull right back in the parking lot to catch up with the second wave of breakfast goers talking politics. Even though we had just eaten, Carolyn would instruct me "Now, don't just order a fruit plate or something get the 'Texan' or something like that," Carolyn said. "You need to get a check." Back then, a check meant campaign contributions. "Or at least a promise they'll have Kay in their home, introduce her to their friends who will give you checks." And that's always the goal in campaigns. To get money.

As I drove, Carolyn would point out some rancher's or car dealers land and explain, "People look to see whose political signs he allows on his fence and that's who they vote for. I made notes of all her pointers. "Call him up!" she'd say. Other times Carolyn would share with me past rivalries and how to overcome those obstacles to get them to vote for Kay. Mostly, Carolyn made me an expert in grassroot campaigning. We formed a friendship over an excess of eggs, bacon, and biscuits that lasted many decades, delivering results, just like she did in my first days working for Kay.

Bob, also a retiree and a precinct chair, put me in his old, dirty, pick-up truck and drove me around northeast Tarrant County, a hotbed of primary voters. This area thought they were the step-child of Ft. Worth and thought deserved more attention from elected officials than they got. After a morning of downloading Bob's knowledge, that he only kept in his head, he'd treat me to lunch at Luby's, where they let him use his senior discount. Senior citizens dominated the precinct chair positions, not young twenty-somethings, that I had come to believe in D.C. were involved in politics.

Bob told stories while pointing out coveted intersections for political signs. "Your gonna have to get up in the dark to get that their spot. Maybe not sleep at all. It's worth it. Prime location," he'd warn me. It was a time when political sign placement was akin to prime commercial placement. That's why the chief of staff, Barry, flew down before the election to spend the entire night with me, driving to one coveted sign location to another. He knew Kay wouldn't be satisfied with my answers or map on the already hundreds of signs I had everywhere. She wanted nothing left to chance and wanted the most important person on her staff, Barry, to personally oversea the extra signs for early voting responsibility. We went to one intersection to another hammering up our signs. Barry let me reminisce Hill talk and we bonded over shared struggles we each had at times with Kay over a drink and meal before we'd start again the next day.

There were twenty-something Republican clubs in Tarrant County alone and about just as many in the other counties in Kay's district. Back in the day, these groups were known to conduct massive phone banks even flying to Iowa—on their own dime—to caucus during the race for president. But despite all the impressive grassroots work they did, their meetings were tedious, sometimes lasting half the morning, while others took up half the night. I struggled interest. In fact, I was tempted to skip it but didn't dare as this was a big voting group I needed on my side. On Kay's side.

The Fort Worth Republican Women, well-over a hundred members, knew how to get things done and every politician worked hard to woo them. They were the hardest group of all for me to win over as a few of their officers were still upset about Kay not "being Republican enough." In Kay's early political days, she was known more for being an "independent" and when it came time to run for Congress, some voters didn't know if she would run as a Republican or Democrat. Both parties courted her. While those days were far behind, they weren't to Ft. Worth Republican Women. I learned a staffer's job is to clean up after their boss's mess and to jump through hoops. I not only won this group over, I was asked to become one of their vice presidents. In the process, they became Kay Granger's biggest volunteer force.

Meeting interesting Republican characters with abundance of stories, learning the district, and gaining knowledge about retail politics were some of my earliest and happiest memoires of working for Congresswoman Granger.

For as interesting and exciting as it was, my job was much more challenging when it came to interacting with the Congresswoman.

It was no secret that Congresswoman Granger blew through staff as many didn't wanted to stay for long. She liked to micro-manage every aspect of everything, had a temper, worried too much about what others thought, and in general had a chip on her shoulder. She called the office constantly to make sure my co-worker, Michael, and I were working, even though most days neither of us left our chairs except for bathroom breaks. We both frequently skipped meals or simply ate at our desk. We were always working.

Office policy, set forth by the Congresswoman, meant time consuming memos to ask permission for every little decision or to address questions Kay had about some matter. She didn't delicate much and instead attempted to be involved in too many details which I found to be quite inefficient. When someone said to us "tell Kay I said hi," these things had to be addressed in memos because if she saw someone and they mentioned to her they had told a staffer to say "hello" and we hadn't put it in a memo, she'd be infuriated. I couldn't understand why this was such a big deal. The reality was that everyone we ever saw pretty much associated us with the Congresswoman, so hardly anyone didn't want to pass on a "hello."

When I asked to have an email address, Kay responded by saying "send me a memo why you think the campaign needs email." I thought it was painfully obvious that staff should have email addresses so that constituents could contact us in a more efficient manner. Because she was an impressive person–successful in business and in Congress, she quickly secured a seat on the powerful House Appropriations Committee. She thought that meant that no one else could offer up a good idea or suggestion. She also thought it gave her the right to dominate one's life.

Congresswoman Granger didn't allow for time off despite one's work load being completed. She liked for us to be "on call" in case "something happens." This meant all our long hours allowed for no vacations. She barked orders constantly and kept the entire team, including me, on high alert for what seemed like most days pointless. Critics used the "b" word to describe her but

I didn't think her being a woman had anything to do with her being difficult, demanding, or demeaning. What I was learning is this is life working for a member of Congress.

Congresswoman Granger was what I would later learn is what personal staff experience when working for a member of Congress. Everything is always important and everything is always a priority and your priority should be them. Like others, I quickly found myself not wanting to hang around either. Like so many staffers, I used the time to build my own network, for what I didn't know.

What was toughest for me though was that Kay entrusted me with a great bit of knowledge and responsibility, but then hated to be questioned. But most elected officials don't like to be questioned. I learned the hard way that Kay preferred to surround herself by people who told her what she wanted to hear, a source of uneasiness and frustration for me. "Leslie, we are only supposed to be Kay's appendages," Barbara, the district director, would instruct me when I would offer up what Kay and her referred to as "new and different ideas." Barbara and Kay were about the same age and had Barbara not worked for Kay, they probably would have hung out together as friends.

Barbara, like Kay, prefer I keep things smooth by always agreeing. "Just think of yourself as an extension of Kay—just be her arms and legs, not her head," Barbara would council me as if I were a kindergartener instead of a campaign manager. "Barbara, I have a mind! Ideas! I refuse to be just appendages!" I would protest with righteous indignation, determined not to be held back.

Depending on the day, our conversations usually ended with Barbara in tears as I was like a misbehaved child that she couldn't discipline. But I didn't much appreciate the district director, stepping out of her bounds to come to the campaign office. Those worlds of tax payer dollar and campaign dollars are mandated by law to be separate but no one seemed bothered by that except for me.

Our "little talks" as Barbara would refer to them would come about when I would question what I thought was best for the campaign. For example, whether it was a good use of campaign funds to fly -in a well-known pollster from the northeast—first class. I thought we had plenty of qualified Texas-based pollsters. Besides, this pollster had expensive taste in hotel and dining. He charged the campaign excessively for his couple of days of consulting.

Another time, a direct mail guy tried wooing me for some of the campaign's business by treating me to lunch at Chili's, spending the lunch hour telling me how great he was and if I wasn't in awe of him that I should be. The mediocre lunch and braggadocios talk didn't woo me enough to change my frustration of how I thought he was a con. I literally could look at a piece of mail and know it was his work. And not in a good way. My co-worker, Michael, agreed. Together, we strongly recommend Kay not use him in the campaign. We were vetoed to the detriment of her campaign. Kay had already made up her mind and wasn't listening to anything we had to offer.

Just as Michael and I expected that direct mail fella billed the campaign for an expensive photo shoot and other outrageous expenses. Worst of all, Michael did most of the work. Only the direct mail fella got over-compensated and Michael got his usual pay. The direct mail guy used the same piece for two-decades, just replacing Kay's photo with different candidates.

Kay tasked me with planning her election night party and she wanted it to be grand. I made sure all the Ft. Worth elite made an appearance, along with a room full of media. The watch party was elaborate in regards to campaign-standards with never-ending hors d'oeuvres, drinks flowing heavily. Everything taking place at a hip just-opened white tablecloth restaurant in Ft. Worth's Stockyards. Big screens were brought in for the occasion. The line of cars for the valet filled the street as Ft. Worth's who's who waited to get into Congresswoman Kay Granger's party. Unfortunately, the Congresswoman barely got to enjoy her party before being whisked away on Lockheed's plane to Austin, that I had arranged, so she could wait for the presidential election results with Governor George W. Bush in Austin.

The results were not clear the next day so Kay returned to Ft. Worth in the early morning hours. Not even 24 hours had passed from Election Day when my co-worker, Michael, announced, "I am going to pay the restaurant today." I didn't see it was necessary to pay so soon and Michael figured as much because before I could ask him about it he continued, "I don't think Kay is going to pay them and I want to make sure they get their money." Michael knew Kay better than I did as he had interned with her while in college at Texas Christian University and continued in the district office, and was now with the campaign. Michael was right, but at the time, I didn't know that politicians were notorious for not paying their bills.

Despite my workload, I wanted more responsibilities and told Kay so. Much to my satisfaction, she agreed. I began doing everything from raising money, representing her at meetings, to assisting her with her Christmas party. Kay liked parties. The Christmas party went off just as she imagined—beautiful invitations, tons of people, tables filled with food, and servers coming by to make sure guests were not empty handed. She got just as upset with me as she did Michael when it came time to pay the bills. I refused to agree that campaign funds should be used to pay for the Christmas decorations. This was a big deal because Kay didn't hold back in her decorating decisions running up $17,000 tab. As beautiful as everything was, I found it hard to believe fake Christmas trees, shiny ornaments, and greenery could cost so much. But they did. Or, was she just paying a friend too much money for their services?

Did the other staff believe, as I did, that the only reason the decorations were so lavish was because Kay thought she could get her campaign to cover the costs? Did they agree with me that she would have never spent that much of her own money? Or was it some kind of pay-back? I didn't know because not one person piped up. I stood my ground anyway and received a tongue lashing for it. This was my first lesson in learning that politics rewards those who agree with the status quo.

The next day Kay sent Barbara over to the campaign office to have one of our "little talks." Still, no one cared that the taxpayer funded district director was so involved with campaign. This bothered me as the law is clear. Barry, the chief of staff, was worn down from these re-occurring situations and "little talks" so he was fine with letting someone else handling things.

"How did you learn of the costs associated with the party?" Barbara asked me with a raised eyebrow. Flabbergasted by the unspoken insult that I had done something untrustworthy, I barked at Barbara, "Kay sent me a memo asking me to have the bookkeeper pay the bill! That's how I know." I continued "Kay's only upset because I insisted the invoice not be paid. It's misuse of campaign funds!" I said, speaking sharply. Michael agreed.

I believed as campaign manager my job was to protect Kay—even if it was from herself. I would tell myself things like "Kay is just so busy she doesn't have time to pay attention to every little detail." Or, "Kay works so hard she just doesn't keep up with all the rules. How could she?" For a while, I believed what I was telling myself. I ignored that a law-maker should know the laws. So, I kept working and kept doing. But deep down, I thought these situations were coming up more frequently. Kay was justifying making small decisions that pushed the limits. Was she making them consciously or unconsciously? I didn't know.

I also didn't know that Kay was just operating like a lot of other members of Congress with power. District directors campaigning, trying to use campaign funds for non-campaign expenses, and simply letting other people pay for things are common happenings for members of Congress as it is all too easy to get away with it. But why was I sticking with her? Just like the voters, I liked her. For now, I protected Kay. But no one was protecting me.

Like so many times in the past, I tasked myself with a job nobody was hiring for. After the Christmas incident, Kay excluded me from more and more meetings. But despite not being in any meetings, I heard the talk of Kay having her son and daughter-in-law join her at President Bush's inauguration on Burlington Northern Santa Fe's plane. When I heard about it, I called Barry. I could feel his exhaustion through the phone line. He used to say years after working for Kay "if I get cancer, I want to work for Kay Granger again, as it was the longest year of my life."

We discussed that federal law says the campaign must compensate fair market value–and that was an exorbitant price tag. I don't think it had always been that way, but probably someone figured out that members of Congress like to travel by private jets. No one wanted the donors or anyone else for that matter to know how much we spent on such. It could cause a problem down the road that we may have to answer to.

I suppose Barry called Barbara to remind her that we couldn't do that because I had another surprise visit that afternoon. Barbara was not the only staffer who asked me to keep quiet. "Why do you always ask questions?" one would ask. Another would say "Can't you just act like you never heard about it?" And so, when I saw the Granger family at the inaugural festivities in Washington D.C., including the Black Tie & Boots party, I did not ask how they arrived.

Becoming more astute in politics, I knew in the scheme of things, the incidences weren't "big deals." They weren't sex and family value scandals. I brought them up because I thought it was the right thing to do. I wasn't sure if some staff didn't know the campaign laws and that's why these issues kept coming up or they didn't care. Maybe because I was new, I was trying to make sure I followed the law. But when Kay's opponent accused her of using insider knowledge to get rich, I knew THAT was a big deal. According to him, she purchased a building in downtown Ft. Worth (which she lived in), used her position on the powerful Appropriations Committee to appropriate funds for an Intermodal Transportation System to be located just across the street from her building. The results? Kay's brilliant real estate choice made her richer.

Oh, sure, her opponent accused her of a lot of other things too—things I didn't quite understand. Like structuring her house under "Jones Street Investments" and having her son rent it. (The house was a duplex.) Really, I didn't remember what all that meant, other than there were several stressful days because of "Jones Street Investments." I didn't tell a soul that Kay had plans of moving her insurance office and her campaign office into the ground floor of her house and making money from them too. "It's not illegal" was a phrase being thrown around often. There were attorneys and closed door meetings that I was no longer allowed in.

The "liberal" Ft. Worth paper even did a potentially damaging piece on Kay, but fortunately for us, most Republicans refused to read that paper. If the story made its way into the *Ft. Worth Star Telegram*, we may just have been in trouble. But as luck would have it, Kay met with editor and he agreed the story shouldn't run. No one ever talked about Kay using insider information again. Meanwhile, her attorney issued a statement saying it was all his fault as he did the paper work all wrong and he was already working to rectify his mistakes. Nothing was Congresswoman Kay Granger's fault.

When bad things happen to a member of Congress, someone else is usually responsible or at least blamed. The standard lines from the member is "Thank you for bringing this to my attention. So and so is no longer with the campaign and this will not happen again on my watch." And while no one used those exact words that day, I would hear them spoken many times in the future. That day everyone was satisfied, including me. But, when the opportunity came to work on Jeb Hensarling's campaign, I jumped ship.

7 THE FAITH, FAMILY, AND FREEDOM CANDIDATE

Jeb Hensarling, a short squinty eyed man whose ambition preceded him, was a staffer for numerous years for Senator Phil Gramm, a kind of political hero to me. Jeb had led Gramm's unsuccessful presidential campaign and now, at 43, he was running for Congress. Boldly, I decided I was going to call up Jeb Hensarling and tell him I wanted to be his campaign manager. Like members of Congress, I too had an ego. Knowing no one would be working late on a Friday, I called anyway. I was on a mission.

The phone was ringing, then an answer, and instead of "hello" the voice on the other end said "Jeb Hensarling!" Confused and shocked, I realized Jeb answered the campaign phone himself. Quickly getting myself together, I began talking just like a skilled telemarketer. "Mr. Hensarling, my name is Leslie Sorrell and I am Congresswoman Kay Granger's campaign manager. Your race for Congress is the most exciting in Texas and one of the most important in the country. I want to be a part of it!" I declared, imagining an audience jumping up from their seats in an "Amen" or "Yes!"

With such a sappy declaration, Jeb began the "thanks, no thanks speech" but then stopped. "What would you want to do?" he asks and I answered without hesitating "campaign manager." Jeb quickly informed me he already had that handled. My gut told me something was going on as he could have hung up but we were still on the phone.

Jeb's reputation of being a successful fundraiser and love of money had been a joke among politicos, so I piped up "What about money? Do you have all the campaign money you want?" I ask coyly, knowing that no one ever has all they ever want. Especially this Jeb Hensarling. Literally over the phone, I could see his ears perk up. "You want to raise money?" he asks and then says "Most people don't like that." Not missing a beat, I answer "You bet. I do." And we scheduled a meeting the next business day and I came on board shortly afterwards.

It surprised people but I did like raising money. I liked trying to figure out the right words, the right information, and successfully getting people to let go of their money. I read every document the campaign had to learn Jeb's voice. In the Combest office, we had a policy to say something positive to the constituent and to let them know we were like them. So we'd say, "Like you, I agree we need to reform the IRS" and then we could talk about what we disagreed about. Buzz words we used were "folks" and "West Texas values." In Kay Granger's office, our phrases were "common sense solutions," "results," and "comes home every weekend." After reading everything I could access, I discovered Jeb's campaign talking points were:

"We did what no one thought was possible, beating five credible opponents."

"Jeb's a businessman" This one was worth noting because Jeb was actually a career bureaucrat, but we were in Republican politics and we needed Jeb to be a businessman, so we said it a lot. In politics, if you keep saying something enough, eventually it becomes true to people.

Jeb did work for a while for billionaire Sam Wyly and Sam Wyly was a businessman. So, that meant Jeb was one too, right? Mr. Wyly wrote letters on

Jeb's behalf, making a joke about Christmas grapefruits and asking for money. Senator Phil Gramm wrote a letter for Jeb too. He said in his "I'd trust Jeb with my life…and the life of our nation."

This was the ammunition that I needed to get money from everyone I met. Jeb had tasked me with what my friend, Kay Granger's chief of staff, Barry Brown, called "an impossible task."

"Leslie, I appreciate your calling, but I even went back and talked to a bunch of guys up here and they said Jeb is setting you up to fail. There is no way you can get to $430k for the June 30 report. I mean, it's the middle of May and the campaign doesn't even have $40k." I asked Barry for sympathy and money now that he was a big-time lobbyist as I had to raise over $23k a day and this was before Super-PACs, which meant I could only ask for up to $1k at a time. I thought if I reached the "impossible task" Jeb would be impressed.

I worked up a strategy to meet Jeb's goal and it required me to arrive at the office at dark to use that time for paperwork to not take away from precious phone time. At night, alone at the office, I studied names of donors, how much they had given in the past—if any— and how much more they could give (in regards to federal limits.) If I ran into someone—anyone—I made sure to know if they had given to Jeb, to thank them, and ask for the amount left they could still give. I memorized people and what they had given.

Intense and dedicated, I knew if Jeb didn't win, I didn't have a job. This race was important to more than just Jeb and me though. Being that this congressional race could go to a Democrat or a Republican—it was an open seat. Just about every important person one could think of in the Republican Party made an appearance for Jeb at his fundraisers.

Karl Rove, the man who was called the "architect of the President (Bush)" came to Dallas. While it was one of our most successful events, it took a while to get it going because no one knew who he was. Jeb and I thought everyone knew Karl Rove. People in politics operate in a bubble. "Seriously," I told Jeb, "Everyone is impressed after I explain who Karl Rove is, but they really don't know who he is." My solution? Put his bio on our invitations "There are not enough hours for me to call everyone and explain who Karl Rove is before getting their money. I need them to see he's a big deal before I call." Jeb agreed and we went through the painful process of having the White House sign off on an invitation.

While I know there is a lot of hate for Karl Rove, I am not one of them. Not because I know him—I don't'—but because when he came to the posh Crescent Club in Dallas, he simply flew in on a Southwest Airlines flight, rented a tiny red car, and drove off to Crawford to meet President Bush afterwards. I would have thought all the passengers would have surrounded him to visit, but no, he said he's pretty much under peoples' radar. I took note. I'd rather be the important person behind the important person because they are out of the fishbowl.

Karen Hughes, Counselor to the President, came in for a luncheon for Jeb and just about every Republican Congressman in Texas joined forces to help Jeb win. Rumor was we might have a shot at getting the First Lady, Laura Bush, to come to Dallas and help Jeb too. While Jeb wanted the First Lady to campaign for him, he was equally concerned that if the opportunity came to us at the last minute we wouldn't be prepared. To address his concerns, I prepared a checklist for the entire office titled "Six Day Notice Fundraiser Check List for First Lady Event for Jeb." Everyone knew what had to happen, Jeb most of all. It turned out we didn't need it that day, but in the future, my firm and staff were masters at putting on a fundraiser with less than a week notice.

Working for "family values" people does not mean observing the Sabbath. We used that day to get ahead. Like most intense campaign staff, I didn't have much of a life outside of work. I did make attempts. After a long Saturday of block-walking, I attend a Halloween party only to have one of my friends "whisper" to the other of my friends about me, "She looks so tired." I responded, "That's because she is."

Almost every night, Jeb had campaign events. I had already missed a "required" Junior League meeting to attend an "Aggies for Jeb event." Not long after that, I missed another League meeting. It was a fundraiser with Jeb and the Vice President of the United States, Dick Cheney. When I first told Lori, our "pledge director" that I needed to miss another meeting because the Vice President was coming in for Jeb she snapped at me "Vice President of what?"

"Of the United States." I answered meekly, realizing "regular people" are not obsessed with politics and its players. "We have an event with the Vice President of the United States at work and I would like to invite you— as my guest." I hadn't told Jeb this yet, but I figured some people give money and wouldn't be able to attend, so I could fill those seats with Junior League girls. Then maybe, they would get off my back for missing a few meetings. "In fact," I told Lori, "I have a table for you if you would like to bring some friends." I was attempting to offer an olive branch to Lori, but I came up short again. "I can't miss a meeting! And you shouldn't either!" she snapped at me.

I was under the wrong impression Lori may want to see the Vice President and would deem that worthy of missing a Junior League meeting. Even though I didn't get kicked out of the Junior League that day, that's when I knew my days in the League were numbered. I couldn't miss any more meetings they told me, "No matter what." Since the election would be over soon, I figured I'd be okay. But instead of attending the Junior League on Monday night in January, I could be found in Kentucky delivering the eulogy of my Grandmother, the one who beat Woodrow Wilson and was the first woman to hold that office. "Well, you shouldn't have missed those two earlier meetings." I was told. I figured that's what happens when you try to get involved outside of politics.

The event for Jeb with Vice President Dick Cheney, held at Union Station, impressed most of those that attended. Red, white, and blue bunting covered the enormous windows making the place even grander than before. All the tables were filled and most importantly so were the campaign coffers.

In five months, I led the efforts of raising over $1.2 million. In 2002, those were huge numbers. Not only did I get my bonus, Jeb became a congressman. On Election Night, Jeb thanked God, Senator Gramm, and me.

Jeb Hensarling, soon to be Congressman Hensarling, knew what his next step was going to be, but I didn't. After all this time, I still don't know what to do the day after the election. But that year the pressure was on, as I was now without a job.

What kept playing through my mind, was what happened just a few weeks before the November election at Jeb's event with Vice President Cheney. A brief exchange I had with a political consultant in attendance asked me "What's your role? (in the campaign)."

"I'm responsible for raising the money," I said. He started laughing. "Not me. I am just a spender," he said braggadociosly. All I could think of then and now is pathetic. Candidates hire him to be "just a spender." I was especially glad he was not the "spender" on Jeb's campaign. His disregard for not understanding how hard it is to raise money means he spends with no appreciation.

This "spender political consultant" reminded me of other consultants that promised campaign staff and candidates "if you would just raise more money I could win this thing." That line always got me. What I heard them saying was they are not smart enough to figure out how to think strategically to spend money, develop a budget, or readjust their plan. Instead, they want to take the easy way out and throw money at everything and hope something works.

A campaign may have a million-dollar budget and successfully raised $850k, and some consultant would say to me "we need more money!" I wanted to fire back "Figure out a way to make it work! Losing is not an option!" But I knew these thoughts weren't welcomed by most candidates. But Jeb, well, he welcomed that kind of thinking. So maybe other did too. As I debated what the heck I was going to do for the millionth time in my life, my Mom's words echoed through my head "you can do whatever your heart desires."

Still intoxicated with campaign adrenaline, I made the rash decision to start my own political consulting firm. I felt passionately there were not enough consultants that had an appreciation for how hard it is to raise money. More than once a consultant didn't give a second thought to how hard I worked for those precious campaign dollars. When someone has no regard for how hard it is to secure funds, then they have little regard for the way they spend those funds. I detested Republican consultants and Party folks that would go into debt, not practicing what they preached on fiscal responsibility. I wanted to show the world my firm would be different.

To be different, I knew I needed a committed group of true believers who dreamed of working in our political system, devoted to our country, and committed to helping good people serve in office. Our own "special forces" unit devoted to political campaigns and causes. I didn't want to be like all the consultants that appeared risk averse—only taking "sure wins." I wanted a team that would work for an underdog and not be afraid that someone just got elected and didn't have any money in their campaign account. If consultants only stood up for what they believe in when it's convenient, they could never effect change. I vowed that my firm wouldn't be afraid to work with the candidate that would make the best public servant—even if it meant starting from nothing. We'd be the David of David and Goliath!

So, Jeb Hensarling was my first Congressional client, quickly followed by Dr. Michael Burgess. Two clients and growing, I hadn't yet found time to buy a computer, name the business, and open a bank account. Scrambling to stay ahead of all the moving parts going on in my new life, I learned to work longer and live with less sleep than before, pulling 17 hour days.

But it wasn't just Jeb and Dr. Burgess, there were an influx of fresh energetic freshman Congressmen in Texas. We were all start-ups and the thrill of starting our organization and theirs from the ground up pumped us full of energy.

"You always fall in love with them—in the beginning," Mom would say to me when I would tell her about a potential client. And it's true. I fell under some type of spell. They shared with me their inner most dreams and goals unpolished and unrehearsed. It's the most real part of the process when they open up about what all they want to do. And they want me to be the one to make it happen. It's our honeymoon.

I gotta tell you though most people aren't wooed by Jeb Hensarling. He comes across abrupt at times and as if people are wasting his time. More than a few people have told me they worried about Jeb's ego getting too big. Everyone calls him slick. Jeb was known on the campaign trail to come up to people working or volunteering on his campaign and say "Am I paying you?"

Despite Jeb's lack of social skills, I liked him. I thought we'd be a team like Senator Phil Gramm and he were—and still are. The story goes that Senator Gramm started out as an economics professor at Texas A&M and Jeb was a student of his. Somewhere along the way Congressman Gramm ran for the U.S. Senate and Jeb came on board with the campaign team, ran his district office, and eventually ran his presidential campaign. Then, Gramm campaigned for Jeb. They were an all-star team.

Jeb and I were too. He taught me his fundraising success and I soaked it up and ran with it becoming laser focused in Jeb's goals being my goals. Jeb asked a lot and I gave a lot. From day one, he paid me for fundraising for his campaign, but expected me to do much more. More than once, I walked door-to-door with Jeb. I recruited a bus full of people to campaign out in East Texas for a fellow Republican running for Congress so Jeb could take some of the credit when the fella won. On Sundays, I would be found celebrating the christening of his first child with Jeb and his family, driving him to the airport, or simply meeting to get ahead of Monday.

During the Christmas season, I threw parties at the house of Jeb and his wife, Melissa. The house could hold 50 comfortably, so it was me who decided which group of people would best mix and mingle together and invite them. Then, we'd host another party for 50, so that their neighbors, supporters, and grassroots activists could all be included. The parties were an open house style and only lasted a few hours. We'd have a short break and refresh everything before the next round would begin. In between the different parties, I vacuumed. I did all this because I figured Jeb would do the same for Phil Gramm.

Jeb told me that Phil Gramm only entrusted him to write hand-written notes to big donors. Jeb entrusted me as well. I enjoyed this task because I thought Congressmen should thank donors more often and take time to send notes without asking for money. I took great liberties and churned out more notes than Jeb ever asked for because I knew when you ask for advice, you get money.

When I was meeting with a big donor he pulled out a hand-written note that he saved. The big donor shared how much it meant to him that Jeb "would just thank me for no reason." I reminded him that he helped out in the campaign early on and that counted. "Yeah, but this really meant something because he hasn't forgotten." The big donor went on to say how the note especially meant a lot to him because of Jeb's reputation as only caring about money. He then offered to host a fundraiser in his home and raise $25k. I left the donor's office beaming with pride that I had made his day. He had made mine too.

It wasn't always that easy. Just the opposite, each day is tough because even though many of our clients were congressmen they literally had zero name recognition. No one thought their jokes were funny—yet. Getting a dozen or so people in a room to hear what they had to say felt like a herculean task. There's a day that always comes that I dread, and it's when nobody shows up. But that's not as bad as when one person shows up. (When no one shows up, no one knows that but the congressman and you.) It happens and you're embarrassed.

Brian, Jeb's chief of staff, and I came up with the idea of simply inviting people to join the Congressman for dinner. We called our plan "Seabiscuit" because no one thought Seabiscuit could do it and no one thought Brian and I could raise as much money as Jeb wanted us to. We'd tell these people, "We don't want you to give now. We want you to get to know Jeb and decide for yourself. If you do, we want you to be a supporter for Jeb's entire career." We only invited select high net worth individuals. We were going for small and intimate. Skeptical on the results, Jeb agreed to the plan anyway.

Most of the time, these dinners worked brilliantly with eight to 16 people attending, leaving with promises of lots of money to come. These dinners worked so well that we had twenty-one of these in one month. But then, it poured rain one night. In Texas, with rain comes traffic. Jeb and I didn't think anyone would come and were just about ready to head out when our worse fear happened—one person showed up—Mr. Lattimore, a well-known Republican donor who drove all the way from Colin County, north of Dallas, to have supper with Jeb.

"No one showed up?" Mr. Lattimore looked around. "Heck, I don't want you to stay because of just me." I looked at Jeb and it is one of many horribly uncomfortable campaign moments that just happens. "Actually, Mr. Lattimore, we were expecting a few more people, but only three and they called regretting they didn't want to get out in this rain." Our room held a maximum of ten, so this could have been believable, but I lied about the three people so Jeb wouldn't have to. Mr. Lattimore offered more than once to "just go home." Not one of the three of us questioned why a congressman's time is supposed to be worth so much more than our time.

Not long afterwards, Mr. Lattimore had his assistant send a maxed-out check. (A maxed-out check is the largest amount allowed by federal law. At this time, it was probably about $2k.) Mr. Lattimore agreed to max out each cycle and that year gave much more to the National Republican Congressional Committee (NRCC) on Jeb's behalf.

Brian and I worked together to try and meet Jeb's goals. So that our conversations wouldn't cut into valuable phone time with donors, Brian called me early each morning interrupting what used to be my peaceful morning walks with my dog, Meg. Brian and I discussed ways to bring in more money. Brian did this because we both made more money if we reached Jeb's goals. He also couldn't call me from the congressional office, as it was important to us to follow the law and keep tax-payer and campaign monies separate.

We had big goals. June 30 is a magical date in the political world by which you are judge. It's the Federal Election Commissions (FEC) deadline for filing the campaign reports required by law. We were only two thousand shy of our goal. Thankfully on June 29, Bo Pilgrim had agreed to give money, but for us to meet the deadline he had to overnight the checks. He chose to use UPS's overnight service. Mr. Pilgrim told me to expect $4k. Since he had reached his federal limit, it would be from different family members. His $4k would put us $2k over the goal. It was close, but it counted.

Much to my disappointment and Brian's, UPS lost the envelope and it didn't arrive until the fifth of July. We therefore couldn't include the monies on our June 30 report although we had until July 15 to file the FEC. The campaign still could cash the checks and take the money. I was physically sick over this as Jeb said he couldn't pay me my bonus because I didn't reach the goal. Brian thought that was too harsh and I should receive it. We were successful, but we weren't. And it was UPS's fault, I thought. Even though I didn't receive any bonuses from Jeb, the NRCC was impressed and rewarded him with a pair of custom-made cowboy boots.

But UPS being late was not the worst of it. Later that year, I retired Jeb's personal campaign debt of $325,000, along with putting over $500,000 in his re-election account, but he felt it was "time to make a change." I had worked so hard and produced results and was disappointed that this is how it was going to play out. Not understanding, I raised concerns. "I know I didn't reach the goals, but we weren't far off. You have tons of campaign money like you wanted, and you didn't even have to pay me any bonuses." I thought he got the best of both worlds. His financial goals met—only a few days late—and he didn't' have to pay for the results.

Jeb gave his side. I continued. "Maybe I made it look too easy. I don't give you all the gory details of how hard it is because I figure I shouldn't bother you with them. All my work is done on the front end. Now, that it may be a little easier you're going to fire me and just let someone else take over the foundation I laid? To this day, the people I put together and introduced and created his Congressional Council and Inner Circle are still with him, giving financially. "You're firing me now?" But as I asked the questions, I realized my usefulness to him was complete.

Jeb explained "It's not personal." I cringed at the words. Because of course it was personal. When he knew, he hadn't satisfied me with a logical explanation, he brought God into the meeting. "I prayed over this, Leslie." I hate it when elected officials think God is always on their side, so I spoke up and countered "I prayed too!" Jeb wasn't expecting that response as his face said he was taken aback. I thought it was one thing for Jeb to decide to make a change, but quite another for him to think God can't be on my side. But a lot of congressmen think they have a monopoly on God. So, Jeb and I did the professional thing and shook hands and parted ways. I waited until I got out of the Dallas City limits to let the tears leave my eyes. They poured nonstop during my hour-long drive home at the realization that Jeb and I were not going to be a team like Phil Gramm and him.

"Good riddance!" my accountant said when I called him. He didn't even know Jeb but said "that man takes up all your time and you didn't get one bonus. It's not worth your time to have him as a client."

"But he is going to move up the ladder—and quickly. I just know it." I whined.

"Let him!" my accountant continued advising me, "and let him monopolize someone else's time."

8 A DOCTOR IN THE HOUSE

My mornings used to start with Brian, Jeb's chief of staff, but my evenings ended with Barry, Congressman Burgess's chief of staff. Barry worked for Congressman Combest, Congresswoman Granger, and now we were working together again now that he was with Dr. Burgess. At times, I would tell Barry "It's late and I'm just now getting around to eating supper," hoping we could talk at another time and I could enjoy a quiet supper.

"That's fine, just go ahead and eat. I don't mind," Barry would say. I do, I thought. But Barry was a friend, and like Brian, he too wanted to do well with his freshman congressmen boss—which meant me raising lots of money. So, I endured dinner over the phone most nights because I wanted happy clients.

"I know you're surprised how I went from scrubs to this slick politician before you," Dr. Burgess would say to constituents in a rehearsed speech Merrie

Spaeth helped him with. It always got a laugh because Dr. Burgess was anything but slick. He was the opposite of Jeb. He wore wire rimmed glasses and was much more at ease in scrubs than in his newly purchased Men's Warehouse suits. Despite me begging him to stop wearing black tennis shoes, he wore black tennis shoes. He was also un-Kay Granger like.

Dr. Burgess's win surprised quite a few people. Like Jeb, he had campaign debt. He worried about his $30k out of pocket expenses as much as Jeb did his $325,000. I wanted to laugh, but knew better. "I can make a couple of calls to the beer people and builders and get this taken care of," I told Congressman Burgess. To his amazement, his debt was retired in about an hour with the help of just a handful of PAC's (political action committees). We were off to a good start impressing our new client.

Despite Dr. Burgess having a consultant, Dr. Burgess performed almost all the campaign work himself. Those things he didn't do, he found a family member willing to volunteer. Dr. Burgess was a sign person, driver, and scheduler. He even filed his own FEC reports through their free software online, rather than purchasing a database.

There is a saying in politics, that the candidate—no matter how tempted they are—can be their own campaign manager. There are several reasons why one should just focus on being the candidate, but the one most candidates agree on—secretly— is so that they have someone to blame when things go wrong. Dr. Burgess had no one to blame.

Dr. Burgess being new to politics didn't know any of this, so when the FEC wanted to issue a large fine, he nervously explained there was no intent to file it all wrong, he just didn't know what he was doing. He hired my firm, the Magnolia Group, to re-file every report, with correct numbers and fix the mess he was in. James in our office did just that. It went away. No fine.

Dr. Burgess was so pleased he began sharing this at campaign events and fundraisers. "One last thing before the evening is over," Dr. Burgess would say "I just have to thank the Magnolia Group—James and Leslie. I mean, I would be in jail if it weren't for James." People would look confused and before they could ask what the heck the newly elected Congressman was talking about I would break out in spontaneous clapping, others would join in. Thankfully, ending the event.

I begged the Congressman to please NOT bring up the FEC situation to anyone. "No one knows except for us. There is no point in telling people about it," I would say no longer being a political novice. "It's public record," he would tell me. "The public doesn't care. They don't look at that stuff. But I'm darn sure your future opponent would like to snag a headline about your breaking the law!" I told him. "Or hearing you mention jail!" I said. Fortunately, for all involved the Congressman stopped thanking us profusely in public about "saving him from the FEC."

Barry and I both expected Congressman Burgess to draw an opponent. Just about everyone, except Barry and I, expected Dr. Burgess to be a one-term Congressman. So, we had exactly one year before an opponent could file to run against him in the primary. His district was drawn where only a Republican could win, so we knew our only worry was with a fellow Republican. The report insiders look to was that June 30 FEC report as it would be close to the last one made public before candidates start campaigning. They look to see if they can compete with that person's campaign funds.

Word was that Texas Representative Kenny Marchant wanted to run for the seat the first time but didn't because he pledged to Majority Leader Dick Armey that if his son Scott ran, he wouldn't. Leader Armey's son, Scott, did run, so Marchant didn't. Others say Marchant didn't run because he didn't think he could beat the Armey machine and name. But, the Armies didn't win. Burgess won instead. So, we were told maybe Representative Marchant would file against Dr. Burgess. But he wasn't the only one interested. There was a long line of office holders who had more money than the Burgess campaign and we knew they considered running too. We had to get money and get it before June 30.

That first district work period, we had a fundraiser every day for nine days straight. Sometime we had three a day. We were exhausted but determined to fill up the war chest for a guy that knew nothing about raising money. We hit every goal laid out for us and ended the year with what no one thought was possible. Congressman Michael Burgess, MD would run unopposed in the Republican primary.

We didn't get to bask in our results though because the Texas legislature did redistricting in a year no one thought they would. That meant they would go after the freshman congressman's districts to redraw as opposed to the more senior members of Congress. Redistricting is when they re-draw the congressional boundaries. That meant the folks we worked so hard to win over, may not be the folks voting for us. That meant the competition may have stronger areas in the new district. With no time to rest, as we ramped up just like it was an election year, raising money to fight off a potential opponent in the newly drawn district. We rose to the task and raised lots of money. But poor Congressman Burgess, was left with a district that spread all the way to Oklahoma by the time the Texas legislature was done with him.

After years of raising money and being in constant campaign mode, we knew this was Congressman Burgess's least favorite thing about being a congressman. I am pretty sure he hated it. I was getting a little concerned having a client that doesn't want to fundraise all the time. I mean, he no longer wanted to schedule fundraisers or make fundraising calls. Dr. Burgess wanted to spend more time on health care legislation, not understanding the system demands more money all the time.

Meanwhile, he had a friend of Barry's in D.C. filing his FEC reports. I was having flash backs from Jeb—all our work on front end, then paying someone else when it's easier. As I am driving Congressman Burgess home, I ask him about hiring another firm to file his reports. "Congressman, I thought you were pleased with our work?" I asked.

"Absolutely Leslie, I am," Dr. Burgess said.

"So, I'm confused. Why would you hire someone else to do the FEC work?"

"You're still in charge of fundraising. Don't worry," Dr. Burgess said, trying to reassure me.

"You're pleased? So you take money out of my pocket and put in someone else's?" I am pulling in the Congressman's driveway now and I notice he has his hand on the car door. "I hadn't thought of it that way," long pause "Barry just said…. well, sorry" and he quickly exited.

That's the day I realized just because you're a Republican does not mean you have any business sense. Even if you call yourself a businessman, and Dr. Burgess didn't, doesn't mean you're good at business. Barry knew exactly what he was doing and I was mad at him for not explaining himself. At the President's dinner, he couldn't look me in the eye. I guess the Congressman didn't find our conversation pleasant because Barry decided it would be inappropriate for the Congressman to ride in a car with a "young woman" after that incident, even though the "young woman" was his political fundraiser.

Depressed and a little irritated, I called Jerry King, who is fond of saying his King Aerospace is the "Southwest Airlines of the defense industry." Jerry knows politics—hates politics—but is a donor and more importantly, a man I respect and admire. We met for an early breakfast at Le Madeline, which is close to his office, and I poured my heart out to him about working hard, doing well, but losing business.

"I am sorry." Jerry said, "But none of it matters." He rattled on how little he thinks of most politicians and the process and all the money involved. Jerry then gave me a bunch of advice I eagerly listened to. "Look, Leslie. You just gotta think of these campaigns as a birth and a death. They are all going to die. Some will have a long life and others a quick death. Don't you think for one second it's you." He confirmed what I already knew that they were just users and it didn't have anything to do with me. It's just who they are or become.

Jerry shared some of his business successes and failures and high maintenance clients then told me to go by his office and "ask Pat (his assistant) for the books. She'll know the ones." After our two-hour breakfast, I headed straight to his office where Pat sent me home with a pile of books I could barely carry with titles like *Corporate Warriors, Special Ops Leadership,* and Herb Kelleher's *Nuts.* Like magic though, Jerry King's words transformed me. Clients coming and going was a reality not a heart break. Using and discarding me was part of the process.

9 THE ATTORNEY VERSUS THE ESTABLISHMENT

We were acquiring powerful congressmen, those running for senate, and many other state legislators, and even some conservative think tanks. We represented lots of powerful people and I enjoyed the intoxicating feeling. When I got a call from someone not running for Congress, I said I wasn't interested. Not at first. When he told me it would make me a lot of money, I decided the least I should do is meet with them.

Now living in Dallas, I made the even longer drive out to Parker County, the place where Carolyn gave me a kamikaze course on politics several years earlier. I met with the candidate, Jerry Buckner, and his wife, Dr. Brandi Buckner—a family counselor, at their shared office building. It was an older home that they converted to an office just a block off the main square in Weatherford, Texas. Jerry, an attorney, grey hair, and little round glasses, spent the next hour telling me he wanted to run for judge and giving me the background and dynamics of the race. Judge? I thought. I don't know about this I thought. Brandi, his dynamo of a wife with long, dark hair and skirts and big colorful jewelry, chimed in with additional background information. Years earlier, Carolyn explained it's more than just votes in Parker County, there is always "all this other stuff." It still holds true today that there's lots of other stuff in Parker County.

What they didn't tell me that day, but I later learned is that Jerry Buckner was a prosecutor on the Cullen Davis trial. At the time, Cullen Davis was the wealthiest man in the United States put on trial for murder. Books were written about it. Movies were made about it. And Jerry made enemies that remain today for his work on that trial. Jerry could have gone on to do a million other things but chose to lead a quiet, content life with Brandi in Weatherford.

They continued telling me about the incumbent, Debra Dupoint, an attractive, young, and energetic woman, who had her Daddy's pocketbook for backing. Getting appointed to this office was a pay raise for her and probably the best job she'd ever held. Jerry, on the other hand, was an older, thoughtful businessman. If he won, he would make less money and it would be his last job. He wouldn't be using this spot to run for a higher position. Jerry didn't need the headache of public office. Jerry had it in his head that serving his community as judge would be the fitting ending to his stellar law career. Earlier in life, he dreamed of being a judge, but didn't pursue it because staying in private practice made more financial sense.

Jerry warned me how Debra's, his opponent, mailers would no doubt show voters a beautiful family with two children. If they didn't have a dog, they would probably get one. In reality, it was a troubled marriage. Rumors in town spoke of an affair with a local man, while her husband had his own homosexual affair in France that summer. After much discussion, Jerry, Brandi and I agreed we could beat the incumbent without having to get personal. We all liked that the other agreed on this issue. We were proud that our team would make the race about results instead of personal issues.

That decision was a big deal because we knew in this ultra-conservative Texas-town; it would be a slam dunk to win that way. Shedding light on their personal problems, especially since they were projecting a far different impression would crush them. All of us were equally excited to win on results and we relished the challenge of a fair fight. Just talking, we already embraced our underdog status and didn't mind a whole bunch of people doubted us. We were already feeling like a team, although we weren't one yet.

Jerry and Brandi were businesspeople but real people with real lives outside of politics. The Buckner's got it. They were willing to invest their money for their dream. They were willing to ask others to do the same. Jerry had been upfront in that while he was a Republican he didn't spend every night going to Republican club meetings. I could completely appreciate that—even after all these years, I'd rather go to happy hour than a club meeting. And if Jerry went to a meeting, it was usually the Chamber of Commerce or something law related, instead of to a Republican club. Most of his free time was spent with his wife, buddies, or hobbies. Jerry enjoyed carving pens.

Some Republican Women clubs are filled with ladies that have the luxury of not having to be in the day-to-day of the work force, so they have time to devote to Republican causes. Sometimes they tend to forget other women who work for a living. Brandi preferred at the end of the day to meet up with girlfriends or family. The Buckner's voted and supported Republicans but running their businesses didn't allow for a lot of free time. Plus, they were on the "billable hour system"—time was money.

What Jerry was telling me (and what I already knew) was our opponent would question his "Republican-ness." Not surprisingly, this always comes up in a primary. And that was what we were talking about—not Democrat Verses Republican like most of our clients. Without fully understanding we were about to commit a sin within the Party. I mean, I knew you weren't supposed to and it was considered the unthinkable. But I still didn't understand. Never being afraid of being called a rebel and wanting to make a bunch of money, I could've been convicted of "premeditation" of committing the sin.

Jerry knew we had a reputation of enjoying a challenge and he didn't think most consultants were capable or willing to take on an incumbent. I didn't even know how right he was at the time. But most of all, Jerry wanted to know "Do you have the guts to do this?" he asked. He knew just how to woo me and so we were a team. Jerry passed a test he didn't know I was giving him in that he knew the environment and was prepared for it. He didn't mince words and he continued to give frank answers to my questions. My standard questions were "Who is going to give you money? Who's voting for you? And who wants to spend their nights and weekends working for free for you? Who are your friends?" Jerri and Brandi both shot back answers at me as quickly as I asked them.

It amazed me when people wanted to run for office and naively they think all these strangers are going to come out of nowhere to give their hard-earned money and time to them. Other times, they are under the impression they have friends, but they don't. Just like the parent with the awkward child, I have thrown Christmas parties, 40th birthday parties, and other stunts to make our candidates cool, likeable, and mostly to secure them some "friends." Thankfully, the Buckner's had lots of friends and people within the Party that wanted to help them. Turns out my friend, Carolyn, was already on their team working and had been one of many suggesting the Buckner's' call me.

Dozens and dozens of people were willing to do whatever it took for Jerry's campaign. It was refreshing to walk into a campaign office full of people willing to roll up their sleeves and work getting Jerry elected. Jerry was fortunate to have people with more Party experience, community experience, and grassroots experience than most campaigns. He had an impressive core group of people supporting him that knew Debra was a bad judge and needed to be replaced. They cared enough about having the right person in office. They didn't worry about "their reputations" or the masses saying it can't be done or even the other elected officials bullying them. Jerry's core group knew who they were. They weren't about to be told what to do.

We walked. We called. We had neighborhood gatherings. We walked. We walked. And we walked some more. We told our story every day all day. It didn't take long for us to realize people "liked" the incumbent and we were fighting inertia. Voters were prepared to re-elect her. It didn't seem to matter that she had broken the law and disgraced the office. During our walks, people didn't like hearing unpleasant things said about Debra and questioned our believability even though everything we were saying was true.

We tweaked our talking points. Whoever was walking with Jerry said "unpleasant" thinks about Debra, not him. We all made it a point to say something nice about her first. "Debra is pretty. Everyone loves her Daddy." We made sure to let them know other people were saying good things about Jerry and put those quotes on our door hangers to connect better with voter's. On parallel tracks, we were running radio ads, newspaper ads, robo-calls, direct mail, and multiple mass communications. Progress was happening but not fast enough. Beating an incumbent was not going to be easy and may not even be doable, but we weren't giving up.

Politics makes for strange alliances. When incumbents worry about their re-election, they turn to other incumbents first. An unspoken pact exists and says "worry about me because if I lose, maybe you'll be next." Big name incumbents started circling the wagons for Debra. We were shocked that the Attorney General of Texas Greg Abbott, State Senators Craig Estes, and even my former boss Congresswoman Granger would feel so strongly about this judicial race and support Debra. I reached out to their staff and some of them personally in an effort to educate them more about the race. Incumbents hate to get involved only to lose as it gives people the impression their support doesn't carry much weight. I leveled with them and said this was not a slam dunk race for Debra and it was dicey for them to get involved. Being fellow lawmakers, I didn't think they should support a law breaker. (Debra had done all kinds of bad things that she had done a good job of hiding from the voting masses, but Jerry and the lawyers in town knew better.)

Knowing no one would rescind their endorsement, the next best option was to ask for them to endorse Jerry too. This would neutralize their support and level the playing field. While most quickly said no, I was most shocked Kay Granger didn't do it. As I thought she of all people knew we were looking out for her. She supported the unqualified Debra because she felt strongly about having more women in elected office. The other elected officials and their staff appeared to not be concerned if Jerry was qualified or would make a great judge. They cared about protecting the all-powerful incumbent and didn't worry about doing their due diligence. Debra's Daddy gave money to their campaigns too. Otherwise, they would have stayed out of this race or supported Jerry if they wanted good government.

We successfully raised money but were still outspent 4:1 as we couldn't compete with Debra's Daddy's money. The folks in the community were contributing to Jerry. But the key, we knew, was for the voting public to see Jerry and Debra side by side, preferably in a debate. Despite her perky image, we knew her weaknesses would be revealed in a debate. We knew the voters would not let her off the hook easily when they could see for themselves. We were confident voters would discover Debra doesn't match her campaign marketing materials. And that's why the last thing Debra and her campaign wanted to do was to debate Jerry Bucker. We kept the pressure on by sending her campaign certified letters requesting debates; made follow up phone calls, wrote letters to the editor of the local paper asking for a debate, and even called into radio stations. We talked about the need for a debate non-stop. This was in a time when debates were still real and not just staged one-liners with no substance. Candidates couldn't talk over or avoid answering the moderator's questions.

Because we were demanding a debate and Debra's campaign didn't want to have one, I received a threatening call from her consultant. The same consultant that treated me to the cheap Chili's lunch years earlier when I worked for Kay Granger. He screamed at me to stop demanding a debate. (I don't use his name because he would be flattered and I don't care to flatter him.)

"Demanding a debate is the oldest trick out of the playbook" he lectured me. He didn't pause long enough for me to say elections are about voters getting to see the candidates, give their case for office, and have the opportunity to ask questions and get answers. No, he just kept yelling over me. "Stop asking for a debate! We're not doing it! Stop!" he yelled into the phone.

When I didn't agree to his demands he threatened me saying "You should watch out for your safety and if you don't stop it I am going to release the dark details on your guy. I have a file on him." He laid the foundation for me to say "what file?" so I refused. By not asking him about it, I infuriated him.

"Did you hear me? Did you hear me? I am going to release your guy's dirty secrets of sex with a 15-year-old! You're asking for it!" There were so many F bombs being thrown around. Finally, he stopped shouting and waited for my response. And with one of Mom's signature long pauses, I followed it by simply saying "All I hear you saying is: "I'm scared.""

"Fuck you! You asked for it!" he said as he slammed the phone.

There was no doubt he would deliver on his promise and attack pieces would be hitting homes soon. A knot in my stomach kept me debating if I should eat something or drink something before calling Jerry as it was a Saturday morning and I hadn't made it out of my robe. While I didn't believe for a second Jerry had sex with some 15-year-old, I knew they had "something" and that "something" would look bad to voters. I knew they were willing to use it and possible embellish whatever it was they had. I couldn't get a hold of Jerry and instead got Brandi.

"Brandi, I need to talk to Jerry." She told me where he was but it was at a meeting or something which meant Jerry would be out of pocket for a couple of hours. "Can you go get him?" I ask pressingly. "I must talk to him now." As far as I knew, there could be a robo-call going out any second with this crazy information and I wanted to get to Jerry first.

"Leslie, what's going on? I can help. What do you need?" Brandi says, trouble-shooting. There was a long silence. While Brandi was completely involved and supportive of Jerry I didn't think I should be the one to tell her. I wanted to talk to Jerry first, then Jerry update Brandi on the situation, not me—not about this. We both could tell by what was not being spoken it was going to be bad. Silence continued. Brandi broke it and softly said. "Tell me. Go ahead and tell me. I will find out anyway." And that's when I had to ask Jerry's wife of twenty something years if she knew anything about a relationship or an incident of Jerry having sex with an underage girl.

"I know it's not true. I just need to figure out what they have so we can be prepared and counter attack." I quickly added. Brandi responded "This is how it happens, Leslie." The grueling campaign life getting to her. "This is how wife's find out about these things." I don't think she thought it was true either but she knew "something" was going on and knew she may have never learned about it had it not been for this campaign. While I never once thought Jerry had an affair, as I knew he loved Brandi, I cringed for the practical family psychologist that Brandi was being instead of the right-to-be-emotional spouse of a candidate. No doubt, Brandi had heard too many of these stories in her family practice, while I had heard too many of them in politics.

We had a conference later that day and it turned out thirty something years earlier Jerry had been asked by his neighbors to defend a relative of theirs being tried for a gruesome murder. Jerry agreed. "It was some of my best work," he tells me. "I was a cocky young attorney excited for trial but wanted to make damn sure I did my neighbors right." He then went into details I have now mostly forgotten. About how they all knew the verdict would not be good for his clients that were accused of chain-sawing multiple people to death. The priority was to avoid a death penalty conviction above anything. I don't know if that means they pleaded "guilty" or not but the family would have considered it a victory of sorts if Jerry could have their loved one's life spared.

During this stressful and mentally draining trial, the family gathered around the hotel pool and decided it would be okay to have a few drinks since there was a chainsaw murder and a family member could be sentenced to death. Among the group was a 15-year-old girl. When the guilty verdict was announced, Jerry recommended another attorney for the appeal process. During that trial, the attorney put Jerry on the stand and asked him if he had worked hard to represent his client, etc. etc. It's my understanding one of the angles in having another attorney do the appeal is to argue the first one did a bad job and the second one thinks it would be a different verdict had he defended the case. It may explain why the second attorney or the prosecuting attorney asked Jerry if he had been drinking and thinking about the 15-year-old girl who was strikingly beautiful and later became a T.V. news anchor and journalist in the Dallas/Ft. Worth area.

And here is what the DuPont campaign did have. Rather than say "no" Jerry's 30-year old self was offended and even amused by the question (since that's the last thing an aspiring young attorney would be doing during a high-profile death penalty case.) Flippantly, and arrogantly, the young Jerry responded "Yeah, that's what I was doing. Having sex with a 15-year-old." It wasn't hard for me to imagine Jerry saying it with his sarcastic and dry wit. So while Jerry didn't have sex with a 15-year-old or anyone during that trial, there was a quote, in a court document, that voter's may not understand.

Depending on what the Dupont campaign sent out and how far the opposition went with their creativity, we may just have trouble getting the voters to believe us with no time to explain. Explaining is not where any candidate wants to be. We were now losing.

Shortly after being cussed out by the opposition, I learned I was receiving this second round of cussing because we had successfully managed to get the voters and media to demand a debate. To our great fortune, the local media didn't think it was fair to not let voters have an opportunity for the incumbent to give her case and the challenger gives his. We got lucky. Debra broke down mentally and physically during the debate. We were now tied.

The so-called sex scandal was our payback in succeeding to get a debate because no incumbent wants to have to defend his record or talk about the dirty tricks they are playing. As promised, the other side went into full slander mode and printed outright lies about sex with a 15-year-old in their direct mail pieces and newspaper ads. It was disgusting that they took such liberty with their lies even putting the "p" word in their propaganda. Even more disgusting, no one held them accountable. A few newspapers refused to print their ads, but most wanted the advertising dollars, and went ahead and ran them despite knowing better. They ignored Jerry and me giving personal pleas and reasoning with them.

We took a big hit the last few days of Early Voting and on Election Day because their story about Jerry was everywhere. It was so crazy that it scared people. Brandi said she could "feel the whispers" in town. We fought back quickly. We were prepared for it. But we were not naïve. Some people would panic and we would lose their votes. Every minute was even more critical than usual. We worked until the polls closed and then held our breaths. We no longer knew if we were losing or winning. Election results always seem to take forever to those of us involved in the campaign, but within hours we learned we unseated an incumbent!

10 THE BUILDER

My former boss on the Hill, Congressman Larry Combest, retired with little notice and a special election was called, where seven candidates ran in the Republican primary. Randy Neugebauer, a jovial builder from Combest's home town of Lubbock, and Mike Conaway, a CPA from Midland made it to the run-off, where Neugebauer emerged victorious. Then redistricting happened. The Texas legislature put Midland in the 11th District of Texas. Mike Conaway became a Congressman, running unopposed that time.

The Texas legislature combined the 17th and 19th congressional districts. That meant two United States Congressmen would run against each other. Congressman Neugebauer was now being pitted against a long-time Democrat incumbent, Congressman, Charlie Stenholm. This race would be the biggest in Texas and one of the biggest in the nation. Money would pour in but everyone knew there was no chance for Congressman Stenholm because the Republican lead legislature made sure of it.

Congressman Stenholm, a tall handsome man with grey hair, was Congressman Larry Combest's Democrat counterpart on the House Ag Committee. So, if the Democrats had control of the House, Charlie Stenholm would have been the Ag Chairman, not Larry Combest. Combest and Stenholm had worked well together for years. I truly believed they liked and respected each other.

I never heard a bad word spoken about Congressman Stenholm from people in the cattle business, so I wasn't surprised when Mom says to me "I thought Stenholm was one of the good guys. Last year at the Cattlemen's meeting they were talking about him and saying good things."

"Well, there's going to be a lot of money in this race, Mom," I say. "The Republicans drew the lines. So even though it will be a close race, they made sure the Republican congressman will have the votes." She said nothing. "I should be a part of it," I tell her. "If you say so." Mom responded which I took to meant she wasn't so sure of what I was doing. I continued to explain. "The cattlemen do like Stenholm. But they like Neugebauer fine. They know the dynamics though and I expect they will give to both sides." They did. Mom didn't say she was appalled but if she did I would have understood.

What was it like working with Congressman Neugebauer? He was an ideal client. He made me feel good working for him as opposed to sitting it out. Congressman Neugebauer asked for another call list when he finished his first one. That meant he worked hard, made his calls, and did what he was supposed to. Then, he called me directly when he had a question and asked it. Sometimes, elected officials go through staff and create other unnecessary inefficiencies. I was told Congressman Neugebauer was a successful businessman. I didn't doubt it because he operated like one.

Congressman Neugebauer didn't worry with the details of the fundraisers we put together because he was a businessman, the kind that delegates, lets you do your work, and pays accordingly. Some clients had staff that thought they were being tough negotiators in not paying a retainer or fee that was already agreed up and in writing. To me, it meant they were bureaucrats playing "business." They didn't understand there is no negation in an executed, agreed upon contract. With Neugebauer's staff, I was always paid on time. In other words, Randy Neugebauer did all the things a good client, a good businessman, and a congressman should do. The results showed, as we raised lots and lots of money. He won his race.

Because of all this, I would have liked to have him as a retainer client. His chief of staff said that wasn't a possibility that they preferred paying per event. "That's not ideal for me, but that means each event will cost more than it would if you were a retainer client." They agreed. It seemed like a great match. And then I was introduced to Toby, the Congressman's adult son.

"Who the hell are you?" an unknown voice screams over the phone. Before I could answer the voice continues. "What do you think you're doing scheduling a fundraiser for my Dad without talking to me?"

In my early days, I put up with screaming, cursing, and other nonsense. I was well past those days and responded sternly "Who is this? And who is your Daddy?" Although I figured it had to be the son of Congressman Neugebauer because I had just scheduled a fundraiser in Houston less than an hour before, I thought he owed it to me to introduce himself. Toby finally tells me his name and proceeds to also tell me his lineage and his financial worth—which is quite high. But I am still confused. The Congressman, his scheduler, and his chief of staff, Gaylord, made no mention of consulting with Toby about dates.

"Look, you need to stop yelling at me. Gaylord gave me the dates the Congressman was available and those were the dates I worked with," staying in my still stern voice mode.

"I am in Mexico and I will be in Mexico then. You need me there. You must have me there! I am calling from Mexico because of your screw up!" Toby screams. "You don't have to call me at all. In fact, I'd prefer you not. You need to talk to someone else, but it's not me," I say realizing the rumors of Toby being a spoiled brat, even though he is an adult are probably all true. Toby tells me he has never been talked to like that and I am gonna regret it. "I'm having your job for this!" he tells me. (I then realize Toby doesn't understand about contracts either.) He says "fuck," "shit," and "damn" to express his level of frustration. In the early days, this type of thing would have ruined my day, cause me to lose sleep, and possibly make me throw up. Now, I had reached a point in my career where I found things like this amusing and pathetic.

"I'm calling my Dad!" Toby screams before he slams the phone.

"Gaylord" I say out loud. "I have to give him a heads up. I have to call him before Toby!" I say sharing with the team. "Gaylord, I just got introduced to Toby. Wow! That was something. Heads up, though. He is calling to yell at you about scheduling the fundraiser when he is in town." As Gaylord talked to me, I realized this was not the first time this had happened. In fact, it was all too common. I never met Gaylord in person, but when he worked in Majority Leader Dick Armey's office, people talked good about him. So, I had empathy as a former staffer putting up with this type of crap. Our conversation was cut short, "I gotta go. Toby's already on the other line," Gaylord says to me.

Not long after, Gaylord called me back. He basically relayed the same story as before, and said Randy (what Gaylord called Congressman Neugebauer) and all of them discussed the dates. While Randy wished it worked out for his son to be there, since there were limited numbers of days to host the event and much money to be raised, he was okay that Toby would not attend. Regardless, Gaylord suspected Toby would have a temper tantrum.

While I was sympathetic toward Gaylord, I wanted to make clear that I would not tolerate Toby calling to bully me. "I hate it for you, but I don't get paid for this." I tell him, as I am not going to take Toby's calls. It was bad enough I dealt with elected officials who thought they were entitled, but the family of—well, that too was common–but I no longer had a tolerance for it. "I know," Gaylord conceded as if it was part of his job description. We hung up and I went back to raising money for Toby's Daddy.

The days leading up to the event, Toby's assistant called to relay he was in Mexico and would not be able to attend. There are a lot of Toby-types in elected officials' families and my gut told me Toby would end up being there. So, we made him a name tag, place setting, and made sure he had a good seat.

During most fundraisers, I silenced my phone as I make sure staff is at the office and others are managing other events, so there's no good reason to not give the client and donors I am with my full attention, or at least for an hour. Looking back, I wish I would have turned it on or at least put it on vibrate. The frantic assistant of Toby's called me dozens of times. She was doing her best to warn me of Toby's coming wrath. She even called my office and had them calling, texting, and emailing me.

Fast footsteps could be heard on the marble floor of the hotel, that I knew had to be that of Toby's. Storming past the registration desk, a man harshly says "No point in me stopping. You thought I wouldn't come in from Mexico. You don't have a name tag for me" as he bursts the door open to the already started luncheon. Before he could do anything catastrophic, I say in front of everyone, a little louder than necessary "Toby, you forgot your name tag. Here's your seat," pointing to his place setting. The Congressman looks up at me, pleased, and introduces his son as Toby sits down and waives his hand to the crowd. Toby then thanks everyone for all the money he raised for his Dad. Afterwards, I called Toby's assistant and thanked her profusely for trying to warn me and apologized and assured her everything was okay.

The next time Gaylord called me to do a fundraiser for Congressman Neugebauer, I doubled the price because I wanted to make it easy for them to refuse. He inquired why our rates went up and I replied with one word "Toby." After a pause, Gaylord responded "I understand." We visited briefly about how each of us had shared war stories of difficult spouses, children, and it comes with working with politicians. Sometimes, the money isn't worth it.

11 THE CONSPIRACY THEORISTS

Just like many of my clients said one thing on the campaign trail to later compromise their beliefs, they made excuses to justify their actions. I was no different. That's what happened when it came to Congressman Ron Paul. He was not someone I thought should be in the United States Congress. I questioned if he even wanted to be a congressman. He had run for president, beginning in the 80's while still serving in Congress for decades. Each time, he was unsuccessful in his presidential campaign but remained in Congress, building a vast nationwide network through his other runs. Worse, Congressman Paul didn't show up for votes most of the time because he was too distracted campaigning for the presidency. On top of that, I struggled with his conspiracy theories and views of returning to the gold standard, thinking we should all run around carrying bags of gold. There were other issues too, more than I wanted to think about.

I swore to a friend back in Kentucky I wouldn't work with Congressman Ron Paul in helping Rand Paul get elected to the United States Senate. I meant it when I said it. But like my clients, it became too lucrative to resist. And on a petty note, I didn't care for Mitch McConnell, the other senator from Kentucky.

"Absolutely not. I am not going to work with Rand Paul," I said adamantly to the familiar accent of a high school friend who called me up on behalf of the Trey Greyson campaign checking up to see if I was working with Paul and if I might entertain working with Trey Greyson and take a call from his campaign. It was assumed by many politicos that Senator Jim Bunning, a Republican from Kentucky, would announce his retirement any day that summer and Trey Greyson and Rand Paul would run against each other for the open-seat.

Trey Greyson, Kentucky's Secretary of State, was Senator Mitch McConnell's hand-picked replacement and considered the front-runner in the race. Mom had hosted both men in her home and raised lots of money for their campaigns for no other reason than they asked her to. I told my Mom in no uncertain terms I was disgusted that the Senate Majority Leader asked her to raise him and his followers a bunch of money but they couldn't humor her in placing a courtesy call to me. My pride was bruised. For crying out loud, this is what I did for a living!

"Mitch McConnell, who you've helped since his first campaign can't manage to have some peon call me back?" I say, frustrated as Mom doesn't seem to "get it." "They have never even given me a courtesy call and they continue to ask you to raise money. You shouldn't do it." I say getting more upset with each word. "You should say 'only if you hire my daughter.' It's not like I haven't done this before! You're not asking them to hire your unqualified daughter. I mean, people running for President of the United States have hired me!"

So, when Trey Greyson's campaign didn't follow through in calling me, I debated. Was I willing to work for the Paul's?

When it came time to vent about Senator Mitch McConnell, I knew just who to turn to—Paige Mullins. I am not exactly sure when Paige began calling

Senator Mitch McConnell "Darth Vader" but I do remember when I did. Right after Mom hosted yet another successful fundraiser for him.

Mom raised almost as much money at her events as people that live in Hoptown. She did this with the help of Democrats, which included the Mullins family. Democrats in Hopkinsville are smart. They understand the political reality that there are no Democrat senators in Kentucky. That means they better get a seat at the table—which means a Republican table. I came in from Texas for the fundraiser hoping to be able to make some inroads.

"I need my name tag bedazzled so Senator McConnell will at least speak to me" Paige says with dread. "He will probably speak to everyone" I say optimistically. "Plus, you're a maxed-out donor." Translation: elected officials always talk to the maxed-out donors because they want to get more money later. "Don't' worry!" I assure and scold Paige at the same time, defending the Senator.

How embarrassed was I when Paige's prediction came true? Senator McConnell did indeed look over Paige's shoulder in search for a "more important" person to talk to. McConnell and his staff hadn't bothered to take the time to know that Paige and the Mullins family were the largest contributors of the evening! I couldn't believe their rookie mistake. But, my business sense left me as this became an emotional family matter for me. McConnell didn't appear to appreciate Mom's efforts, appreciate the Mullins, and never once reaching out to me. Greyson's campaign never followed up from my friend's phone call.... Well, why not work for the Paul's? That's how it happened. Like my clients whose kids felt entitled, I felt entitled. Like them, I thought I was different.

When Don Huffines, a well-known long-time Republican donor and businessman in Highland Park, who also served as Ron Paul's National Finance person for his presidential campaign, called and asked me to manage an event for Rand Paul, I took a deep breath and said "Yes. Yes, I'll do it!"

Even after I said "yes" I still couldn't believe I was going to help Rand Paul win a senate seat for my home state. I couldn't bear to share the news with Paige either. We both might start calling me Darth Vader, Jr.

This event was unlike any I had ever done before. Mr. Huffines insisted, smartly, that we put "business" as the dress code on the invitation. I never knew anyone to wear anything other than business suits at fundraisers, but this was going to be a different sort of crowd than the "country club republicans" as the Paul family calls them.

My husband, Will, a CPA who audited auditors, continued to ask me for updates about Ron Paul's, and now Rand Paul's, "audit the fed" campaign. Auditing the federal reserve has long been a subject that is important to Congressman Paul. Continuing to hound me on the subject, I grew frustrated, but really, just frustrated with myself for working with the Paul's.

"I know Congressman Paul is kind of crazy, but what's so wrong with him wanting the Federal Reserve audited?" I ask Will. "I don't' know much about it, but that sounds like a good idea to me!" I fire back.

"Leslie, the Federal Reserve is already audited." Will says calmly. In disbelief, I ask "How can that be true? If it is true, why do the Paul's keep saying it? Why do they get all these people worked up?" I ask not knowing what to hope for. I knew better and prepared myself as I listened. "Deloitte audits them," Will says coolly and continues "so do the Paul's think they did a bad job?" he asks, knowing I have no idea and continues. "If so, the Paul's should say we need someone else to audit them or say they should be fired. But they shouldn't say we need to 'audit the fed' when it's already being done!"

"I agree. Why don't you ask them that question?" I say to Will. Many times, I found elected officials appreciated questions, especially if people were sincerely interested and willing to have a meaningful discussion as opposed to trying to publicly embarrass them. I continue "I mean, don't bring it up in front of everyone, but one on one. I bet they know the fed is audited. Maybe it's just a way to grab people's attention on the subject and they mean more. I am pretty sure they both are well versed on the subject and could talk intelligently about it." I say, hoping that is indeed the case. So, Will looks forward to going to the fundraiser and getting an answer to his question. I am interested too.

Our team got there early and Ron Paul and his wife were just making their way from the Huffiness' stairway. (They had arrived much earlier and taken a brief nap at the Huffiness' home as they were all old friends by now.) Congressman Paul appeared thinner than when I had last seen him as his suit hung differently on him than in years past. Rand Paul, who I had only spoken to on the phone a few times, looked exactly as I had seen him on television—short, with unruly curly hair. I sympathized because of my own hair being curly. Both thanked me and shook my hand and then the elder Paul listened as Mr. Huffines talked policy and politics distancing themselves from the rest of us. As they walked away, I could hear Mr. Huffines saying "a few years ago these Congressmen would never have signed on to your bill. Now, they all agree with your 'audit the fed' campaign…"

From the beginning, I knew this would be a different kind of cocktail reception. On the phone, when someone says they are going to support and contribute to one of my clients, I always try to get a credit card right then and there. Why wait? Getting the money in is important. But forgetting the type of crowd I was dealing with, they adamantly objected. People feared the government tracking them and all kinds of other things. Almost everyone I talked to was anti-credit card. "A check is fine then," I'd say exasperated by such talk.

When I am in charge, we make sure we have the money BEFORE the event. Sure, we collect a few outstanding pledges and some walk-ins, but the money is in the door before event day. But not this event. No one would give a credit card. Then, they were reluctant to send a check as almost no one wanted to send anything through the U.S. Postal Service for fears I am still not clear about. That meant, we would have to collect all the money at the event.

As we set the registration tables outside I instructed the team, "Not one person goes through the front door of the Huffiness' house without us collecting their money. I don't have to tell you that we have a high number of outstanding pledges." We had to collect this money in person or I feared it would be impossible to collect with the credit card and mail challenges. Almost everyone wanted to pay in cash as they had crisp $100 bills in their wallets and pocket books. Only we couldn't accept it. The federal law only allows individuals to give $100 in cash. Interestingly, $100 is the amount a person can give anonymously in cash as well. No one wanted the FEC to know they were giving. Person after person wanted to give in cash. At this point, I was prepared to not be shocked if someone pulled out a sack of gold.

"I am sorry," I say to an elderly man and his wife. "You have to give the campaign a check or credit card. We cannot under any circumstances allow you to give $2400 in cash!" ($2400 was the maximum an individual could give by law at the time.) "It's against the law!" I tell the couple and the ever-growing crowd at registration waiting to pay.

"We've been Paul supporters for years and we always pay in cash!" someone shouts from the back to me. The staff looked at me in disbelief. Surely a United States congressman is not breaking the law and taking large sums in cash. We think maybe these people are confused as surely they didn't give that type of money in cash when it's illegal. Worst, surely the Congressman didn't accept it. We don't want to say as much because that would put us and them in an awkward spot. Besides, the goal was to collect the money.

"At this fundraiser, it can't work that way." I explain. There is talk among the crowd that they only have cash. I hear them asking each other "how will this work?"

"This is crazy," I whisper to the staff, and tell them "We need to get this money to the campaign. We can only take $100 cash from a person. Perhaps, they have relatives that sent a contribution with them or something like that. Surely, we can find a way." I head toward the house to take a break from the madness outside.

Before I get inside to the event, I meet Robert, Rand's brother who has the same short build as Rand but straight dark hair. Within seconds of meeting Robert, he eagerly shares with me that he'd like to run against my former boss, Congresswoman Kay Granger. Before I can ask him why he would run against her, he explains how she's a "country club Republican." Robert goes on about her liberal ways and I caught myself defending her. "I used to work for her and I've got to tell you. Ft. Worth loves her. She used to be their mayor. While more and more people are frustrated with Republicans, Kay Granger is not one that can be beat. She has more name recognition than most members of congress," I say feeling compelled to prevent another Paul from running for something. Robert chimes in "Yeah, I think you're right. We did a poll and her numbers are high. She can't be beat in a primary. It's a shame." I am in disbelief at hearing they have already paid and done a poll. Polls are expensive. I think that means either his brother or daddy paid for it with their campaign funds. What will Robert end up running for, I wonder, and when?

Inside the Huffiness' home, "Three Fools and a Stool" played upbeat music and recited poems. A man in costume as George Washington read from the constitution. This man never got out of character causing me to wonder if he thought he really was George Washington. The man was very convincing.

The dining room table is filled with delicious platters of food, including patriotic red, white, and blue pimento cheese sandwiches. Starving, I eat one as I survey the room of brightly colored and patriotically dressed attendees carrying books they want signed by both Rand and Ron. There is an unusual number of vests. Mrs. Huffines and I are the lone people in black dresses and heels. Trying to get the motivation to mix and mingle, I overhear peoples' conversations. "In Texas, the legislature wants to track us by installing smart meters, but we're fighting it." Another says, "Thank God for the Paul's. We've been fighting this fight for decades and we're starting to really make progress." I eat another sandwich and prepare to enter the fray. Then, I see Will and head straight for him, instead. "Thanks for coming," I say relieved to see someone I can relate to.

"Here, come meet Congressman Paul and ask him your question." I say leading the way, fingers crossed, hoping that Congressman Paul is the expert I want him to be on the Federal Reserve. After all, he did run for the president three times, surely he knows his own economic policies. It's his strong point, right? I need Congressman Ron Paul to nail this question because I am working on getting his son elected to the United States Senate and I already know that if he wins, he will want to follow in his daddy's footsteps and run for president. Despite what the Pauls' don't say, there is no doubt in mind that there are already presidential aspirations. I am not comfortable that I would help put him in a good position to run for president. I refuse to let myself think about it as it makes me hate myself.

I introduce Will and Congressman Ron Paul to each other. They shake hands. After a few formalities, Will says "Congressman, I am a CPA and I have a few questions about your 'audit the fed' campaign." Congressman Paul perks up as it is clear he likes to talk about this subject. "The Federal Reserve is already audited by Deloitte …" Nothing prepared me for what happened next. Ron Paul doesn't wait to hear Will finish his sentence but instead he mutters under his breath some words we can't make out and he quickly shuffles across the room. Will and I look at each other in disbelief. It's not as if we can't follow him across the room. But we don't. We already have our answer. I am physically shaking, but know I can pass it off to others in the room as having too much caffeine. But what am I doing?

Will then goes up to Rand Paul to ask about his position on auditing legislation, specifically Sarbanes-Oxley. Rand indicated he was in favor of repealing Sarbanes-Oxley because the legislation's requirement to implement fair value accounting was causing a crisis in financial markets. Will suggested that the legislation had no such provisions. Paul cannot satisfy Will with his answers and Rand can see this. Finally, he thinks Will may be pleased when he says "I get my policies from my Daddy." I don't ask Will if he is disgusted, I know he is. Quietly, Will leaves the fundraiser. I never get headaches but at that moment I was questioning if I may not be getting a migraine. I am shakier than before. "What have I done?" I ask myself, where no one can hear me.

When the speeches begin, I step to the back of the room as usual. Instead of staying to the bitter end like I typically do, I tell the team I must leave. "We have it covered" they responded. I knew they did. Outside and away from the Huffiness' homes, I called a cab. When it arrived, I say, "to the Granada, please." The cab pulled up to the music venue just in time. Inside, Will spotted me, waiving, both of us knowing I wasn't about to miss the Keb Mo concert we bought tickets to before I became a part of the Paul crew. After the night I experienced, I didn't even feel guilty about attending because I wasn't doing any more damage by helping anyone with the last name Paul build their brand to run for president.

12 THE BILLIONAIRE

W ho do you think should be president?" people would ask Mom and she would answer: "My daughter thinks Mitt Romney." That ended any potential for conversation as not another word would be spoken. "I don't think anyone knows who he is, Leslie," Mom would say in the early days. And, she was right.

Believing in Governor Romney, I naively did not pursue any other candidates for president—not a smart move for someone in the business of politics. But a typical move for someone who suffers from bouts of idealism. Despite having close ties to those working in the McCain campaign, I continued to obsess over working with the Romney team. Despite many people telling me, "Give Carla a call," I didn't. They were referring to Senator John McCain's national finance director, Carla. Carla worked for Senator Phil Gramm. One of the interns under her was Jeb Hensarling, now a congressman for the fifth district of Texas. Carla's hometown—Forney, Texas was in that district. The political world is incestuous.

In fact, for years when I drove through Forney, I'd think of Carla and give her a call. If I would have called, she would have taken the call. But I didn't call because I didn't think John McCain was the best person to be the Republican nominee, even though he was winning at the time. I happily put all my efforts toward Mitt Romney because I thought he'd make a great president.

Having never met Governor Romney I only knew about him through my research. He impressed me right away. His business acumen, serving as governor in a blue state and getting things done, and turning the Olympics around. I liked that Governor Romney was successful. To me, the country needs to be led by someone who has experienced success and knows how to create it. But this time, Mitt Romney would have a title unfamiliar to him— underdog. I wondered how that would affect him and his campaign. Never being afraid of an underdog as a client, I thought I could be an asset, so I cold-called his campaign headquarters in Boston and left quite a few voice mails. I didn't know what else to do as I had no Boston or Romney connections. I didn't know at the time many of the Bush Pioneers would support Romney and put in a good word for me.

Crazymaking. It's when you know you are sane but the people around you make you feel crazy. If they would just acknowledge they were crazy it would be of some comfort, to me. Even though I experienced this with each and every campaign, nothing prepared me for the overdose our team received during the 2008 Mitt Romney campaign. By now, I should've known better.

When I got the call from Romney's headquarters in Boston they talked to me as if we'd been long friends. "So, we got your calls and talked with some people and we want you to come up," the unfamiliar voice said over the phone. "Great. I'd love to! When were, you thinking?"

"Day after tomorrow" the voice answered without hesitating. I shook my head, irritated at how demanding campaigns are, and more irritated because I had a client flying into Dallas for meetings I set up about a month in advance. Sure, had I known, I could have made something work, but changes this last minute would not be fair for my current client. Hoping not to blow things up, I went on to tell the only presidential client I wanted to work for I can't. "Congressman Mike Conaway, one of our clients, is flying to Dallas and I am already committed to being a part of those meetings."

A very long pause. Figuring I was about to be lectured to about didn't I know Mitt Romney was running for president of the United States and so forth, I wondered if the line was dead. Still, only silence. I didn't dare say a word out of fear of retribution. I wanted to be on Governor Romney's team. Instead, the voice finally comes back on the phone and says "There is a 5am flight out of DFW tomorrow. Be on it. We will have someone pick you up."

I received a follow up call with a few more details, but not many. My flight routed me to Charlotte which meant I was barely arriving for the scheduled time they wanted to interview me. It also meant I may not make the connection back to Dallas to meet Congressman Conaway at 8am. I didn't sleep for the next 48 hours. I didn't think I could share the truth with Congressman Conaway and his office either because at that time they were for Rudy Giuliani.

"Campaigns are like fast-moving trains," I'd tell newly hired staff and clients. "No matter how much planning goes into something, there is always something that can't be planned for. If you want it, you just have to jump on because the train has already taken off." That's exactly how I felt about the Romney campaign. Hired on the spot in Boston to be the regional director for the southwest United States, they told me about an event they had scheduled for the next week in Dallas. Next week?! We had no choice but to jump on board and hope like heck to perform accordingly. We did.

Mom was right when she said she didn't think many people knew Governor Romney. But that didn't stop headquarters from constantly wanting our numbers to be up there with President Bush's. The Boston staff couldn't comprehend that people would say to us on the phone. "Romeney?" We'd answer "No, it's RomNEY." Still confused, they'd respond asking us to spell it. "Sure, it's R-O-M-N-E-Y." When we'd say Governor Romney again, after spelling, people would ask us "Governor who?" or "Governor of what?" When we'd answer "Massachusetts" it didn't help matters. Apparently, Massachusetts doesn't mean much to most people living in the southwestern United States.

In those early days of 2007, the American public didn't yet want to think about the next presidential race. That was hard news for the Boston staff to hear. Plus, they had a hard time believing us when we presented them with the challenges we faced. Of course, "everyone" knew the Romney name in Massachusetts and Utah, but not the rest of the country. Not only did they not want to hear that people didn't "know" Governor Romney yet, they were offended. We only shared such stories with them to give them an idea of the landscape and what they—we–were dealing with. Instead they responded by preaching to us that Romney should perform equally as well as George W. Bush or better.

Comparing Romney to Bush in 2007, well I saw that as silly and unrealistic. When I brought up that it was ludicrous to think at that stage we could outperform Bush, who was the son of a president, governor of Texas, and later president himself, who was the ultimate Texan, they simply responded by asking "What's your point?" I mean, a Mormon from Massachusetts simply is not going to outperform a Bush during that time. It wasn't being mean or negative, just realistic. Campaigns hate reality. Of course, this was well before the Super PAC's and creativity in fundraising that came about. This was raising money with limits of a few thousand bucks.

Reality wasn't welcomed and the Romney staff didn't take time to listen to what we said, take our input, and adjust accordingly. Of course, this is not a Romney-only challenge. Presidential campaigns are bureaucratic monsters that move slowly. They cannot turn on a dime. Campaigns by nature require nimbleness. Mass conference calls, a pet peeve of mine, apparently are a favorite of presidential campaigns. My friends who'd worked on other presidential confirmed. To me, they simply slow things down and do not allow for people to make decisive decisions. Large numbers of staff, rules, processes, and procedures encourage people to miss the bigger picture—the goal of raising money.

"Leslie, why weren't you on the conference call today? Everyone at HQ (yes, they would say "HQ" for headquarters and I quickly took note) is talking about it. I mean, you've missed them all! We didn't say anything to you when you missed the first couple. But now, you're in serious trouble. A lot of people are pissed at you," a Romney staffer scolded me.

"What conference calls?" I ask. "I am happy to be on every conference call, but I wasn't aware of any. Did you email me? My office? Call any of us?" asking as my stomach turns to knots at the realization I've already managed to quickly anger just about everyone at HQ in a short time.

"I just don't have this information," attempting to explain, hoping that they would respond with a "that's okay," or "It's our fault." But no such luck. "We emailed you!" The Romney staffer exclaimed. "Are you sure?" I said knowing I did not have any email with such information. "Could you check the email? Really, I would have called in. And if I couldn't make it, I would have had someone else on my staff be on the call," I continued. "We sent it to Leslie@MagnoliaGroup.com"

"That's not my email address—its .org. There should have been an error message. Or someone should have called when I wasn't on the first one."

"Well, you better be on the next one!" the Romney staffer said not hearing, caring, or making any acknowledgement of the insanity of his remarks. "How can participate when I don't know the call-in number, the time, passcode, or any other information?" I asked, frustrated. "If I have the information, I will be on the call."

Next week minutes before the conference call, I get a call from HQ "Hey, we just want to remind you about the call." (Since of course, I had missed the prior calls.) "I still don't have the call-in information!" I shouted. Finally, after many more missed conference calls, I received the information needed to join the daily conference calls without ever getting any satisfaction of anyone acknowledging that they kept sending everything to the wrong email address. The conference call episode foreshadowed the year ahead.

The hundreds of conference calls were maddening because they were devoted to questions like "how many calls have you made? And how much money have you raised?" They took valuable time away from us (and everyone) from actually getting work done. To me, who cares if I made one thousand or one hundred and one calls. Obviously, we had to make lots of calls, but it's not like we would stop at a certain number. And if we had called one thousand and weren't at our financial goals, we knew we had to call a thousand more.

Our newly hired intern, Chance and I never spoke a word on his first day because I was literally stuck on the phone all day with the Romney team, sneaking away at times for a quick bathroom break. I resorted to passing him post-it notes to communicate with him. It was horrible.

On the calls, HQ would give us "helpful tips" like "raise money in chunks of $25k and $50k." As if we wanted to raise money in small increments. Then, on the call they would take a few minutes to tell us about a new feature in the ComMITT system. (ComMITT was their campaign's database that they wanted everyone to use—consultants and some bigger donors as well.) "We now have all your events programmed in and it will notify everyone in the system about the event and allow them to rsvp directly. This makes it more efficient, saves you time…"

Meanwhile, I am logging onto the system to check it out as our Dallas event is the next event on Governor Romney's calendar. I am excited for anything that will help speed the process up and create more success for us and them. I click on "Dallas" and there is an error message from the link. I write a post-it note and pass it for someone else in our office to continue to try while I remain focused on the call. It's not me, they have trouble too they tell me in a note passed back.

"This is Leslie Sorrell in Texas," I say on the call. "We have just tried the new link and it's not working." Again, we just want HQ to understand despite them telling us they are giving us tools they haven't. An I.T. person came on and confirmed it was not working. The original caller told us they would talk to us "offline." As usual, no one resolved the problem before our Dallas event at the Crescent took place, but it didn't stop their finance director, or the "sixth son" as some call him bragging that he was providing us with lots of "tools."

I constantly felt I was in a non-fiction version of the *Emperor's New Clothes* as many days I was the lone voice. It reminded me of Congresswoman Kay Granger's staff who encouraged me to agree with whatever was being told to us and just be the appendages. I refused then and refused now, but my life would have been much easier had I just went along. They even flew another regional director down from Missouri, who chomped gum like my family's cow graze on grass, to give me a talk like Barbara used to, demanding me to make her life easier by "just say what they want!"

While Governor Romney's opponent, Mayor Rudy Giuliani, was eating ice cream at *Wild About Harry's* on Knox Street in Dallas shaking hands and visiting with voters, another presidential candidate was having a pep-rally at Ft. Worth's Billy Bob's. The Romney team took the opposite approach by only meeting people who contributed the maximum and agreed to raise lots of money. Sometimes, Governor Romney hadn't even been to that particular city, so he had never met anyone, nor had they met him. But that didn't stop anyone from expecting people who had never met Governor Romney to decide not only they wanted to support Romney for president in a highly contested primary but to also send him a maxed-out contribution, and commit to raising $25k to $50k. No one saw any irony in this.

My team and I knew how to do our job well, but this crazy-making was making me, well, crazy. I called Jim, a Bush Pioneer, and asked for his advice and insight. Jim was a go-to person for me because I respected him, he didn't hold back, and had experience on a presidential race. More than a few have said "Jim elected George W. Bush, not Karl Rove." Regardless, he knows what he is talking about and was serving on Romney's national finance team.

Jim's office, Turtle Creek Plaza, was conveniently located just two blocks away from my office, so I could pop in easily. Interestingly, our Magnolia offices had been Jim's first office space and I always placed more importance than one should on such—as if it brought good luck or something. After I caught Jim up, I asked "So what do I say when they want a specific number for a specific city? Or ask how many calls I've made? That's important to them. I get we all want to raise as much money as possible but they think we should predict and give them an exact number. We don't even talk about goals or what we want to achieve. It's just give me an exact number. They want a new number every day!" I say exasperated. And in this Bush Pioneer's typical bluntness he said so loud and fierce that my shoulders jumped back a bit. "Tell them you are going to raise as much God-damn money as you can. Screw giving them a number!" I instantly felt better. Jim knew what I knew. No one needed to motivate me to raise more money and it was pointless to try to come up with some number out of the sky every single day. Who cared how many calls I made, the question should have been how much money did you raise? Or did you get anyone on the phone. I understood the most important thing was to raise money.

I then told Jim about all the conference calls preventing me from actually raising money as there were several a day, in addition to all the calls and emails. Jim laughed. He went on to tell me to keep in mind the very people going ballistic had never done this type of thing before. He'd seen stressed-out politicos before. He made me feel better in a matter of minutes. I never took up much of Jim's time because I knew when he was talking to me, he wasn't making money. He had a business to run. I had what I needed—reassurance that I wasn't crazy. He would have told me too. No doubt about it. Jim doesn't hold back.

So, while I didn't say Jim's words verbatim, on my next call I did say surprise a few when I cursed. "Jim says we're going to raise as much damn money as we can. We're not going to get caught up in giving you a number every hour." As usual, my comments didn't go over well. HQ didn't understand. I just wanted our time to be freed up to do our job. I hated talking about our job—I wanted to do it. They didn't seem to comprehend we clearly understood Romney's goals and wanted to reach them.

I am not sure what specifically I was saying the day the sixth son blew up on a mass conference call, but I do remember he was yelling and cursing at me and I finally cut in and said in a matter of fact tone, "If you are yelling because it makes you feel better, continue. But if you are yelling because you think that motivates me, please stop." Not only did he continue yelling, but yelled louder. I responded by saying, "Good, I am glad this makes you feel better."

When the conference call was over, I received a call from Herb, a consultant on the team who is now an assistant vice president with Baylor College of Medicine, telling me "I just wanted to let you know I thought he was offensive and I was proud of you. You held your own. You were professional and thought you should know." Herb had been in the business for years and was well respected so his call meant a lot. Other regional and state directors, who I didn't know or hadn't even met called me too. They introduced themselves, told me the region they represented, and shared thoughts like Herb's. "I don't know why he hates you but..."

"Oh, no he doesn't hate me." I cut in. "He's just stressed out..." (I didn't like the fella, but I knew it had nothing to do with me, just the pressure of the job.) "Oh, he hates you," they interrupted. I had developed a pretty thick skin over the years, but I wasn't prepared to hear that because as much as I respected Governor Romney, I found it disappointing that some of his closest advisors didn't focus on results or reality. It appeared they mostly ran around with an over-dose of nervous energy, yelling constantly, and never caring to see if what they were doing was effective or helping the campaign reach its goals. Some senior staff were willing to cut their nose to spite their face and none was as obvious as in the decision to take Oklahoma away from our territory that we managed.

Governor Romney had not gone to Tulsa to raise money before and they were only allowing for an hour in the city at an awkward morning time to host the fundraiser. Despite having a strong Oklahoma list, we wanted to ensure the best event possible so we brought on Karma Robinson. She is the go-to person in Oklahoma representing almost all the state's members of Congress. Karma and my team worked well together over the years

She had worked presidential politics before and didn't want to go through that experience again. Thankfully, she did so because I wasn't above begging. After all, I knew selling Romney in Oklahoma was not going to be easy at this point in the campaign.

With Karma's help, the event was as successful as it could've been given the time constraints and dynamics. Senior Romney staff disagreed and removed us from Oklahoma. While I was disappointed, there was no doubt in my mind anyone else could have performed better. When the Romney campaign returned to Oklahoma and we had a conference call, the new guy reporting his numbers said he had "almost $1500 in pledges." I figured he would be fired on the spot, right over the conference call, or even resign from humiliation. When I reported such an embarrassing amount to the team, they were in disbelief. We all agreed we simply felt sorry for the new fella and knew his days in politics were numbered.

One of the big headaches that contributed to the crazy-making for us was that we were instructed not to print any materials, like invitations, but let those types of things come from HQ to ensure a consistent look and to protect the Romney branding. In theory, I would agree with that decision, but not in implementation. HQ staff were willing to have the perfect invitation and spend the time to make sure that happened, even if it meant going out only a few days before the event day. That type of thinking hurts attendance and money. We weren't going to share with people HQ didn't run like a well-oiled machine, but we sure were tempted when people complained to us their invitation arrived only days before the event. I didn't like taking the blame for something that was out of my control, but I did it anyway. I did it for Governor Romney.

For the next event, we adopted the Southwest Airlines motto of any employee has the authority to act if it's in the customer's interest even if HQ didn't give us that authority. We printed and mailed the invitations ourselves so they would go out on time. We raised money, had a successful event, and asked for forgiveness afterwards. We also took the liberty to include Governor Romney's bio telling people who he was and what he accomplished. Our techniques were effective. In the next presidential election, that I was not involved with, we received our invitation for a Dallas Mitt event the same day the reception was being held. I was relieved not to be going through that again, but felt sorry for whoever was because it appeared the campaign was operating with the same inefficiencies.

Just like most campaigns, we were asked to pull rabbits out of our hats. Miraculously, most of the time, we did. At the last minute, we secured an additional private plane to fly Texans up to Boston for the "America's Calling" event. Only minutes later, HQ insisted the plane fly to Utah to pick up people to go to Boston. HQ didn't see why I shouldn't mind picking up the phone and telling the Dallas businessman, who owned this plane, we changed our minds and don't want to use his campaign for fellow Texans to volunteer and raise money in Boston but instead for dignitaries in Utah. I dreaded making the call, but did so because I was ordered to.

"Mr. Muse envisioned his plane being used for Texans," his assistant told me. "He isn't really interested in it going to pick up people he doesn't know in Utah." She went on to explain what I already knew and understood. I just wished it made sense to the people in Boston.

I had earned a reputation of telling it like it was, so maybe that's why some of the greener HQ staff would call and share their frustrations with the Magnolia team. We did our best to boost their spirits as we needed everyone focused on doing their best for Romney. One twenty-something fella panicked before the "America's Calling" event in Boston, where people flew in from all over the country to raise money. My phone rang at three o'clock in the morning. I took the call because it's part of the job and we don't get the luxury of not answering regardless of the time. When I see the Boston area code, I manage a non-groggy voice and said "Leslie Sorrell." The caller on the other end doesn't apologize for the time of even acknowledge it and instead gushes out "I am too young to die! I am only 23 years old. I don't need this. I can't take it! It's all too much!" I am relieved to realize the fella is not suicidal, but just super-anxious.

I spent close to an hour playing therapist. Each Magnolia staffer has a story of a Romney staffer needing a pep talk from difficult, pressure-cooker experiences. Two fellas had slept for weeks under their desks. Others thought they were having nervous breakdowns and others simply wanted to quit. Since we needed them on our team, we needed them to be at peak performance and we understood none of them had done this before. But we never once shared with anyone in Boston their confessions.

"Who is Mitt Romney? Tell us about him," people would ask when I would try to pry money away from them. "Governor Romney is a businessman. He'll break apart the government, streamline it," I said to potential supporters. "But what do you think of him as a man?" While I answered their question with what they wanted to hear, it's when I realized that while I admired Governor Romney, I could not say in good faith I knew the man. I did not want to share with anyone that I found him…. well, guarded. I didn't tell them I got the impression he reserved sharing his real self only for certain people.

This bothered me, so I called people who did know him-the Bush Pioneers on our team. These of course are not all the same people and can't be put into one big lump, but all of them I have known over the years and have met with are amazingly generous with their time and astute to politics. I shared with a few of them my struggle as they would be discreet. Many of those same people were on the Romney team and had the opportunity to meet with Governor Romney one on one. These were men that had met many presidents, so they would have a good perspective I thought.

Over a hamburger at the Stoneleigh P a Bush Pioneer say to me "Do you know, Leslie, I have met with Mitt Romney now over a half a dozen times?" I didn't know. "And?" I ask. "I don't know him any more goddamn much than I did the first time. Hell, I think he should be president, but I don't know him. You could meet George W. Bush one time and you could walk away saying you knew him as a man. As a person."

He wasn't the only Bush Pioneer to say it. I heard that kind of stuff all the time. The people I most admired in my business just had so much respect for President Bush that I believed there was a time where they were working for a cause bigger than themselves and all of them put the country and patriotism above everything else. They made me believe it was the real thing. I wanted that too. I hoped to have that experience with Romney campaign.

While I learned a lot of people didn't "know Romney" I moved on and continued sharing with potential donors what I did know about him. I had a close relationship with a good many of donors across the country and if I personally put my stamp on something it helped them feel more comfortable in supporting that candidate. Since they didn't know Governor Romney they expected me to do the vetting for them. They too wanted to believe and I told them I did.

No matter what I said and did, and no matter what Romney did, no one wanted to talk about the connectivity problem. When I mentioned it, someone would just shout back at me "Don't you worry about that. Your job is to get money." But it's all related," I unsuccessfully tried to explain.

I was an even bigger failure at trying to get the campaign to address the "Mormon issue." In fact, they would hardly use the word. Instead, they would say "LDS" which took us non-Mormons a little while to realize that stood for Latter-Day Saints. Somewhere along the way they stopped using "LDS" and changed it to a new word altogether that I can no longer remember.

They must have got tired of telling me "Stop focusing on that and focus on raising money," because I certainly got tired of hearing it. I only kept bringing it up because I felt it would help the entire team raise more money. I didn't care that Romney was a Mormon but a lot of people did. The consensus of the campaign was to ignore the issue. On deaf ears, I would say "Look, I am not asking for some detailed document or secret church doctrine, just some general information. Maybe some talking points. Or a Mormon memo."

Someone in our office whispered "Did you just ask for a Mormon memo?" both scolding and laughing at me, while the rest of the team poorly tried to suppress their giggles at my awkwardness. I was while still on the phone with the Romney crew. I should have chosen my words better, but I did think we needed some talking points. "People just don't know. I don't know. And they are asking us all kinds of questions. When I can't answer, the more questions they ask. We don't need a whole bunch of details. Just something—anything."

I guess voters across the country didn't call up to Boston and ask fellow Mormons these questions, but people from Texas, Mississippi, Oklahoma, and all the other states we represented for Romney didn't hold back. Worse, there was some crazy show on HBO about Mormons that didn't work to our benefit. I didn't have a clue as to what they were talking about since I had long ago cut off cable, but I figured it was probably a disaster people learning about Mormonism on HBO. I thought we could educated them rather than some reality TV show.

Voters had questions and they wanted them answered. They asked us things like "Why don't Mormons drink caffeine?" Which led to debates about hot and cold drinks and such. They asked us about magic underwear and then to more serious questions of "What are Mormons fundamental believes?" I couldn't talk intelligently about this and neither could anyone on staff. We needed to be able to talk about it with some sense so we could get voters to focus on what really mattered about being president. I tried to explain to the campaign that ultimately I believed these questions were good signs. It meant people were curious. That they were interested in Mitt Romney. That they wanted to support him, but they needed a few answers before committing.

Finally, someone told me "We'll get you some information," but after days passed I realized it was only to get me off the phone. It appeared to many of us that the illogical staff of the Mitt Romney campaign pretended they weren't Mormons by ignoring the issue. They also said Romney is winning. I said otherwise and suffered for it. In 2012, Mitt Romney talked about his faith at the George H.W. Bush Presidential Library at Texas A&M University. It was well received and long overdue.

Election Night 2012, I arrived early evening at the Fox 4 Station in Dallas, where I gave commentary on live air or radio until midnight. My day started with radio interviews beginning at 6am and it was spent discussing Romney and the election results.

"At the core of people's being, I tend to believe they ask themselves 'is what we're doing working?' and for that reason alone I believe Mitt Romney will be our next president," I said. So even with all the challenges Romney faced, I believed that people would want a change from President Obama.

Along with the regular news anchors, Clarice Tinsley and Steve Eager, they brought former Texas state representative Alan Vought on with me for the Democrat perspective. Tablet in hand, I am trying to find the Florida results. At the time, I am holding out faith that Romney can pull out a victory because the Florida panhandle had not yet come in. Like a lot of people, I believed those were Romney votes.

Then, Mark Jones, executive producer, comes in and says in a voice we can only hear, but not viewers "I think Ohio is called. Checking." Steve, Clarice, and I are not sure of the results. Alan, beside me, is obviously at ease as I glance over seeing him sitting back, comfortably as we wait for more information. I go back to my tablet to double check. Alan knows what I am not ready to accept–his guy won.

In disbelief, I keep asking, whispering to the others "Ohio is called? Ohio's called?" tired of the suspense but having a bad gut feeling. Mark Jones comes running in behind the cameras confirms "Ohio goes to Obama!"

I say in agony, on live T.V., "It's over!" I didn't even want to work on Mitt Romney's campaign this time and I thought he had come to say and do anything and had become negative as opposed to the first time having solutions. So why did I feel so miserable? The next hours passed much too slowly. Now, we had to talk about the results.

"I believed Mitt Romney would win because what we are doing is not working," I say. "It doesn't matter if people connect with him or not. They know what we're doing is not working. I thought the voters would do something different." I sound like a broken record by now.

Representative Alan Vought goes on to say something about the "47%" and the "War on Women" didn't help Mitt. I try to ignore him. I have no energy to say "how come we can't say the truth anymore?" Elections almost always come down to the women voters, so I know those talking points were effective. But all I can think is why am I so upset? Even though I constantly felt frustrated with Romney staff, and liked the Romney in 2008 better than the one in 2012, I wanted him to win.

Finally, it was time to go home. In the parking garage on our way out, Alan laughs. "Hey you're in a Smart car. I' m in a gas guzzling SUV! Isn't it supposed to be the other way around?" he asks jokingly. I am so darn tired of Republicans not successfully sharing their message. With little enthusiasm, I go on defense.

"Actually, I have always cared about the Earth. So do a lot of Republicans. I recycled long before it was cool. Every piece of paper is used twice at Magnolia. Cattlemen, like my family, are some of the first environmentalists. I never understood why Democrats think they own these issues. It only makes sense to me that I'm the one driving the Smart car!"

Alan gives a friendly laugh and I realize I took years of frustration out on him. We shake hands but before getting into his SUV Alan shouts "I can't wait to tell the guys in the office you're a Republican driving a Smart car!" I'm the fiscal conservative, but I say no more even though I know Alan has thick skin.

I came home to an empty house, television on Fox4, my dog Meg already fast asleep. I crashed, still in my suit after 17 hours. When Romney came out on the stage, I believed it was true he didn't have a concession speech prepared. All I could think about was that he's still surrounded by people telling him what he wants to hear rather than what he needs to hear. Before he speaks, I think about the work his family and he put into the campaign. The years of his life he poured into running for president. I went to bed without sleeping.

13 THE CPA

I wanted to work for the "good guys," but even my do-gooder ways wore me out at times, so I would put them aside. That's what happened when I worked for Congressman Don Young who was on the Center for Responsible Ethics in Government's "Most Corrupt" list. He did things like get a $931 billion earmark for special projects and a $231 million earmark for the "bridge to nowhere," but I happily worked on his team because he was a good paying client and surprisingly easy to work with. I justified my actions the same way elected officials justify theirs.

But, when I landed Congressman Conaway I felt like I was back wearing a white hat. He represented part of the old Combest district, with the biggest cities being Midland and Odessa. In one our early days of fundraising, I scheduled all day meetings in Fort Worth. I expected the day to be a success in terms of money. Then, I got a call from Dee Kelly, Jr's assistant that the meeting must be canceled and rescheduled, she apologized. I didn't doubt her as the Kelly's always participated in politics, responded quickly, and their assistants were amazingly on top of things. I found it mindboggling as they were some of the biggest names in Ft. Worth, with plenty of buildings named after them, yet they always took my calls. Still, I panicked, knowing it was too late to get another meeting scheduled. I hated to disappoint a client. I didn't know how Congressman Conaway would take the news.

"The meeting with Mr. Kelly needs to be rescheduled. Maybe we just eat lunch early and then get back to our schedule." I was nervous because it is a sin in politics to eat without having someone to pitch too or to pay for the meal. The day wasn't as I had planned.

While I wouldn't take most members of Congress to a hamburger joint like Kinkaid's, I knew Congressman Conaway appreciated a good burger and wasn't afraid of eating at a restaurant without a table cloth. In fact, Congressman Conaway actually preferred casual, something that I admired in him. But when I pulled up at Kinkaid's front door, car still running, the Congressman looked at me with an odd expression on his face that I couldn't read. "What are you doing?" he asked. "Letting you out," I answered. "It's pretty crowded and parking is hard to find. I will need to park a few blocks away, so you may want to go ahead," I say. "You're going to let me out and you're going to walk?" Conaway asks. "Yes," I say slowly to him, confused. "There's something wrong with this picture. Show me where you're going to park." Conaway demands.

Now I am more confused as I can't just point to where I am going to park. I have not yet found a parking space. So, I pull away from the front door and luckily find a spot I can parallel park into rather quickly. "Will this be okay?" I ask Conaway, not sure what's going on with this relatively new client of mine. He looks at Kinkaid's and then back at my car, then to me. "You think I can't walk that far?" he asks. "Oh, no. No, sir. I just thought you would want me to drop you off to make efficient use of your time. So, you wouldn't have to be bothered. And..." Conaway cuts me off. "Who has done this to you? Is this what my colleagues ask of you?" I want to answer him but I don't want to insult his colleagues. "I don't mind. Not at all. I like happy clients," I say. "That's ridiculous" Conaway tells me. "Besides this is great weather."

We make our way the two blocks to Kinkaid's where we order two enormous burgers and hand cut fries. We share a picnic table with strangers inside the former grocery and no fellow customers suspect there is a United States Congressman dining among them. When we go to leave, on autopilot, I jump up and say "I'll be right back with the car." As I move away, going as fast as one can go in three inch heels, Congressman Conaway shouts— as I am far ahead. "Leslie, wait!" I stop where I am and begin beating myself up. It's a known fact that staff should gobble down their food, retrieve the vehicle ahead of time, and have it waiting. I made a rookie mistake of enjoying and actually eating lunch. I had wasted valuable time and couldn't believe I dropped my guard as this Mike Conway fella kept me confused most of the day.

"I'll walk with you," Conaway says. I stood still until he reached me. Preparing for him to raise his voice and lecture me, he said nothing. I'm ready to apologize the moment Conaway speaks. We go ahead and walk to the car. When we get inside Conaway tells me to "Elaborate on what just happened." I go into great detail of how I know the protocol…. he interrupts me "I'm disgusted at my colleagues. I can't imagine the day I would send someone to fetch the car for me." This guy really is a freshman from West Texas. West Texans aren't afraid to do things themselves, eat hamburgers at dives, and wear cowboy boots with their suits.

We go to our next meeting and when we are done, we exit the elevator, Mike—who tells me to call him Mike now, looks to me and says "I'll wait here in the lobby and you go get the car," as he points outside. With cat-like reflexes, I am in sprint mode to the car and just as quickly Mike says "Leslie, I am joking. My colleagues really do, do this!" he says shaking his head, smiling. "I still can't believe it," he says to me. "And you really do this! I am coming with you to the car!" Mike announces. It's at this moment I let Mike know I don't get jokes, surprised I hadn't already shared this nugget as I usually get that information out to a client pretty fast

Quickly, Mike Conaway became one of my favorite clients because I trusted he was one of the good guys. I admired how he "traveled light." I found it fairly easy to raise money for him, so I made money. He didn't get bogged down in all the details, he let my staff and I handled things. I think he saw we could introduce him to other donors outside of West Texas that he didn't know. We could also encourage people in his district to give easier than he could.

"He might be a good client but you have to go to the Permian Basin," people would say as if it were some terrible far-away place in Siberia. But I really liked West Texas. I am bad with directions but can successfully navigate my way around Midland and Odessa and that was nice going someplace with one less worry. I enjoyed all the Tex-Mex and liked that I could find a parking space without having to go into a multi-level parking garage. I entertained myself by playing a game-would I live in Midland or Odessa? The two cities were competitors like Ft. Worth and Dallas. I am one of the few that lived in both Ft. Worth and Dallas and found them each a great place to live. It was the same with Midland and Odessa—I thought I could live in either spot.

But most of what I liked about West Texas were the people I got to hang around because of Mike Conaway. I admired them. They don't have time for pretense, suits, and small talk. In a time where a lot of people act like they have money–we call them $30k millionaires–that's not the case in Midland. They have more money than anywhere in the country—second only to Greenwich, Connecticut-but act like they don't. And many of them are fun and interesting to work with. And no one was more West Texas than Congressman Mike Conaway.

During the presidential race, Congressman Conaway switched his support from thinking about Mayor Rudy Giuliani to Governor Romney shortly after meeting them both in person. He hadn't planned on getting so involved, but I wasn't surprised he did. He's from West Texas and they don't sit on the sidelines in politics. His wife, Suzanne and he hosted a breakfast fundraiser in their

Midland home for Romney. They raised a bunch of money, but not enough to satisfy the Romney team.

The Romney staff were frustrated I hadn't convinced some of the Bush Pioneers to raise hundreds of thousands for Romney like they did for George W. Bush when he was running for president. I explained, to deaf ears, that these people got calls from George W. Bush. They expected to hear from not just me, but from Romney too. They wanted to know the man. This made sense to me.

So, the Romney staff ran around the Conaway's home like chickens with their heads cut off trying to locate Bush Pioneer, Joe O'Neill, a successful oilman that they had not convinced to join their team. When the Romney staff took a second to stop buzzing around, they panicked thinking he hadn't shown up. I spoke up "The man you whizzed by and brushed on the shoulder, the one in the plaid shirt, that's Mr. O'Neill." The look on their face was priceless as they weren't ready for West Texas.

A Romney staffer characterized my work as "sloppy" in reference to the Midland briefing papers I prepared that listed everyone's employer and occupation. "You listed just about everyone on your briefing forms as involved in oil and gas. And self-employed. Everyone can't be involved in oil and gas!" I laughed. "In West Texas they most certainly can," and those that overheard the conversation sympathized with what I was dealing with. That day I laughed about it. Much later, on another Midland trip to their home, Mike Conaway and I laughed about it all again, while Suzanne and I enjoyed a margarita poolside.

I not only liked Mike Conaway and his wife, Suzanne, I liked just about everyone I met and worked with raising money in his campaign. There were all kinds of people in West Texas that I talked to even when I wasn't trying to raise money. I helped their kids get jobs, I sent cards for their birthdays and anniversaries, and went to supper with them when I was in town. I even got to meet one of my childhood heroes, Clayton Williams, who they call "Claytie" in West Texas.

I couldn't remember what Clayton Williams looked like or many details. All my memories I had were that he ran for Governor of Texas and that my parent's and those in the cattle business supported him over Ann Richards. I couldn't have told you who ran for governor of Kentucky back then but I knew the entire details of the Texas race and overheard a few tacky jokes that I still remember.

I cried when I learned on the nightly news what Mr. Williams said in a debate. But most of all, what I knew about Mr. Williams was the grand deals Daddy had with him. Some grand successes and others grand failures. He bought thousands of cattle. Daddy always talked about us going to the poor house, which I always imagined was close by. To me, Mr. Williams kept my family out of the poor house. I was grateful and all this led me to imagine Mr. Williams as the Marlboro man. (I grew up admiring cowboys and the American west.) When I met him as an adult, working with Congressman Conaway, I was not prepared for the small, petite, man that stood in front of me.

I felt silly because I was nervous about introducing myself to him. But, I did it anyway. He was still talking to some other people so I approached Mrs. Williams, Modesta as people called her, and told her my story. She was moved and reached out for her husband's arm. "Go ahead," she nodded to me in one of the most soothing voices I have ever heard. "Mr. Williams, I am Leslie Sorrell," I say feeling like a small, awkward child. "Oh, yes. You invited us tonight," Mr. Williams says, referring to Congressman Conaway's dinner. "Yes. But…I am from Kentucky and my Daddy and you…" Before I finished, Mr. Williams says "Oh, yes. Your Daddy is Gene Sorrell." He laughed. "We had some good times. How long has it been since he died? How is your Mother? Is she still in the cattle business?" Modesta leaned over and whispered in my ear "See, he remembers." We talked a few minutes more as I didn't want to take up too much of their time. They both gave me a hug. None of this would have happened if it weren't for Mike Conaway.

Mike Conaway has a unique relationship to Clayton Williams that goes way back, and because of that, somewhere along the way, I mustered the nerve to ask Mike Conaway about Mr. Williams's comments he made decades ago that no one seems to let him forget. "He just opened his big mouth and made a mistake," Mike said matter of fact. "He doesn't believe what he said. It was a mistake and he certainly has had to live with it." Of course, people make mistakes. And I could continue to be proud of my childhood hero and my parents' interactions with him because of what Mike Conaway shared with me.

As good as things were with Mike, his donors, and West Texas, things were not always so smooth with his staff. Mike had a loyalty that sometimes worked against what was in his best interest, mainly when it came to his campaign staff. Both of his chief of staffs agreed but they didn't have any better luck convincing Mike otherwise.

None of us thought it smart that Mike let Bill, his well-paid accountant with whom he shared office space as a CPA, also serve as the de facto campaign manager. To make matters more complicated Bill's wife worked in the district office as the scheduler. Neither had worked in a campaign before but that didn't stop Bill from lecturing the Magnolia staff on his so-called expertise. It frustrated my team that Bill would moralize them, all the while it was public record Bill was filing the federal election reports incorrectly and constantly having to amend them.

Bill kept silent when a contribution would come in that we were expecting and pretended to not understand why that bothered us. (I needed to know so we could either thank someone for their support or make sure they kept their pledge of sending money.) We needed to know whose arms to twist. We could have raised more money had it not been for Bill's shenanigans. He simply made things unnecessarily difficult.

Worse, I worked hard to bring money in the door and Bill worked as hard to keep it from entering if he didn't approve of that individual or their religious beliefs. We had heated conversations over people he believed might be "questionable Muslims." Bill couldn't comprehend someone could be a Muslim and want to be involved in politics and their community and not be part of a terrorist plot. It didn't occur to Bill that these were grateful immigrants who started with nothing, made something, and employed lots of hardworking

Americans. He mocked their customs and ultimately refused to deposit their money. I was humiliated because of his ignorance.

But despite all the head-butting I did with Bill, I didn't bring it up with Mike, only with his chiefs. Looking back, I think it was because I wanted Mike to not have any faults and I didn't want to have that conversation with him because I knew he would choose Bill. Mike appeared emotionally attached to Bill. The chiefs must have thought so too because while they disagreed with what Bill was doing they didn't want to take him on either. Meanwhile, I went back to battles I thought I could win.

I thought I could win the "Ways and Means battle," but I was wrong. When Mike Conaway told me he wanted to serve on that committee, he thought one of the best ways to get selected was to raise a bunch of money for the National Republican Congressional Committee (NRCC) and other Republican campaigns across the country. His chief of staff, Jeff and I agreed. Jeff shared with me the other campaigns they identified to support and such.

Mike didn't particularly enjoy raising money but considered it a necessary evil and usually left the heavy lifting to me and I was fine with that arrangement. So, I was surprised at his new-found energy converted to constant fundraising mode. I took this to mean Mike Conaway genuinely wanted to serve on the House Ways and Means Committee. Of course, it made sense as a CPA he would be interested because the Ways and Means Committee is the head tax committee charged with revenues and making budget recommendations. That fit Mike well and much better than the Agriculture Committee, which was one of Mike's committee assignments.

Conaway was not the only one wanting to be on the Ways and Means Committee though. He would have to go against one of his colleagues, Congressman Kenny Marchant, in his battle to secure a seat on this powerful committee. Jeff didn't share any details about the dynamics of the race between the two and neither did Conaway, only to say they knew it was going to be a tough race. For reasons unbeknownst to me, Kenny was the Party's choice and anointed one—not Mike. But that didn't stop me as I went to work right away and organized a meeting at the Claydesta Towers in Midland, named for Clayton and Modesta Williams.

"Anything for you, Mike" more than a few said at our meeting. True to form, Conaway supporters dug deeper into their pockets and gave in ways they hadn't since George W. Bush was running for president. They were proud that Mike Conaway was their Congressman. And they wanted him to increase his power. So, we didn't have to explain it twice when Mike told them raising and giving money increased his chances to secure the seat on the committee. This was a savvy group of politicos and they knew what needed to be done and rose to the challenge. After all, this is a group of kingmakers that made presidents. Surely, they could get Mike on the Ways and Means Committee.

One of the more practical donors correctly predicted some in the room may hesitate in giving to the national Party. Many Republicans don't like giving money and not getting to control who gets it and how it's spent. They get frustrated with hearing every election year that the Party needs money to get out of debt. These are fiscal conservatives.

"Look, I know many of you prefer not to give the national Party, but this is for Mike. We think that if he sends significant funds to 'em he can get on Ways & Means. That's good for him and good for you. We need him to get credit for your money," said a loyal Conway supporter.

So they gave, not necessarily approving of what races the NRCC got involved in and didn't get involved in, but they did so because like me, they believed in Mike Conaway. We raised over $100k for the NRCC in a few days. For individual campaigns, we raised about the same amount. Congressman Robin Hays who served on the Ag Committee with Mike, Pete Olson, a congressional candidate in Houston, and many more candidates and congressmen from across the country came to Midland leaving with thousands of campaign dollars from people they had never met. All for Mike.

While the D.C. team did their part inside the beltway, we worked on an aggressive campaign outside the beltway educating and informing Mike's supporters of the situation with meetings, conference calls, and other updates.

All this happened in days. In one letter, Mike shared with them "As we discussed, I am continuing to work hard on moving up the food chain to get on the Ways and Means Committee and feel like I am making some progress." When Mike Conaway didn't secure a seat on the Ways & Means Committee and Kenny Marchant did, I was left with more questions than answers. They were questions I would never get the answers too. I got the impression the chief, Jeff, left over this. Suzanne, Mike's wife, said "it's the most upset and disappointed I've ever seen him." It was taking him longer than they thought to get over the loss of not being selected.

Much later, we had a golf fundraiser at Horseshoe Bay, my Will asked Mike "With your financial background, I know we would all like to see you get on some committees like Financial Services or Ways & Means. What can we do to help make that happen?" Many piped up in agreement, nodding their heads, anxious to hear the answer. I realized Conaway supporters were just as optimistic and doggedly determined as me. Disappointedly, Mike answered as a man who had been beaten down by the system. I didn't recognize this Mike Conaway. "It doesn't look like that's in the cards for me. We tried a while back and we shouldn't have." Why shouldn't we? I wondered. What did he know that I still didn't know? Mike continued. "I am on the Budget and Agriculture Committees. One day, if I am lucky, I may be the Chairman of the Ag Committee."

Mike the chair of the Ag Committee? I thought that would be all wrong. By the looks on everyone's faces they thought so too. Mike didn't have the enthusiasm I saw in Congressman Larry Combest when he summoned us into his office and excitedly told us Speaker Gingrich personally called him to say he would be the next ag chairman. I stood dumbfounded and waited for Mike to elaborate. He didn't. My husband, Will, looked over at me. He knew exactly what I was thinking and says to me "I'm sorry."

"The day I am no longer excited about my job; I will come home. I don't have to go to Washington to figure out what I believe. I love this job but I don't have to have it," Congressman Mike Conaway said numerous times on the campaign trail. But I no longer believed Mike Conaway loved his job. But clearly, Mike Conaway wasn't ready or able to walk away from the power.

Word travels fast in politics. I had just decided to work with Grant Stinchfield, who wanted to run for Congress. Working with Stinchfield meant working against Republican Congressman Kenny Marchant, a former client. Shortly afterwards, Congressman Mike Conaway called me. "I have to let you go because you're working with Kenny's opponent." Shocked, I simply say "I am sorry to hear that." This did not seem like the Mike Conaway I knew.

"Me too, but that's the way it is if you are working with Kenny's opponent," Mike says as if he is suddenly became close friends with a man he didn't think that much of not so long ago. I confirm I am indeed working for Kenny's opponent and share with Mike his name because I don't even think that Mike has any idea who is running against Kenny or any details. "I am working for Grant Stinchfield and he is a good guy. In fact, some of your supporters here in North Texas are disappointed with Kenny and the job he is doing."

"Well, it wasn't right you had that group 'We the People' do those robo-calls. I was told they were traced back to Magnolia." I have no idea what he is talking about but take note he says "Magnolia" as opposed to me—maybe trying not to make it personal or something like that.

"Mike, I have no idea what you are talking about and I can tell you we have done no such thing. I am not aware of any calls anyone is doing. And on those calls, it is supposed to state who paid for them. That's simply not accurate what Marchant is telling you. When you heard about it and had a question you should have called me," I said.

"Well, that didn't sound right to me," Conaway conceded. "I don't even know how they would trace it back to you. But, I just wanted to call you in person. I wanted to do that. We've had a good run," he says sounding a bit like the fella I knew. What I wondered but didn't ask was what does Kenny Marchant have on you? But instead simply said "Yeah, we have had a good run," agreeing with the Congressman. "It's been a good run. A good six years." Conaway repeated. "Yes, it has." I agreed again. Enjoyed working with you," Conway said. "And so have I," I tell him. There was nothing more to say. Really. Conway ended the call with "Good bye." And I knew we would never talk again.

This call came before the filing deadline, meaning there could be a chance Stinchfield wouldn't file and run. Word got back to me that Marchant's campaign wanted me to change my mind about Grant and that if I did, they could get my client, Congressman Conaway, back. I only needed to get Grant out of the way. I was sickened they could get Mike to call me and then were so confident they could get him to hire me back. I wasn't interested.

While I did appreciate Congressman Mike Conaway calling me directly, I did find it odd I hadn't heard from the new chief of staff, Richard Hudson. Two days before Mike called to let me go, Richard had asked me to reach out to some people on behalf of Conaway to raise money for Speaker Boehner at an event the Speaker was headlining at the Austin Club. Most of the folks I knew in the 11th District of Texas were not Boehner fans, but some people may give a little money to attend the event and "give Mike credit" for helping the Speaker out and being a team player.

I had several messages into Richard about Speaker Boehner's event. It was unusual for someone to be fired and not hear from the chief, at least with a follow up courtesy call. Plus, I wanted to follow up from my email about Speaker Boehner's event in Austin that Conaway would be attending as I still wanted to close any gaps and keep things running smooth for both him and Congressman Conaway.

When Richard and I finally connected, he apologized and said "I've been so busy I haven't even had a chance to catch you up. By the way, I was surprised Mike would let you go just because you're with some other challenger's campaign. When Mike talked to me about it, I recommended against it." I believed Richard.

Richard apologized again and said "I've been a little out of it. I spend most of my days at the NRCC. I'm running for Congress in North Carolina's 8th." Not terribly shocked, as rumor had it years before that Richard, then chief of staff for Congressman Hays, was responsible for Hays narrow loss and that Richard wanted to run in that seat. It went to the Democrats, but now it was an open seat and he had his chance. I was in disbelief that Congressman Conaway would let Richard remain as his chief and run for Congress simultaneously. Was that even allowed? Obviously, a lot had happened in the time Richard and I hadn't connected. And while more than a few chief of staffs wanted to be a Congressman, not as many are so bold. Not approving of Richard's actions, I did admire his gumption and told him so. "Good for you!" I exclaimed. I even said I would help him, but I knew he wouldn't dare as he wouldn't want to upset Congressman Marchant.

Richard went on to say that through redistricting in North Carolina, the 8th Congressional District became significantly more Republican. It always comes down to redistricting, I thought. These elections take place before Election Day–the deal before the deal. "While several candidates entered the race, there weren't any strong ones," Richard tells me. "I was excited the Republican leadership approached me to run." Why would leadership approach Richard? He had to be talking about Leader Cantor, my client I also admired, and I kept thinking I was tired of always being disappointed. I mean, why would they choose to get involved when it would definitely be a red seat? And when I get involved it's a sin. I only had questions, no answers.

Literally, Richard was the chief of staff for Congressman Mike Conaway one moment and now he was off and running for Congress. Richard had done something right because even with four opponents many members of Congress got involved in his Republican primary campaign. But none of it made sense to me.

But let me be clear, this wasn't an easy race for Richard. Club for Growth, a nationally known political action committee that prides itself on supporting fiscal hawks and economic freedom candidates, attacked Richard. They brought significant political power and clout into the race. Club for Growth had hard-hitting ads touting their guy as the real small businessman in the race. "Small businessman" are magic words in a Republican primary. Everyone fights to get to labeled that in voters' minds. The Club attacked hard saying Richard was not a small businessman as he claimed, but in reality, a Washington insider. They called him a career bureaucrat who was married to a fellow staffer who happened to be a chief of staff for another member of Congress. (His wife, Renee, was chief for Congressman Quayle.) The Club said that Renee and Richard weren't residents of North Carolina liked they claimed, just there for the campaign. Everything that they said was true of course, but voters have trouble determining what is fact and fiction in politics.

All of Richard's hard work paid off as he overcame their attacks and won in the Republican primary run-off election the following July against Club for Growth backed candidate, Scott Keadle. Richard was not a Congressman— yet. He still faced Democrat incumbent, Congressman Larry Kissell, in the November general election. Thankfully for Richard and the Republicans, the North Carolina legislature drew the district from a "competitive" one to a much more heavily Republican seat. It was almost assured Richard would be the next Congressman from the Eighth District of North Carolina. Sure enough, that November, Richard defeated Democrat Kissell with 54% of the vote.

No one had to ask how I felt about Richard becoming a Congressman and what Conaway and the Republican leadership's role was in the race. But the Magnolia staff couldn't help but ask how I took the news about Conaway. They knew how I felt about him. My answer surprised them. "Deeply disappointed," I said. "Not over losing a client so much as losing faith in one of my most favorite Congressmen." I mourned the loss of another good person falling victim to the system.

14 THE INCUMBENT

One way to get to Congress is to decide to run, hire a good team, raise a bunch of money, and win. But there are more Machiavellian ways to get there. A quiet, and some would say boring secret is redistricting. Like what Richard did. Redistricting, required by the constitution every ten years, ensures the population is equalized per member of Congress and means the district lines are adjusted accordingly. Redistricting is the ultimate insider's game. Elected officials hope people don't pay attention to it. So far, they have got their wish.

The unusual and controversial Texas mid-decade redistricting efforts were led by Majority Whip Tom DeLay. DeLay's reputation as "the Hammer" was further earned as many credit him for single handedly pushing through new congressional districts and taking out Democrat strong holds using the redistricting process. DeLay's audacious plan worked and resulted in the Texas

Republicans securing a majority in the U.S. House of Representatives for the first time in 130 years.

Traditionally, redistricting was good for my business. Even though we weren't directly involved in redistricting, I made sure staff and interns understood the process because it was important to our bottom line. If you were in one of our meetings, here's what you would've learned.

In many states, like in Texas, it is the state legislature that draws the lines. The Republicans controlled the Texas legislature at that time, so they got to draw the lines. The Texas legislature does not act independently. U.S. Representatives lobby and consult with the state on how they would like the lines drawn for their districts. In fact, most of the Congressmen from Texas use monies from their campaign accounts to hire an attorney for the redistricting process. Several of them deploy their chief of staffs to Austin, Texas's state capitol, to look over the state legislatures' shoulders.

The Texas Legislature does an interesting dance of keeping the current group in office happy, while balancing their own ambitions of going to Congress and having the power to draw the lines accordingly, and making sure it follows the constitution. Texas got two of the three right as their redistricting efforts went to the U.S. Supreme Court more than once because they didn't follow the law and submit their maps for pre-clearance. That mistake cost the state several millions, but Republicans thought it was worth the price tag.

The better the Congressmen and his staff are at lobbying their state legislators, the better district they get and the less competitive election they'd have. Coincidently, Kenny Marchant not only was a member of the Redistricting committee in the Texas Legislature, but chaired it.

Rumors were that Representative Marchant regretted not running for the 26th District of Texas, the one represented by Congressman Burgess. Some of the most drastic changes happened in that district. It went from a concise district, with most of one county and a few parts of the surrounding to something very different, stretching to Oklahoma. Was it because Congressman Burgess and his chief of staff were not good at lobbying the

Texas legislature? Or was it because Representative Marchant had the power to carve out his own district? Or both?

While the redistricting played out, our team would call donors and keep them apprised of the process and get money. "Congressman so and so has been campaigning for the past two years to his constituents, only to learn the legislature is giving him a whole new set of constituents. That opens the door for an opponent. We need more campaign dollars to tell this new set of folks who the Congressman is and keep someone from filing against him."

Not only did the redistricting process help us to raise more money for our clients (and us), typically it created opportunities for more clients. Word got out that the Texas Legislature was going to create an open Republican seat. The 24th Congressional district changed drastically from a very safe Democrat seat that Congressman Martin Frost held, now to a very safe Republican seat. A Republican could now run and win and become a United States Congressman. Interestingly, the very same cities Representative Marchant represented in the legislature all got included in the new 24th Congressional district. Even the city of Carrollton, the city he was mayor of before going to the legislature got included.

Just like Congressman Charlie Stenholm ended up having to run against Congressman Randy Neugebauer because of redistricting, something similar happened with Democrat Congressman, Martin Frost. He decided the Republican Texas Legislature made it impossible to stay in his current 24th District, so he choose to run in the 32nd District of Texas, represented by Congressman Pete Sessions.

Republican Congressman Pete Sessions and Democrat Congressman Martin Frost's race was one of the few competitive ones in the country. PACs poured in about $3million (those were large figures back then. It was still pre-Super PAC days.) Media from across the country covered this race, including NBC's Grant Stinchfield, an investigative reporter. Congressman Sessions beat Congressman Frost 54% to 44%. During that race Grant Stinchfield got bit by the political bug. But because of Grant's work at NBC5, he was not allowed to "participate in political endeavors" so instead he watched closely from the sidelines.

While, Congressmen Sessions and Frost were running against each other, Texas state Representative Kenny Marchant ran for the United States Congress. Marchant had all the advantages of an incumbent. The other three people in the race didn't have a chance and were not serious opponents, not raising money, and actively campaigning. The only concern was with so many people in the race and a low turn-out, there was always the possibility Marchant may fall short of winning by 50% and go into a run-off.

Regardless, it was a forgone conclusion that Kenny Marchant would be the next congressman from the 24th District of Texas, representing seven hundred thousand people. Maybe that's why voters stayed home—only 9,073 people voted. Congressmen represent about 700,000 people. But, Kenny Marchant became Congressman Marchant with 9,073 votes!

I know all this because I worked on this race with Kenny Marchant. He was one of the first clients I didn't know well but all my D.C. buddies and lobbyists friends told me "He's gonna win. You need him as a client." Or they would say "Client for life." Austin was hard for me to break into, more so than the D.C. scene as Austin never thought I was "Texas enough," "old enough," or "man enough." I figured having Marchant as a client may help as Kenny Marchant was considered the poster-child for Austin-insiders.

Debating whether I should try to get Representative Marchant as a client, I couldn't help but do think what it would do for Magnolia's bottom line. But even with our successes with other congressional candidates, Kenny Marchant didn't return my calls. Since the whole world told me I needed to land this fella as client, I was determined to do so. Finally, I decided to ask for help from a well-respected Bush Pioneer about not having any luck even getting in touch with Marchant. (I am not using the Bush Pioneer's name because he is still one of the good guys out there.)

"You bet," the Bush Pioneer said without hesitation. He went on to invite me that afternoon to attend Representative Marchant's Annual Texas-OU fundraiser at the Melrose Hotel as his guest. The fundraiser took place the fall before Kenny Marchant made his public announcement, but no one doubted Marchant was running. Optimistic I could make some inroads; I took the Bush Pioneer up on his offer.

Within minutes of arriving of me arriving in the ballroom, the Bush Pioneer walked over to Representative Marchant, spent about 30 seconds with him, walked back to me, and said "It's done. You should be getting a call next week." I hadn't seen a business deal go down so fast! In awe that the Pioneer could speak to the Representative Marchant, tell him to hire me, and get it done all so quickly and effortlessly, I did the only thing I knew or could do. I simply said "Thank you!" and shook his hand.

Kenny Marchant and I worked together because he was told to hire me by a very powerful person. I worked for him because I wanted to make money on a race with a guaranteed outcome. It was business. Otherwise, we didn't enjoy working together.

I broke Magnolia's cardinal rule of working on "commission only" but I didn't think I had much bargaining room. I couldn't imagine going back to the Bush Pioneer and say "I blew it." Besides, I knew money would pour in relatively quickly, so it was a safe bet. Normally, we require a retainer, plus commission, plus bonuses. I share this because it meant if I didn't raise money, I got a percent of nothing. So, I made darn sure we had a packed schedule. We could sleep when we were dead.

The message to potential donors was simple. "There's no doubt Kenny Marchant is going to win. Do you want to be on the early train or the late train?" I would take a pause and then add "and the late train costs a lot more." Money came in at record speed.

Just as quickly, I learned Kenny Marchant doesn't "do breakfast" or mornings. After scheduling a late-night dinner meeting with a group of donors at the Indo-Pak restaurant in Carrollton, Representative Marchant made an appearance and left shortly after arriving. It didn't go over well with them, so I did my best to cover for Marchant, staying through more courses than I could count and never-ending cups of chai. Not only did I learn I have an endless appetite for kabobs, the chai gave me plenty of energy to listen to the passionate debates on our country. But the biggest take-away was that I discovered Marchant doesn't do late nights either.

When I confirmed a meeting with Bush Pioneer Dan Cook, a billionaire who speaks loudly because he is hard of hearing, I was thrilled at the potential possibilities. His advice and ability to raise money was priceless. More interesting, Mr. Cook got to know a young go-getter named Shawn Terry when Shawn ran against Congressman Martin Frost. Shawn lost, but impressed a whole bunch of people with his hustle and his fundraising skills. Mr. Cook assisted Shawn in starting MHT Partners, which managed a couple of billion dollars. And now, Kenny Marchant and me were in their offices. All we had to do was to listen and learn. The money would follow.

But Kenny Marchant wasn't used to people telling him what to do. Kenny Marchant had made a bunch of money too and typically had people coming to him. It was in this meeting, that I realized Kenny Marchant was not like any client I had ever had. He wasn't about to ask Mr. Cook for anything. Mr. Cook realized this and said rather gruffly, "I'm not giving you a dime unless you ask me for it." To my surprise, Kenny Marchant did not. I can't remember experiencing such and an awkward silence. I couldn't believe it. I thought I may die right there. I couldn't take the silence anymore and blurted out "Mr. Cook, thank you for taking the meeting. I know your time is valuable. Of course, we would appreciate your contributing to the campaign." Before I could continue, Mr. Cook says "he needs to be the one to ask," as he pointed to Kenny.

Mr. Cook had helped get a man elected to president and a whole bunch of other people in office. Like so many, he personally wanted to be asked. That's why he took the meeting. He was prepared to contribute. But Kenny refused to ask. I thought it couldn't get any more awkward, but I was wrong. Thankfully, that's when Shawn popped in. Not witnessing what had gone on, I went ahead and said "It sure would mean a lot to us if Mr. Cook and you would write a letter on Kenny's behalf." He agreed. I knew exactly who to send it to have the letter perform well and it did. But we never did get money from Mr. Cook. I blamed Kenny.

American Airlines had a strict "incumbent only" rule. It meant their PAC only gave to someone already in office, not any candidates. So, I was quite pleased with myself when I succeeded in getting American Airlines to bend that policy by Gerald Arpy, the CEO, hosting a roundtable luncheon at their offices. While the American Airlines PAC didn't contribute directly to Kenny's campaign, several of their executives gave us nice size checks. They did this because they knew they should get in good with the member that would be representing them.

Afterwards, in the parking lot of the American Airlines headquarters, Representative Marchant told me, while pointing his finger at me, "I am not doing that again." Immediately, I felt sick at my stomach. Shocked, I took a moment to process what he was saying to me. "We just had a fundraising meeting where we raised several thousand dollars, got a tour, and ate lunch in less than two hours. They're the largest employers in the district. You don't think that's a good use of your time? They agreed their PAC would max out after the election."

Most members would relish in such an efficient use of time—eating lunch, collecting money, and leaving with more pledges. Not Representative Marchant. "They should come to me!" Marchant said in a booming voice that made me feel quite little. It was quite the opposite of his typical soft voice that defied his large self. "That's the way we've always done it. And that's the way I want it done now. You're running me all over the place."

"Of course I am! We have a small window to take advantage of. You're running for Congress! You're complaining about working too hard? I am not asking you to work harder than me!" But I said all of this only to myself. What I said out loud, and in the nicest way I knew how, was to point out the obvious. "But you're a Representative in the Texas House. You're not a Congressman. Not yet."

I said what no one else around him was willing to say. Clearly, everyone else from Marchant's Austin circle refused to speak so boldly to him. I knew he was going to win, but I thought he needed to be humbler and appreciative to be more successful in fundraising. But Marchant didn't care because he didn't need anyone. He could fund the whole campaign without any help from anyone and I believe he was prepared to do just that. My response probably was not what Representative Marchant was looking for from me. He exploded.

"Leslie, I am not going to keep doing this! You're working me too hard. I don't have to do this. "

"Okay" I whispered, quietly conceding, as we each headed to not only our separate cars, but our separate ways. I knew we wouldn't be working with Kenny Marchant for his general election campaign. And this was the same day I was okay with that because some campaigns last longer than others. Jerry King told me years ago "campaigns have births and deaths." This death just came a little quicker than most.

In the seven or so weeks Marchant and I worked together, we both were successful. There were no hard feelings. It simply didn't make sense for us to continue for the general election. And over the years, Congressman Marchant would hire us for a one-time event as needed. Surprisingly, he'd even give me hug at times. We were both okay with how everything turned out. It was business.

"After my primary, I knew the general election would be easy. My district is overwhelming Republican. I thought, well, I could just coast to November. But Senator Phil Gramm told me I had an obligation to work on GOTV (Get Out The Vote) efforts and help turn-out Republicans for the general election." Congressman Burgess told me. "Before that conversation with Senator Gramm I hadn't looked at it that way. But it made sense." Senator Gramm must have not had the same conversation with Kenny Marchant because he simply coasted to November and left the other Republicans behind.

Meanwhile, Grant Stinchfield continued to enjoy his investigative reporting. However, he was growing frustrated that the news business had become nonsense. Instead of meaty investigative pieces, reporters were relegated to standing on the snow-covered bridges telling people "There's snow and ice on the bridge. Go slow." Grant said "That's common sense. People don't need to be told the obvious."

Worse, stories Grant pitched were not deemed newsworthy because the viewers no longer were interested in "real news" but preferred sensational stories of diets, celebrities, and other non-sense. The tipping point was during the auto bailout. Grant was working on a story where the auto industries were asking to be bailed out while simultaneously in negotiations with Jerry Jones's new Cowboy Stadium on purchasing suites. Grant hadn't even shared what he was working on with anybody; so, he was surprised when his boss summoned him and demand he kill his story because it would hurt their advertising dollars.

"That was a wake-up call. The news business has been bought and sold." Grant told his friend Jeff, also in the news business. Grant also shared his temptation of wanting to run the story anyway. "I'm not naïve. The story won't run regardless–if I quit or not. They wouldn't let it." Jeff agreed. That wakeup call was a catalyst for Grant to figure out what he wanted to do next. I knew Jeff and he would be the one to set up the meeting at the coffee shop where I met Grant for the first time.

Grant had always been entrepreneurial. He sold t-shirts in college, later had a tree trimming business, a production company, and simply worked on filling a niche and turning it into extra money. Grant visited with many people about his next business venture. A close friend of his shared his success story and enjoyment of his Kwik Kar business and how he had now acquired three stores. Grant researched Kwik Kar and with his friend's encouragement purchased the Kwik Kar Oil Change of Irving and left the news business behind him.

That's when Grant and I got together to talk about his grandiose plans of "fundamentally changing the way Washington works." While I thought Grant was little crazy, I fell for his infectious energy and enthusiasm. Working on Grant's race meant I could get back to the basics. Grant's ideas meant I'd have the opportunity to do something different after years of clients simply being content in staying with the status quo. I knew I'd have fun with his campaign.

Grant spent our first meeting and follow up conversations talking about what he wanted to do and what he wanted to accomplish. He didn't spend a great deal time talking about opponents, not yet. Finally, I asked "So, which district would you run in?" Without hesitation, Grant answered, not with a number but a name. "Kenny Marchant." I cringed, as I wanted to work with Grant, but didn't know if he could win or I had the stomach for what would follow, if I joined Grant. I shared some of my concerns, but I held most of them back. Instead, I focused on how hard it would be for Grant instead of for me.

"Grant, people tell you they support you now, but what does that mean? You need to find out if they will actually give you money, vote for you, or put a sign out, knowing Kenny Marchant could see it." I continued my doomsday talk. "Then, you think you have all these friends and people who want to help. But Campaigns are cruel in that you learn you don't have as many friends as you think and they are hard on marriages. And that's just if you're running–it's worse if you're running against an incumbent in a Republican primary."

Grant, as determined as ever, kept pace. "I've been in the news business. I 've got thick skin." That didn't mean much to me, but Grant assured me it meant he could handle whatever happened. It proved to be true.

Texas was going through the redistricting process as required by law again in 2011 for the 2012 election cycle. While Grant was willing to take on an incumbent, I still wasn't sure I was and asked "Why don't you entertain running in one of the newly created districts?" For me, Grant reluctantly entertained such. But as the redistricting process continued it became clear there would not be an open seat opportunity for Grant. The Texas delegation drew the lone open seat as a safe Democrat seat. That only happened after the courts rejected the newly created 33rd being a Republican seat. (The courts said all of Texas's population growth was from minority populations and therefore there needed to be drawn a minority seat and that became the 33rd District of Texas.)

Grant went back to his original plan of running against the weakest member of the Texas delegation—Kenny Marchant. Grant and I had talked plenty about Grant— his strengths, his weaknesses, and his vision. Now, Grant was ready to talk about his opponent. He wanted to run against Congressman Kenny Marchant because he was an entrenched incumbent who had lost his way. Grant rattled off many of points, some I'd heard about, some I ignored, and some were new to me.

- Kenny Marchant went from $25million to $50million between 2008-2010, the economic collapse, while serving in office.
- Kenny said he was against ear marks–but made an exception for a company he owned stock in.
- Kenny had never spoken on the House floor.
- Kenny never introduced a piece of legislation.

"Kenny Marchant didn't even do the things a Congressman is supposed to do," Grant told me. For these reasons and many more, Grant believed Kenny Marchant was ineffective and his time had passed. While Grant Stinchfield successfully convinced me he would make a great Congressman, I hadn't yet convinced myself to go against a former client and Republican incumbent. The same thoughts went over and over in my mind. Ronald Reagan declared "thou shall not talk ill of a fellow Republican" and somewhere along the way this became known as "the 11th commandment." Somewhere along the way it meant, Republicans cannot challenge Republicans. I was a little girl when Reagan was president and I wondered how come no more Reagans had come along? Where were the Reagans? Maybe, it's because no Republican challenged anyone and we'd been stuck with the status quo for much too long.

Between Grant's fresh energy and ideas and Marchant's sleaze, I was prepared to do the unthinkable. To make sure Grant was, I grilled him for another round. "I want to make sure you fully understand Kenny Marchant is considered to be a "reliable conservative vote." Grant was about to start with why Marchant wasn't conservative and I refused to let him get his argument in.

"Regardless of the reality and all the reasons, you think Marchant is no longer fit to serve, you are going to have people tell you over and over they'd prefer a reliable vote to an unknown," I said to Grant. And those words–reliable conservative vote–are words I came to hate because we would be told that even more than I imagined. I wanted to make the point of what the number one push back may be from other Republicans. It wasn't that they thought Kenny was effective it was simply that he was "a reliable conservative vote." Even as I spoke to Grant I saw the words "inertia" pop-up in my mind. And make no mistake. We were going to be fighting the status quo and inertia in the biggest battle of our lives.

"So what does a "reliable conservative vote" really mean?" Grant asked even though he knew what it meant and wanted to hear my answer. "The short answer is that it means Kenny Marchant is not a liberal Democrat. It means he can push a button like a robot and that he is good at getting in-line. It does not mean he is a leader. Or, a person who has ideas." I say harshly as I am not upset at Grant but already worked up at all the people I am going to have to have this conversation with, very soon.

"But he doesn't even take advantage of having a safe Republican seat." Grant said. "And I could argue he has quite a few votes that are NOT that conservative. He should go on the offensive –I would–and share the conservative message. He needs to bring more conservatives into the primary process." I agree with Grant, while imagining what kind of Republicans we could get if more informed people participated and got involved in primaries. No one votes in them, so practically no one is making the decisions in our country and people are under the impression it's the majority.

"Agreed," I replied "And win over the hearts and minds of undecided or independent voters. But being viewed as a reliable vote means they can count on him to do what they want and not rock the boat most the time. We both know you want to rock the boat." Grant smiled as we already knew each other's personalities.

Rocking the boat by playing in a primary was a big deal to me, but not that big of deal. It didn't seem much different than to than in some past campaigns: enthusiastic candidate having well respected people in the community supporting them because they were disappointed in their current elected official and thought someone else could do a better job. No one in the group was under the impression the task at hand would be easy. Many were prepared to contribute money, go door to door, make calls, and do all the things it takes in to have a successful campaign.

After a bunch of wooing, Grant asked me to run his campaign and I said "Yes. Yes, I'll do it." There had been a few rumblings that Kenny Marchant may retire. It was too good to be true, but I thought Grant should check it out. "Grant, it's only right to call and ask Congressman Marchant if he is retiring. You need to personally tell him you are running against him." I advise clients to do that because it's the gentlemanly and professional thing to do. In fact, I advised Grant to call "everyone" as I didn't dare want to give anyone the excuse they would have supported Grant had only he asked.

It was no secret that Congressmen and their staffs shared frustrations over the years how they were expected to raise money for themselves, for others, and the Party but somehow Congressman Marchant got a pass. Many had even complained to me, about Marchant in the early days, hoping I would have some influence over him. All of this was a secret though they kept because with the public they praised Congressmen Marchant. It's just the way it is. Incumbents support incumbents.

Grant's call took Kenny by surprise and somewhere in their conversation Congressman Marchant suggested to Grant "Why don't you just run against Joe Barton?" (Joe Barton is a Congressman that represents Texas'6ᵗʰ District.) I had tried to prepare Grant for all kinds of scenarios, but Congressman Marchant suggesting Grant run against one of his colleagues wasn't one of them. But Grant simply told Congressman Marchant he'd made his decision.

I went to work expanding and building our team to take on this herculean task of fighting the status quo. We needed a team that was not so loyal to the Party they ignored everything else. We needed people who believed person over Party. Country over Party. We needed a team filled with critical thinkers, not litmus-test voters. One that was smart, full of spirit, and not afraid to put in the long hours required of a campaign like this. We needed a team that believed as Grant and I did.

15 THE CHALLENGER

On the corner of Main Street and Wall Street in Grapevine, Texas the Stinchfield/Magnolia team kicked off to what was supposed to have been only a four-month campaign to Election Day against Congressman Kenny Marchant. Instead, the campaign went on for twice that long. Redistricting was to blame.

We could not have scripted a kick-off any better, with the sunny weather and media turning out for Grant's big announcement. Our supporters filled Liberty Park waving American flags, while curiosity brought out potential supporters. A sitting member of Congress would have been pleased with such a turn out, as a challenger Grant was ecstatic. So was I.

The crowd, as I had hoped, filled with people who didn't know Grant, but were against Congressman Kenny Marchant and looking to switch horses. "I supported Kenny in his first election," one man shared with me "only to be disappointed. I want some new blood." Others said they never liked Marchant. A handful attended because the Congressman told them one thing and voted the opposite. "He broke his promise to me," a woman said as if she were still in shock. But mostly, this group of spectators looked forward to putting some energy into a race that was long over-due to have some injected into it. After all, Kenny Marchant had been an elected official longer than most our team had been alive.

I planned for everything. Working on a million "what if" scenarios, but I didn't plan enough because what I hadn't counted on that day was Congressman Kenny Marchant treating Grant Stinchfield challenging him seriously. I thought Marchant was too arrogant. Marchant's decision both impressed and disappointed me. When I saw a Marchant spy attending Grant's campaign kick-off, I knew I had been wrong in thinking Marchant would dismiss Grant.

"You either run unopposed or scared," Senator Phil Gramm says. "There's always one member of Congress that wakes up the day after the election surprised that he didn't win. It's because they didn't take their opposition seriously." That wouldn't be the case with Marchant.

"How do you know it's a spy?" Grant asked. "Simple. He's young. Young people don't go to these things. They have to be at work. He's dressed like a politico–wearing a dark suit in this heat…his dark sunglasses. And he hasn't talked to anyone since he arrived."

"Leslie, you've been doing this for too long. That doesn't make someone a spy!" Grant says. "Watch," I shoot back as I make my way to the stranger. Upon me approaching, the fella he immediately put his phone to his ear, pretending to talk. A "regular person" would have just said "hi." There was nothing secretive about Grant's campaign kick-off. Any person could have showed up, even someone in a Marchant t-shirt and it would have been their right. This was open to the public and broadcast on the nightly news. I didn't care that a spy showed up. But it meant Congressman Marchant was not taking Grant lightly. I had hoped Congressman Marchant and his team would be like a typical incumbent, with too much arrogance.

Confirming my fears, a Carrollton precinct chair shared with Damon on our team, that Marchant's staff was all too familiar with our reputation as dogged campaigners. The Marchant campaign was paying attention. When we took Grant Stinchfield as a client, many of the initial reactions felt like a replay of when we took on Republican incumbents in the past... the threats, emails, and occasional call from the person who thought it couldn't be done and tried to talk me out of it. Being underestimated my entire life, I ignored the naysayers. But, it was harder this time. I kept telling myself and our team "almost no one thinks anything can be done, until after it is done."

While the rest of the country was debating if there was a "War on Women," those of us at the Magnolia Group had no doubt Congressman Marchant declared a personal war on us. We barely got Grant's campaign started and were dodging bullets. I had no idea Congressman Marchant would go to such lengths as making personal calls to Texas's congressional delegation, known clients, and to anyone saying good things about the Magnolia Group. Congressman Marchant demanded they severe ties with us. With me.

A different Bush Pioneer than the ones I mentioned earlier, who also I want to leave his name out because he is one of the good guys, had no doubts about Congressman Marchant taking such action. (The Bush Pioneer asked me not to mention the Congressman's name to avoid further strain on Marchant and the other Congressman's relationship.) The Congressman confirmed that his colleague, Kenny Marchant, indeed placed a call to him. That same Congressman promised to the Bush Pioneer's message to Marchant that "a number' of high net worth donors were not happy with Marchant because of this. Meanwhile, that Bush Pioneer said to me "I am debating on whether to contact the Justice Department and send a note to a reporter sharing with him of Marchant's disdain for women and thirst for power." The Justice Department? This was all bigger than I imagined.

A friend and colleague that I worked with reached out to me and awkwardly asked me to remove his association with the Magnolia Group. "Kenny Marchant tracked me down about the quote I have on Magnolia's website. I know you don't have to but it would make my life easier if you would take it down....at least until after the election." Sympathetic that my friend was potentially going to be punished in his career because of his relationship to my firm, we removed his glowing remarks about us from our website.

Part of me felt flattered Congressman Marchant would go after me. A much bigger part of me felt very small, like a skiff out on the open waters with no one around to rescue me but myself.

Congressman Kenny Marchant even convinced a reserve marine to go against his self-professed motto of trustworthiness and loyalty. "I am loyal to a fault. I am a Marine" announced Kenneth Sheets, after he got elected to the Texas House. Sheets was one of our clients, who was still in shock we gave him the time of day when most consultants, he told me, didn't return his calls. Months after his election, Sheets was still full of gratitude and went to profess his love for us.

"You were there for me when no one else was.... we're a team all of us. I am loyal," he gushed. He may have seen me roll my eyes or just my cynical face as he said one more time for emphasis "No, Leslie. I am loyal to a fault. I won't forget this," Kenneth Sheets said firmly.

It didn't seem real or genuine. It reminded me of when a fella gives you flowers to soon. It just seems weird. I shared with Andrew, on our team, "I've never had a client go on and on about how loyal they planned to be. I wasn't even challenging his loyalty. I don't believe him," I told Andrew. "Really?" Andrew asked in disbelief.

And then, Representative Kenneth Sheets had his loyalty tested. "Kenny Marchant has people trying to strong arm me," Kenneth tells me. "And?" I ask, knowing that he would succumb to the pressure, as he just wasn't that strong. "I talked to everyone else on the team (meaning consultants, staff, and such) and their all against it." I laughed to myself. It only mattered was what Kenneth Sheets thought. He would be the only one making the decision.

Kenneth Sheets called me many times, seeking empathy, with all the pressure he was under with the Marchant team. One time, he shared how "one of Kenny's big supporters keeps promising me he'll contribute and raise lots of money. If I just let Magnolia go," Sheets says, almost as if he wants me to give him permission to. I don't and instead, play along.

I reminded Sheets that this fella contributed to his Democrat opponent during the election. Only after Kenneth won, and only after Kenneth placed multiple phone calls, did that individual bother to contribute to Kenneth's campaign. "How'd you know who it was?" Kenneth asks. "Who else would it be?" I said, laughing as it takes a person of certain lack of character to make such offers. With Congressman Kenny Marchant demanding that our clients fire us, I knew it was only a matter of time before it would happen.

On a Friday afternoon, Kenneth Sheets called and announced "I want a meeting at 8am Monday to talk. I'll come to your office," in such a commanding voice I wasn't sure it was him on the other end of the phone. That Monday morning, I knew Kenneth wanted to "talk" to terminate our contract. I told Mom "it's just like in a relationship. When they say 'we need to talk,' it's never a good thing." Mom didn't think there was anything funny about the situation though. "I didn't realize it until Kenneth refused my offer of coffee and water," Andrew would later say, calling "it" being fired. Andrew took "it" hard.

Kenneth Sheets struggled to get the words out. He struggled more to make eye contact. It was understandable because when we came on board his campaign had less than $10k in the bank. In four months, we had raised about $400k. "I need to make a change and let Magnolia go," he said as if Magnolia were not me but someone else not in the room. "Oh," I said. "I didn't' realize you were beholden to Kenny Marchant." Not denying it, Kenneth explained that the "big Kenny supporter" just wouldn't stop calling him and was going to contribute a lot of money to his campaign. This wasn't the first time Kenneth had relayed this conversation to me, so none of this came as a surprise. What did surprise me was that Kenneth was so upfront about admitting he had just been bought and sold. But he didn't have the money in hand, not yet. I wondered how Kenneth thought he could collect on such a promise and why his reputation could be bought for so little.

But I didn't have time to play detective, I had a race to win and it wasn't Kenneth's anymore. I stood up and nonchalantly said "Okay, well best of luck" and held out my hand to shake. Kenneth remained seated and appeared startled that I was ending the meeting. I saw no need to waste time on him as I needed to get back to Grant Stinchfield. "Well, I have work to do for clients and there is no reason for us to continue our meeting. You've accomplished what you set out to do," I said thinking Jerry King would be proud of me.

"Thanks for making it so easy on me," Kenneth said sheepishly. "That wasn't my goal, but all the best," As we shook hands, I gestured my hand toward the door of our conference room for him to leave.

I will never know the promises made and deals cuts but we all witnessed a quick friendship developed between Congressman Marchant and Representative Kenneth Sheets staffs. They even began going Dutch, sharing tables at conventions, straw polls, and GOP gatherings. Kenny's "big supporter" did make good on his promise and hosted a fundraiser for Kenneth Sheets.

We weren't alone in thinking Representative Kenneth Sheets crossed to the dark side quickly. Becky Oliver, a news anchor at Fox 4 in Dallas, was suspicious of Representative Sheets filing legislation that appeared to benefit insurance companies rather than his constituency. She grilled him an interview that Andrew and I watched.

"A Dallas lawmaker claims his bill will help lower rates for homeowners but a consumer advocates says it will penalize homeowners. Under current Texas law, damage due to natural causes or Mother Nature does not count against you if you file a claim on our homeowner's insurance. But that could change." Becky Oliver says.

Alex Winslow of Texas Watch, a consumer advocacy group tells Oliver it is a dangerous bill designed to intimidate policyholders. "Insurance companies want to take your money in premiums but they don't want to pay out in claims," Winslow says.

"Who wanted this bill, the insurance companies or your constituents?" Becky Oliver asked. Kenneth Sheets didn't answer her question. Instead, he gave a canned statement. "This is a bill that's about good policy," Sheets said. "This law will not apply to the regular person," Oliver disagrees and responds "This WILL apply to the regular person, she counters.

Oliver then tells viewers that it was an interesting interview because Representative Sheets seemed "pretty confused most of the time." After watching the news report, Andrew and I smiled as if we were reading each other's thoughts. We were proud to be able to say Kenneth Sheets was not our client. The more entrenched politicians are in the process, the more often they believe they know better than the very people they are tasked in representing. Representative Sheets filing a bill that helps insurance companies over his Dallas constituency shows just how quickly elected officials can be turned.

But we weren't paid to worry about Representative Sheets being beholden to insurance companies, Congressman Kenny Marchant, and others. Our energy went into helping Grant Stinchfield get into Congress.

16 THE BEGINNING OF THE END

G rant, a challenger to the old guard, miraculously kept pace with the Marchant machine when it came to raising money. I was a little taken aback that people were giving Grant as much money as to a sitting Congressman, but they were. Congressman Marchant's individual money was mostly from political insiders and lobbyist as opposed to the average citizen. As good as that made me feel that Grant was making progress, I didn't celebrate.

Instead, I prepared myself and the entire team. "Because we're keeping pace with Marchant on money, we should now expect to get crushed with an influx of PAC (political action committee) money to make us less competitive." No one said anything. "It means, no matter what we do, how good we're doing, we will never be able keep pace." I continued to pour on the bad news. "It means that no one is going to notice how good Grant was doing with individuals—

over 500– in a pretty short period of time." Grant was proving to me and others he was a good candidate for Congress, not to mention a good client.

Grant had a committed and motley group of about 20 that met regularly to discuss, advise, and help in the realities of what Grant and all of us were doing. Some of those 20 were originally Kenny Marchant supporters, but it was a newbie who asked "Don't you think some of the PACs would give Grant money?" Before I could explain the depressing reality of the PAC system, Grant jumped in and was about as blunt as a person could be.

"No! No PAC is going to go against a Congressman in a primary. No PAC is going to give me money. They support who is in office. They aren't going to tell Congressman Marchant 'no.' So we aren't going to waste our time on that."

I had similar conversations with Grant and was equally impressed and saddened that the message got through to him so quickly. Behind closed doors, Grant and I did make a list of Hail Mary PACs we called on. Because of Grant's economic views, he thought Club for Growth might get involved. Everywhere Grant campaigned, he proudly carried a gun on his hip as he was long-time NRA member, so he was convinced he was "more NRA" than Congressman Marchant. Everyone wants the NRA on their side. We couldn't help ourselves. We didn't spend significant time on PACs, but maybe a few hours. It did prove to be pointless as we didn't get any PAC money.

For most of the campaign, Grant Stinchfield raised as much money as from individuals as Kenny Marchant. The folks back home didn't rally by giving campaign cash to Kenny. Grant Stinchfield was holding his own. On this front, I allowed myself a brief moment of pride, but only for a few minutes because of the harsh reality of Congressman Marchant holding a seat on the powerful Ways & Means Committee meant that even though individuals didn't step in to save Marchant, the PACS would. They quickly pumped Marchant's campaign full of cash to make up for his lack of individual fundraising success. PACs made up 65% of Kenny's war chest.

Not only did PAC's give money either, the bullied their employees into giving money too. A businesswoman showed up at one of our receptions for Grant and told us she was sold on him. "I am impressed. I want to help!" she said. "My PAC director cannot believe I give to our PAC and personal money to candidates, but I think it's important. I don't give large amounts, but I know every little bit helps," she said blowing her cover as a newbie to the scene. She told our group she had already "liked" Grant's campaign on Facebook and "friend" requested him—just while at this reception.

At about that same time, her boss responded to her earlier text telling of meeting me and how excited she was to get involved in Grant's race. (I was personal friends with her boss and hadn't been aware this woman had texted her. I knew she wouldn't approve of her employee's actions. Still oblivious, this woman had no clue. So, I go along and say "Oh, tell her hello for me! It's been too long."

"I will!" the woman says over enthusiastically, high on the political energy in the air. Not being able to help myself, I ask "and what else does your boss say about your helping out?" She didn't respond right away and was reading intently from her IPhone. While she hesitated, not knowing what to say, the expression on her face confirmed my thoughts about her boss. She was receiving orders to back away. I already knew they were with Marchant. Shortly afterwards, a group of their top executives contributed heavily to Congressman Marchant and the PAC gave $10k, the maximum allowed.

That woman didn't show up at Grant's next campaign event like she said. I hoped on Election Day, this woman would realize she's alone in the voting booth.

Grant, full of energy, didn't miss an opportunity to personally introduce himself and ask people for help, whether at the gas station or Starbucks. Valets loved Grant. In just a few seconds, he managed to give them his name for his ticket, spell it, and somehow let them know he was running for Congress, and ask for their support. "You bet, Grant. You got our vote," they would say. I knew if it were left to valets of North Texas, Grant would surely win.

Of course, the race wasn't up to the valets. This race would be decided by those who voted in the Republican primary—which isn't that many—

about 60,000 voters would determine who represents 750,000 people. That's who would decide my fate. Voters aren't used to contested primaries. They are trained to be familiar with Republican verses Democrat. Red verses blue. Voters, brainwashed by their Parties to blindly vote straight ticket, contributed to voters not knowing the name of their elected representatives.

"Don't worry," voters would tell Grant as he stood on their front porch, their television almost always blaring *Fox News* or *ESPN Sports* in the background. "We're Republican…voted that way for years." Grant and I would do the delicate dance of explaining that our opponent was also a Republican. That meant they couldn't wait until November because our race would be over. They had to vote in the primary. Worse, because of the redistricting process, the primary Election Day had not been decided. We were campaigning, telling people they had to vote in the primary, and could not tell them when that would be. How crazy is that?

Many times, we were talking to a person who had voted in the last four Republican primaries. In my world, we called these people "4R's." They are the Holy Grail in a Republican primary because it is almost certain they will turn out to vote. In theory, they are the most educated of voters. But even 4R's would say to us "I don't even know that Marchant fella. But, I think it's because Kay Bailey Hutchison is our person." That meant that even the 4R voter is confused about politics because they didn't understand Kay Bailey Hutchison w and embarrasses most people—not a good way to win a voter over.

Because most of these 4R voters go to the polls in the primary, and contested primaries are not common, they may vote for someone without really knowing or learning about them since there is only one name on the ballet. In November, the voter would just vote straight Republican without having to look at anyone's name. So, it is understandable that voters don't know elected officials' names or what office they hold. In other words, voters didn't really "know Kenny Marchant." My state-wide office-holder clients were under the impression "everyone" knew them because they got millions of votes, forgetting a whole bunch of people hit one button, not having any idea who they are voting for or their name. Grant and I had to educate voters before we could motivate them. Grant would wait until we were back on the sidewalk, heading to the next house to vent his frustrations.

"They don't even know the way this works and they are deciding elections?" Grant asked, venting his frustrations, understandably, before we approached our next house. (We were block walking.) "That last voter was a precinct chair and they didn't know the difference between who represents them in the Senate verses the House? How the hell does that happen?!" Campaigns are humbling for everyone involved.

I tell Grant a story. "Several years ago, I shared a cab with some ladies that had short permed hair and sparkly clothes. They told me they were not only precinct chairs, but had come to the (Republican) convention for decades, and worked on more campaigns than they could count." I told Grant as he wondered what this had to do with him, but I continued anyway. "I told them about working with newly elected Congressmen Jeb Hensarling. Before I could tell them about my other clients, they asked me to tell them about Jeb, since they were not familiar with him. Instantly, I rattled off his resume, including the part about working for Senator Phil Gramm."

"Oh, I love Phil Gramm!" exclaimed the woman with the red sequined vest and the other woman, carrying a big elephant purse and matching red orthopedic shoes chimed in. "Me too! I am so glad he is my Congressman!" The first lady with all the pins and buttons on her vest said, "Oh, I love Phil Gramm, I wish he was my Congressman, but I have that new fella…. uh… John, John."

"Cornyn," I chimed in, thinking of the stark contrast of our outfits and deciding to call these convention types unbeknownst to them button people. "Yes, that's who's mine," she said nodding her head in agreement. "Grant, there was no way I could say to them. Phil Gramm was your senator. He's retired. Senator John Cornyn replaced him. By the way, every state has two senators and the number of representatives is based on population. Well, I could have but not without insulting them. They were clueless. And these were people with 'decades experience,' I explained, raising my voice.

My story didn't cheer Grant up, nor was it supposed to. But it did make clear that Grant should always assume that no one understands how our government works. Much less, we shouldn't expect them to know what district they live in and who represents them. Unfortunately, ignorance benefits incumbents like Congressman Kenny Marchant.

At one of our meetings in the Magnolia office over lots of caffeine, I laughed that my prediction of Congressman Marchant not hosting any town halls during the district work period came true. Typically, congressmen hold town halls during their district work period to provide a setting where they can share what happened in Washington, what's going to happen, and people can ask questions. It was no secret that Congressman Marchant was known to be lazy, so I had boldly predicted Marchant, without an opponent, would forgo a heavy workload. I was right. In contrast, Congressman Mike Conaway didn't skirt his civic responsibility and hosted 18 town halls in three months.

"I am not going to wait until I get into Congress to do what a congressman should do," Grant announced to us. Without being asked, Kelsey and Andrew on our team began finding locations in every city located in the 24th district of Texas for Grant to host town hall. They created flyers, electronic invitations, and much more. They jumped into action.

We had the first town hall in Grant's campaign office, located in a small strip center on Main Street in Grapevine. We borrowed some folding chairs from a local lion's club. Our banner, with Grant's name and picture was secured with rope covering up the last business, a nail salon that rented the space before us. With every seat filled, and standing room only, we were bowled over by the turn out. Some Congressman's town halls I've seen have had less than ten people attend.

"I got into the race simply because I felt I could do a better job. North Texas deserves a better leader and fighter," Grant announced and then without dominating the conversation, turned it over to those attending. "At Congressman Marchant's office, he told me he would not vote to raise the debt limit," a woman said forcibly dressed in black pants, white blouse, and black leather jacket. "When he did vote to raise the debt limit, I never heard from him or his office with an explanation." The woman's name was Konni Burton. She would become one of Grant's most vocal supporters. Fired up, Konni was getting involved in politics, full speed ahead. The next election cycle, she went on to serve in the Texas Legislature.

While I didn't recognize everyone in the crowd, I did know Mr. P.J. Tillery and went up to him at the end of the evening. Ten years earlier, his pick-up truck pulled into the parking lot of the scruffy little campaign office of Jeb Hensarling, who was running for Congress in Texas's fifth district. Mr. Tillery hadn't made an appointment. He claimed he was driving by and thinking about whether to volunteer for Jeb or not. Mr. Tillery, being about 80, said he needed something to do. After visiting with a few skeptical staffers, I was invited to speak with Mr. Tillery. It appeared to me they were tossing him off to me as they thought he was wasting their time.

Always willing to engage someone, I went out to meet Mr. Tillery. We exchanged pleasantries and before I knew it he asked what the campaign needed and what he could do to feel useful. Without hesitating, I answered. "Well, we could always use money!" I saw a few staffers look up from their work at me. "How much?" Mr. Tillery asked. "$1,000 is the federal limit, but we have to raise well over a million for this campaign to win as it's one of the top races in the country the Democrats are targeting."

"What else?" Mr. Tillery asks. The rest of the staff continued to listen, curiously. "If you're up for it, you could ask your friends for contributions too."

"How would I do that?" asked Mr. Tillery. "You could call them. Write them a letter. Or, if you want to give me their names and numbers and I will call them." I said, thinking I liked Mr. Tillery. "Whatever you think would be the best way to reach out to them," I continued. Mr. Tillery stood up "Just a minute. I need to go to my truck."

While he was fiddling around in his truck, the Hensarling staff found it humorous I would think this guy could give and were saying as much in a whisper. But I had goals to reach, had read *The Millionaire Next Door*, and had nothing to lose. Mr. Tillery walked back in. "I found my check book. Here ya go," he said, tearing out a check out. "Now, I am going to go home and work on my letter. Then I'll come back so we can go over it. And I would like to work in the office some too. Oh, one more thing. Promise me you won't hit my friends up for more money after I get them to give." I accepted Mr. Tillery's $1000 check—what we called a "maxed out contribution," shook his hand, and kept my promise. He raised just over $10k in the next few weeks while coming into the office regularly.

It had been a decade, so I wasn't expecting Mr. Tillery to walk in when Grant held his first town hall at his campaign headquarters in Grapevine. Turns out, Mr. Tillery's neighborhood in Dallas was in the newly drawn 24th district and his political juices were ripe again.

"Mr. Tillery it's been years! So good to see you!" I said ecstatically. I turned to Grant and my entire team and announced enthusiastically "This is Mr. Tillery!" Mr. Tillery was astonished that everyone knew of him—he was legendary in our office. I talked about him in every training session, demonstrating taking people seriously, treating them with respect, and to always ask big. I also talked about Mr. Tillery to every candidate, to ensure they don't blow anyone off, like Senator McConnell did to my friend, Paige. And Grant was no different.

Everyone on our team stood, staring at a man they were not sure existed, thinking I just made up for training. Until now. Grant spoke first, "Mr. Tillery, it's an honor! Mr. Tillery broke out in a big smile. "I haven't worked on a campaign in while and heard you needed help. I want to get the crooks out!" he said matter of fact. Grant and I both looked at each other in disbelief. Mr. Tillery, who helped Jeb and me early on, was coming out of his political retirement to work on his second campaign.

That night, I learned ten years earlier, Mr. P.J. Tillery was driving around Dallas doing anything to avoid going home. After numerous trips, up and down Abrams road, he saw Jeb Hensarling's campaign sign and randomly decided to pull in. Not sure if Jeb was a conservative or not, he asked lots of questions as he sure didn't want to volunteer on some liberal's campaign. "Working on Jeb's campaign with you, raising money, and writing letters...

that saved my life. My wife had died the previous week and I just didn't know what to do with myself," Mr. Tillery told me. That evening at Grant's event, Mr. Tillery introduced me to Janice, his newly-wed wife. I took Mr. Tillery's involvement as a positive omen.

In addition to the team's heavy workload, most everyone put in a few hours every day to walk neighborhoods, but the weekends meant marathon-walks with volunteers and staff. Kelsey's Matt helped and Andrew's Dee did the same for him. Everyone's significant others volunteered and worked for Grant because they knew how much it meant to the one they loved. Or maybe, campaigning for Grant was the only way to see each other. Our friends and our families got involved and invested in Grant because we asked them too. Regardless of where they lived, what their beliefs, they supported us— and in turn supported Grant. They heard first-hand how high the stakes had become for their loved one working on this campaign. They wanted to win too. They were willing to do their part in whatever way they could. Everyone went out on a limb for Grant and got personally involved because the Marchant campaign had made the race not only personally about Grant, but about each one of us as well. Not one person involved in the campaign had a "hall pass" when it came to Marchant's wrath. Because of the overly personal attacks, we prepared our volunteers.

Marchant supporter, Kensley, badgered Grant at more than one town hall and had no interest in hearing Grant's answers. Instead, he preferred shouting over Grant. Blindly following Marchant, Kensley would spend considerable time giving Kelsey and Andrew headaches with his antics over the course of the campaign. Kensley, apparently retired, spent his days following our group around always on high alert to harass whoever represented Grant at an event. Despite his efforts to try to rile Grant, Grant remained the statesmen he was trying to show the voters he would be in office.

At one town hall, a man sat in the front row poorly hiding he was recording Grant's town hall. I signaled to Grant as much as that meant he was a Marchant spy. "We're recording this town hall, so you don't have to," Grant said, catching the fella off guard. "You're welcome to though. That's what Congressmen are supposed to do—host open town halls. I want the public to see this. We will put it up on our website, have a link on Facebook…." Grant continued in all the ways we would share it. The fella mumbled something awkwardly. Later, we confirmed he was a Marchant campaign staffer.

Congressman Kenny Marchant didn't like Grant Stinchfield going around telling people that he didn't host any town halls. But it was the truth. After months, it appeared Marchant's team was determined to prove Grant wrong. Rather than just host a town hall, Kenny finally had an "invitation only" town hall. It was held at a big corporation for their employees, conveniently a company that Kenny held stock in.

"That's an employee meeting—not a town hall. A town hall meeting requires having a meeting in a town and in a public place," Grant would say as he campaigned, mostly dressed in kakis, jeans, campaign shirt and on cool days a pull-over. In other words, he left his suits behind—a stark contrast to the Marchant team and their stiff suits.

While we advertised in community newspapers, on Grant's website, and many other club calendars about Grant's town halls, Kenny bragged about his one already-over controlled board meeting on Facebook, claiming it was a town hall. "Did the employees of the company even have a choice to attend or not to attend?" Grant asked. Between the town halls, knocking on doors, people shared their personal stories to not just Grant, but to each one of us. How Kenny said one thing and did another. More than once, Kenny told people "I don't do earmarks." One of those times was on Kenny's own "town hall conference calls" he hosted on tax payers dime. Andrew always participated in those calls to listen first-hand to what Congressman Marchant was saying to the constituents of the 24th District of Texas. No one could talk on the call, as they were muted, just the Congressman spoke. Andrew wished he could have because he wanted to ask Congressman Marchant what was he thinking when he did a $2.4million one for a company in Carrollton that he coincidentally held stock in. It appeared to us Congressman Marchant made exceptions for earmarks to make money.

As Grant and our team talked about Congressman Marchant's lack of leadership, Marchant's campaign wasted no time attacking Grant. Of course, Kenny Marchant was never the one directly attacking. Instead, a carefully orchestrated whisper campaign spread throughout the district. One of the secrets shared was that Grant was born in New York, thinking their fellow Texans would conclude that all Yankees are liberal. The hypocrisy was almost laughable, being that Kenny Marchant was not born in Texas either, but I was in no mood to laugh.

Other secrets Marchant's team whispered to voters was that Grant was best buddies with Ted Kennedy and the Kennedy clan. Campaigns tell these types of lies and exaggerate because voters believe them. Voters typically don't fact check. That's what Susie, Congressman Marchant's district director, counted on when she warned voters. "Grant was a member of the media for more than fifteen years during which time he was a spokesperson for the Kennedy family and contributor to MSNBC."

At Grant's town halls, people were constantly asking Grant about his connections with the Kennedys, which meant the Marchant teams whisper campaign was working. While that frustrated me, I did like it when a voter would approach Grant and ask him about his involvement with the Kennedy's. It gave Grant the chance to tell his side of the story. The expression on their face was priceless.

"Lauren and Carolyn Bessette were dear childhood friends of mine. Their parents were as close to family as you can get," Grant would explain. "When JFK Jr's plane went down, the Bessette family asked me to speak on their behalf because they were besieged by media. I made a nationally televised statement for Lauren and Carolyn's mom and dad, NOT the Kennedy family."

When they asked specifically about Senator Ted Kennedy, Grant would shrug his shoulders and casually respond, "I met Ted Kennedy a few times during the week of the funeral and in the process of making arrangements for the service. During that tragic time, he was a gentleman, even though I disagree with his politics."

Like I said though, campaigns count on voters being too busy to search for the truth. Susie went on spreading rumors, trying to defend her boss from Grant's attacks. The liberal Kennedy connection didn't make much progress in the over-all campaign. *The Dallas Morning News* did NOT endorse Grant because they called him a "Jim DeMint Republican"—a golden nugget campaigns seek in a Republican primary. (Translations: they were calling Grant too conservative). We no longer had to concern ourselves with anyone thinking Grant was a liberal—a Kennedy—now that the largest paper in the district proclaimed otherwise.

Susie devoted countless hours trying to keep Congressman Marchant in office. We hit back hard. "Sadly, this is politics as usual, as Susie twists the truth and manipulates the facts to mislead the people she is trying to win over," Grant responded. According to the law, the one Congress passed, taxpayer staff and campaign staff are supposed to have separation. The idea behind it is that taxpayers should not fund elected officials' re-election efforts. Despite being a self-proclaimed fiscal conservative, Kenny Marchant had Susie campaigning for him.

"District staff shouldn't be hired for the campaign, giving supplemental incomes. Taxpayer funded employees are permitted to take "time off" and "volunteer" for their bosses. It's not realistic to have a full-time campaign and full-time constituent services office with the same staff." Grant rightly told people.

But these types of messages never made sense to voters as it was too much insider politics. It wasn't sexy enough, crazy enough, or simple enough. In reality, these things should be pretty big deal. No one seemed to care, so we moved on to other points.

Our team constantly talked about Congressman Marchant reporting his average net worth went from $25 million to $50 Million between 2008 and 2010 and that Congressman Marchant had no explanation. Susie defended the Congressman saying "that part about Kenny doubling his net worth is absolutely false." Another time, she shouted out from the back of a meeting hall "That's a lie!" Grant, coming across as a cool reporter, not like some hot-head, said matter of fact, "Those are Marchant's own financial disclosures. Our information was from Kenny's own financial reports." Grant said again for emphasis. He continued. "It was confirmed by *The Washington Post*, the *Fort Worth Star Telegram*, and Open Secrets."

"Look," Grant said to the crowd. "We just want Congressman Marchant to explain how he managed such terrific returns when the country was in the worst recession in recent American history. He refuses to debate me or hold any open town hall meetings—so no one is able to ask him any questions about it," Grant told the packed crowd at a Republican club meeting.

There were so many of these meetings, we had a team of people attending and representing Grant. And for the most part, everyone dreaded them because of the visceral environment. Kelsey, Andrew, Matt, Stuart, and Ben were on the front lines, as I spent more and more nights analyzing data, reviewing questionnaires, or other tasks while the rest of the crew got beat up on by the Marchant team.

Grant educated voters on the STOCK Act (Stop Trading on Insider Knowledge) that was first introduced in 2006. Kenny Marchant was never a co-sponsor of the bill. With Americans growing frustration with Congress and corruption in Washington, most members of Congress knew that they had to act—despite Congress not wanting to end something that has benefited them so greatly. Grant encouraged voters to call their Congressman, Kenny Marchant, and ask him to sign on to that legislation. For over three months Congressman Marchant refused. When it became apparent that the STOCK Act was going to pass, overwhelmingly, Congressman Marchant conveniently signed on just days before it passed. (It was a water-down version but at least it was a step in the right direction.) By Grant running, he had already made Kenny Marchant a better congressman by getting him to sign on to the STOCK Act. "But, why did he wait?" Grant kept asking voters.

Congressman Marchant continued to refuse to participate in any debates with Grant. He made sure to skip meetings and events that he normally might attend, like Republican meetings and forums. Instead, he sent a team of people in his place. There was no doubt in our minds that Kenny Marchant didn't want to be in the same room as Grant Stinchfield. If they were in the same room, Grant would ask the questions Kenny Marchant didn't want to answer.

Throughout the campaign, Marchant's campaign focused on minute details to distract voters from the more important issues. Marchant's team took exception that in a big metropolitan area, like the Dallas/Fort Worth metroplex, that Grant lived about five miles outside the district-ignoring that the Constitution of the United States never made it a requirement that Congressmen live in the district. I wondered, did it bother Congressman Marchant that the Chairman of the NRCC (National Republican Congressional Committee), Congressman Pete Sessions, didn't live in the Texas district he represented either? Marchant's team didn't share with voters that Grant owned a business and a property in the district.

When the Marchant campaign attacked Grant as someone who just recently got involved in politics or who never attended Republican club meetings, Grant fired back. "My role as a watchdog did come with some drawbacks. News guidelines forbade reporters from taking part in political functions or organizations because we had to give the perception to the public that we were unbiased. Because I was one of only a handful of conservative reporters, I tried to always take a 'John Stossell' look at stories."

Then, Grant would use the opportunity to share with voters about himself, instead of just fighting off the attacks of Marchant. "I was one of the first reporters to expose ACORN and I was one of the first to raise the TSA privacy issues. I reported on countless government waste stories. I was well known for doing stories that would take a pro-business, capitalism approach few reporters were able to see."

The entire team worked on tight responses to all the crazy accusations and attacks flying around. Andrew was the best at drilling Grant because his hard follow up questions caught Grant off guard. Grant expected such from me, but Grant could never get used to Andrew's hard lines. "It's just that he's so nice and I never see it coming. And you, well I expect that from you," Grant said, embarrassed that he didn't nail all the questions as he should have. Grant vowed to never let it happen again. So we drilled him constantly, making his answers concise, tight, and interesting.

We wanted to make sure our team and volunteers had all the facts straight too and not be caught off guard when they went to a meeting or knocked on a door. We did this because there was always someone trying to see if our team would take the bait. Club after club meeting, night after night, the Stinchfield team would show up with campaign materials, signing people up, and courting those 4R voters, while I continued to stay out of the spotlight. Our staff was young, as Marchant had been in office longer than most of them had been alive. We recruited more senior volunteers.

Meanwhile, Grant happily answered Marchant supporters' questions at events, before spreading his message of doing things differently in Washington. When a Marchant fan shouted to the crowd "Grant voted in the Democrat primary," hoping to shock the all-Republican crowd into thinking he was a closet Democrat, Grant didn't miss a beat Andrew and Kelsey would report back to me.

"I proudly tell people I voted in the Democrat primary in 2008!" Grant would say enthusiastically. "Like so many conservatives, we followed Rush Limbaugh's "Operation Chaos" advice. Since McCain had the nomination locked, the goal was to hand Hillary Clinton Texas to keep Obama from winning the Democrat nomination. Surely, we can all agree Hillary would have been easier for John McCain to beat."

Marchant's campaign struggled to come up with any dirt or anything substantial on why Grant shouldn't be the next Congressman. Finally, they discovered Grant hadn't paid $120 in taxes to Dallas County on a production company he owned. "I didn't even know you had a production company, Grant!" I said. "Why am I just learning about it!" Grant answered, equally frustrated. "I mean, it's more of a hobby."

Marchant's consultant went over-the-top when he called Grant a "liar and tax cheat." Grant was wrong in that he hadn't paid the $120, but he didn't know he owed it. As soon as he learned about it, he paid it. When I told David

Childs, the former Dallas County Tax Assessor for 17 years, he responded to me by saying "Leslie, it's not a big deal. People are tired of only the rich guys being in office. They are ready for real people who are trying to do the right thing. Grant paid it. He can tell people he's not some multi-millionaire who has someone who handles all this for him, like Marchant."

I agreed and was glad the latest fire drill was so easily resolved. Just like David Childs, several people saw through Marchant's attacks and viewed Grant as someone like them. We also learned most people are confused by the over-complicated legal morasses we call our tax code. They were willing to give Grant the benefit of the doubt.

Andrew and Kelsey said Marchant's consultant going extreme helped us. "When the story ran, we got more calls than usual to volunteer for Grant," they both announced when I returned from a donor luncheon. Thankfully, Marchant's petty attacks didn't resonate with voters and helped our grassroots movement grow.

What kept nagging at me though, was I knew no one at the tax office took the time out of their busy day to dig up a hundred-dollar mistake about Grant. "Grant, no county employee gives a damn about you. This is Kenny Marchant. He has influence deeper than I realized." Grant thought I was being paranoid. So did I. But, my gut knew no one would just come across this information at the same time Grant decided to run for Congress. I knew better than to believe in coincidences. Before I could elaborate, Grant had the Dallas County Tax office on the phone. They hesitantly told us they received "an anonymous tip."

"It's the first time someone had ever called us to inquire about someone else. They were very persistent and curious about the status in our office. They were pushing us. They called daily." The Dallas County Tax office never said who "they" were, but we all knew.

While on the phone with Grant, the tax office guy realized, what we already knew. He was a pawn in the Marchant camp. Grant had speaker-phoned the poor fella so I could hear too. The voice on the other end said "I'm sorry," to Grant. "I hate the way the situation happened." Grant tried to cheer the poor fella up as we didn't question how bad the guy felt.

At this point in the campaign, Grant and I managed to find humor in knowing that his $120 hiccup caused the Marchant team to devote so much time and energy to something that didn't get them very far. The message played well on the campaign trail. Grant constantly talked about how the tax code is too complicated and needs to be simplified. "Our more than 44,000 page absurdly arcane tax code is just one glaring piece of evidence of the travesty of the American democrat ideal of government for the people, by the people." Grant would say, with people nodding in agreement.

Of course, Congressman Marchant agreed with Grant that the tax code is overly complicated. But Kenny Marchant was already in Congress, sat on the tax writing committee, and could do something about the tax code. Why didn't voters wonder the same thing I did? It would mean Congressman Marchant would actually have to introduce a bill and get it passed. Most people didn't know that Congressman Marchant never had any legislation pass and only introduced four bills. We did our best to raise awareness but if it is not a sex scandal, it's hard to get people to care.

I felt like I was the only person that noticed Congressman Marchant talked about Congress in third person, as if he is not a member of the body. All his campaign and congressional office materials talks about what's wrong with Washington and Congress, but offered no solutions. With only 9% of Americans approving of the job Congress is doing, perhaps it was understandable he did not want to claim being in Congress. But why didn't someone ask the question?

As much as I hate yard signs, I didn't doubt their importance to candidates and voters. Voters can figure out who's winning the sign race easier than complicated issues they find boring and time consuming. We had over two hundred 4 x 4 signs go up in less than 48 hours and hundreds more locations for future signs. Any congressman would be impressed with the results, for a candidate it spoke volumes. I guess that's why Marchant' team made a conscious decision to eliminate our signs.

Matt, our super-walker, also became Grant's super-sign person as well. He understood it's the small things that amount to big things in campaigns. Andrew and Kelsey took Matt's data and worked their magic with it. Poor Matt was on the front lines though, which meant took the brunt of the Marchant shenanigans. Like the time Matt repaired a Stinchfield sign located in a high-traffic area that had mysteriously fallen off the fence of one of our supporters. While Matt was working, a gang of Marchant lackeys demanded that Matt take down the Stinchfield sign, while they arrogantly replaced it with a blue Marchant sign. "These are our supporters!" they shouted at Matt, but he knew better.

Matt knew we had permission for every single sign and identified who had given us permission and tracked all that data. Meanwhile, another supporter, Sally, saw this going down from her vehicle and pulled over to facilitate the situation as well. Matt and Sally simply called the people. Turns out they were home and shortly made their way down their driveway to resolve the situation in person. Andrew, Kelsey, and I listened as Matt told us "You should have seen the looks at the Marchant gangs' faces when our supporters said they were voting for Grant." Marchant's guy whined "but you our supporters!" They went on explaining they supported Congressman Marchant during his first campaign, but have not been with him since. "I wish I would have recorded the conversation!" Matt said regretting he didn't capture the moment via video for us. He wanted us to see how un-congressional the Congressman's team acted. Sally told us the same story when we saw her at the next political event.

We think because of that day; poor Matt became someone that Marchant could "put a name with a face" of someone they saw regularly working for Grant. Just like Congressman Marchant had tracked down my friend and told him to get his name off my website, Congressman Marchant pursued Matt, in a parking lot, after a political event. Matt recounted to us "The Congressman tracked me down and accused me of stealing his signs!" We could all tell Matt was still in shock, and we were too.

"How does Congressman Kenny Marchant even know me?" Matt asked. I could only conclude it was because Matt had been so visible with door walking and putting up signs in high profile areas, they saw him everywhere, while we were confined to our computers. Understandably, Matt grew uneasy and a bit paranoid, even taking down his Facebook and entire online presence as he didn't want Congressman Marchant and his thugs going after him or trying to hurting his future Olympic dreams. (Matt was in his off-season and was scheduled to return to training after the election. He had dreams of being an Olympic speed skater as he had barely missed the team the time before.)

So, not only was the Marchant campaign following us around they spent a great amount of time stealing Grant's signs everyone told me. "What?" was my standard response to all the reports of such. I just couldn't imagine running for a legislative office, being a law-maker, and demanding your staff to break the law. Plus, it was childish. But several of our supporters witnessed it first-hand.

Bobby, served on Grant's leadership team and lent his centrally located office in Irving for phone banks and team meetings. He had a big 4x4 Stinchfield sign that commuters could easily see at the busy intersection. Bobby was furious when Grant's sign had not only been stolen but replaced by a Marchant one. He called me to vent "I can't believe their nerve!"

"I can," I say to Bobby. "I am beginning to no longer be surprised—which is a first for me."

"I'm gonna cut it down!" Bobby says furiously. "That's fine with me, "I say. "We'll bring you a new sign." I did try to be the bigger person asking Bobby to not throw it away. I knew how expensive those darn signs were, and in a moment of sleep deprivation, I offered to call Marchant's office to let them know they needed to come get it. "Good idea. But I'll do it instead!" Bobby says enthusiastically. I cross one item off my list.

By the time Election Day had ended most Stinchfield signs had been stolen or vandalized. Gene, a Stinchfield volunteer and a veteran to politics discovered us early in the campaign and devoted a full work week to manning the campaign office and managing his zone for Grant. Gene mesmerized us with stories of his younger days when he piloted for Caroline Rose Hunt, the famous hotelier and philanthropist. Because Gene flew the same type of plane as John Travolta, when he saw him, they briefly connected over pilot talk.

Gene called Andrew regularly, reporting in. We weren't expecting him to tell us some signs in his neighborhood had death threats on them. "Death threats?" Andrew asks, getting my attention with no effort. "One sign even has Grant's eyes cut out!" Gene says, obviously shocked. Gene thought I had "seen it all" when it came to politics, but even I didn't share with him death threats aren't typical. I didn't take it lightly, even reported it to the police. It wasn't long before Andrew had filed a report in almost every city in the district Grant was running.

During the election, we couldn't get the media interested in a story of hundreds of Grant's signs being stolen, death threats, and vandalism. Every time we pitched a story and every time it got rejected we kept hearing the cynicism of the business.

We digressed with all the crooks we knew....Congressman Wallace Jefferson who had money in his freezer and was not in jail....Congressman Charlie Rangel not paying taxes, still serving in Congress and successfully secured contribution to name a public policy center after him and Majority Leader Mitch McConnell who basically did the same thing.....Congressman Don Young and his bridge to nowhere...John Wiley Price who the FBI had investigated for decades but was waiting for a perfect case before prosecuting.... Senator Vitter who hired prostitutes while embracing family values....and there were so many we just got depressed. "No wonder we can't get Grant any earned media!" I say "how can we compete?"

We effortlessly named politician after politician that had broken the law but nothing much happened. We stopped, overwhelmed by our conversation. I realized we could have spent the rest of the day, as these were just political crooks off the top of our head, brainstorming with no effort. I poured another cup of coffee as it was too early for alcohol.

While it may not be sexy, stealing signs is illegal. We had spent $12,000 on those signs and we wanted someone to be held accountable. Twelve thousand meant nothing to anyone other than to the Stinchfield team. We had worked hard for that money, but it was chump change to the millions elected officials are screwing taxpayers out of, so there was no way any reporter was going to cover such petty crimes. Ironically, after the election, a local TV station requested an interview with Grant discussing his experience with his signs being stolen and vandalized. Where the heck where you a few months ago? I wanted to say still carrying some anger around. Instead, I said "Grant, probably best you speak with the reporter."

Grant's momentum drew attention as he was making waves in a world where rocking the boat is not allowed. It was not a secret that many in the Texas delegation didn't hold Congressman Marchant in high regards, but we didn't expect fellow Congressmen to spend their time and energy intimidating and discouraging Grant's supporters. I can only conclude they wanted to continue the days of running in a Republican primary unopposed. No one could dismiss that serious people were supporting Grant. The same people that supported other members of Congress in the Texas delegation and other Congressmen didn't like it one bit.

Congressman Jeb Hensarling told Don, a supporter of both Jeb and Grant, at one of his inner circle meetings "You shouldn't contribute to Kenny's opponent. I just don't think you will get a return on your investment," Don recounted Congressman Hensarling's conversation to me. "Well, it's a good thing you didn't let anyone intimate you when you supported Jeb Hensarling in a five-person Republican primary!" I said disappointed in Jeb once again. I was proud Don knew how to walk the tight rope of supporting Congressman Hensarling and Grant.

But that didn't mean we all didn't admire some qualities of Jeb as a congressman. That's why Grant attended and contributed to one of Jeb's fundraisers. Grant, ever active on social media, mentioned Jeb's successful fundraiser on his Facebook, thanking Jeb for a great event and posting a picture. This upset Congressman Marchant as we were receiving calls from Jeb's office requesting Grant take down his post. Apparently, Marchant's office was giving Jeb's office a hard time about Grant's posts. We thought it should be obvious to Marchant's office that only Grant and Grant's team oversaw such, but apparently, Congressman Hensarling's office was still getting requests. Grant simply said he supported Jeb, who was unopposed, and contributed money to his campaign. "I am not taking down anything or giving in to Marchant's demands," Grant said.

Marchant's office was afraid the perception may be that Jeb endorsed Grant. I didn't know anyone who was under the impression Congressman Hensarling endorsed or would consider endorsing Grant. But I did wonder if in any of those conversations between the two congressmen if Jeb asked Kenny why Grant was at his event, while Kenny was a no-show.

17 THE CAMPAIGN THAT NEVER ENDS

When Nancy Ann and Ray Hunt hosted a fundraiser at III Forks restaurant for Grant, the North Texas heavy-hitters turned out in full force for Grant and his campaign for Congress. The people who gave hundreds of thousands of dollars to Republican causes were betting on Grant. Names like Simmons, Staubach, Hill, Westcott, Bramlett, Cooper, and many other who's who of Dallas were with Grant.

When America's quarterback and legendary businessman Roger Staubach endorsed Grant, Kenny Marchant's former colleague, Texas State Senator Florence Shapiro, gave Mr. Staubach an earful. Kenny's buddy, Representative Shapiro said Staubach would regret supporting Grant. Roger Staubach was in the district Florence Shapiro was representing. To me, her actions were typical of most other 30-year incumbents. They want to make sure voters stick with the status quo. There had been talk for years that Shapiro would like to run for Congress, but only if a seat "opened up."

Chad Hennings, former Dallas Cowboy and businessman, also supported Grant. Hennings has had much success in his life and I wanted him to do something in politics. I spoke to him about running for Congress against a different incumbent. Quickly, I realized he was intrigued but not going to run. He answered to a higher calling that I admired. I was so proud there were strong people willing to stand up against the Marchant bullies and Chad Hennings was one of them.

While Grant had so many notable, prestigious and successful people we "all know" he also had people whose names voters may not know, but that we were excited to have on board supporting Grant too. These were people who live in our neighborhoods, take their children to the nearby park, and splurge taking the family out to eat on Friday nights after a ballgame. They were looking for leadership. In contrast, Marchant's bench was filled with false and make-believe support.

"Endorsements only matter in regards to what that individual is going to do. What their support means in terms of delivering you money and votes," I told Grant. We understand the importance of an inspirational hero or exceptional people that come along in life that you look to as guidance and those were some of Grant's "big names" as opposed to other elected officials simply kissing up to each other. While many of the current Party people were afraid to go against Congressman Marchant some of the older guard felt differently.

When former Texas Secretary of State George Strake told me he would support Grant and his campaign for Congress, I was overwhelmed. For the "twenty-somethings" on the team, I had to elaborate, telling them Mr. Strake served under the legendary Gov. Bill Clements, first Republican governor in Texas for almost 100years…Republican State Chairman…family has Camp Strake that is a Boy Scout wilderness retreat…. sits on many boards and is very generous of his time and money for good causes…" Being thoroughly impressed, they began googling him and discovered they felt small just reading about him. Meanwhile, I was truly moved. I believed just like all these men were underdogs at one point, they overcame hurdles, and won. They were trailblazers. It made me think we could win. That Grant could win.

The media usually loves anything with football and controversy. But these Texas legends supporting Grant over long-time incumbent Kenny Marchant were stories no one in the media would cover. Most of the time, I resented the media including everyone that came out to support someone in office. Endorsements like Grants would typically get picked up effortlessly. But no one did in this case. Why?

One big Republican donor and activist later revealed to me he was scolded for supporting Grant in a private meeting with Majority Leader Eric Cantor. "We're going to have to be on opposite sides on this one," he said to Leader Cantor. He went on to share with Leader Cantor how many of the grassroots and heavy- hitters he visited with that were supporting Grant, naively trying to influence him in supporting Grant. "It didn't work," he told me. Leader Cantor's answer was interesting, he said "I can't afford to have any more rebel Republicans on my team."

I had boasted to people about Congressman Eric Cantor for about a decade. "He's a rising star," I would say. Years before it ever happened, I predicted he would be the Majority Leader if not Speaker of the House or even vice president. Congressman Eric Cantor is a sharp-minded political junkie, who worked as hard as anyone I knew. But now, I realized since being Majority Leader he operated in constant compromise of who I wanted him to be.

When Leader Cantor came to Texas we were his team. Like Jeb, Cantor appreciates one's ability to raise money and there are many jokes about each of them and their love of it. While Cantor's office shared with me that "Kenny Marchant was not happy with the situation," (of Cantor still hiring us to raise money while working for Marchant's opponent.) But the Cantor team was not about to walk away from a couple of meetings and hundreds of thousands of dollars we raised for him. They didn't want to miss the opportunity to be introduced to someone that would later give them over $5million to their various Super-PACs.

Hours of negotiations took place between Marchant and Cantor's team. Cantor's office kept me updated. They did concede to Congressman Marchant that they would make sure I did not attend the luncheon I oversaw and that Congressman Marchant wanted to attend. (Congressman Marchant said he didn't want me there.) The compromise was that my staff would be allowed to attend the fundraise we were putting on for Cantor. "Since we are in charge of the event, I would hope so!" I said sarcastically over the phone, in disbelief at such petty conversations existed between congressmen and staff.

"Eric is in the business of keeping members happy," his campaign manager told me as if I didn't get what was going on in the negotiations. Appropriate words, I thought. Cantor had sacrificed himself for a bigger cause, but not a greater one. "He won't win his next election," I told a donor friend of mine. "For me, he has become the Tom Dashel of Virginia." (Tom Dashel was very powerful in Washington, became majority leader of the Senate, but lost touch to most of the folks in South Dakota, losing his seat.) Majority Leader Cantor, who had once been on the short list for vice president of our country, lost his next election for Congress. He now works on Wall Street.

As the campaign to determine Texas' next Congressman from the 24th District continued, being longer than any of us imagined, we became exhausted and operated on adrenaline. The second Tuesday in March was the original Election Day, but because of the redistricting debacle in Texas, Election Day and the district lines continued to move. Eventually, it was scheduled for May. More than a few days, I started work at 5am and finally sat down for supper around 10pm. I was not alone in maintaining a rigorous schedule. The entire crew discovered how much work they were capable of with little sleep. I drug myself out of bed each morning, and so did everyone else, as we knew every hour was precious and we couldn't afford to lose any time sleeping. Some of us took this to more extremes than others. Amy, on our team, had been found at the same spot for almost three days, with little food or drink as she was determined not to leave her computer until she produced the voter data report for Grant I said we needed to win. I, on the other hand, still managed time to shower, eat, and change clothes every day.

Meanwhile, the Stinchfield team kept expanding. One fella, David, worked part time at Starbucks and became the official Stinchfield barista in addition to his field director duties. Ben, was a student at TCU. Thankfully, our volunteer force was large and growing. But the workload continued to be overwhelming. Andrew and Kelsey became masters at working on their laptops, in their cars, in between phone calls, events, and meetings. Campaigns are physically hard on people and it was beginning to show on everyone. The constant campaigning resulted in Grant losing too much weight. It wasn't the first time a client had lost weight campaigning.

"You don't look good, Grant. You're too thin. Gain some weight!" I demanded, frustrated and exhausted with everything except Grant, but knowing voters typically like attractive candidates. Grant responded genuinely "I am no longer doing any cardio, only weights. I am carb loading…" and I start laughing at hearing the words "carb loading." Meanwhile, the rest of the gang—including me— were trying very hard not to eat every meal in our car or to remember to find time to eat. The healthiness of our foods had been long tossed aside until Election Day. Grant, on acute fitness alert, made us laugh when we all needed a laugh. He certainly wasn't going to the Nation's Capitol and turn into a Washington fat cat.

That's when we got the idea to turn Grant's weight loss, health obsession, and fondness for P-90X (A program I hadn't heard of before Grant. It's a high-intensity, interval work out) into a way to get earned media coverage. For ninety days, Grant highlighted his strategies to cut the fat in Washington and produced some videos on it.

Our hard work and creativity paid off in the Tarrant County straw poll—a first indicator into voters' minds. With the presidential elections still in play, the straw polls were largely attended. The Tarrant County straw poll lasted an entire Saturday. The entire team was up early, functioning on coffee and doughnuts. Securing votes took president over real food and lunch.

Each candidate running for office, from president to dog catcher, had a reserved space at the newly built Hurst Convention Center. The most exciting races, other than the presidential ones, were the congressional races. Candidates' booths became decorated and filled with campaign paraphernalia and staff courting voters as they walked around assessing the candidates.

Congressman Marchant didn't show up. Instead, two dozen of his people, dressed in dark blue Marchant t-shirts, came out eagerly handing out candy, pens, emery boards, and recyclable grocery bags. On a much leaner budget, we opted for red, white, and blue Mardi Gras-like beads. All their toys were shiner and appeared in endless supply, which I knew meant money flowed easily in their campaign. They even gave the expensive totes to Kelsey, despite being dressed in her Grant Stinchfield t-shirt. She happily accepted the Marchant bag, turned it inside out, and filled them with Stinchfield supplies. Other Stinchfield supporters followed her lead and secured their free tote too. Straw polls and polling locations get eerily like middle school elections.

We didn't even try to compete with the thousands of slick over-sized mail pieces they handed out to attendees. Afraid people would glance and toss it among all the other campaign materials that day, we took a more frugal route of printing thousands of inexpensive business cards with Grant's "Stinchfield Standards" hoping that voters might put them in their purses and pockets and make it home with them. Just like when I met Grant in the coffee shop, I hoped when voters heard from Grant, he could win them over. I prayed silently that Marchant and his expensive toys wouldn't drown Grant out. I prayed "please let Grant win this straw poll."

Marchant's team hired a photographer in attempts to capture Grant in a not-so-camera-ready moment, one they thought would happen when it was announced Marchant won. This is a typical gimmick in politics, catching your opponent in an awkward and disappointing look on his face, so it was pretty much to be expected from the Marchant group. We had our own photographer too. Both captured Grant's exuberance when it was announced that Grant won the Tarrant County straw poll 57% to 43% and my prayers were answered–that day.

I were not the ones claiming support we didn't have. Your anger needs to be directed toward Kenny Marchant, not me." I told Wade.

Of course, Wade wouldn't dare talk to Kenny Marchant in the same tone he talked to Grant or me. His anger was probably more at himself for not being strong or bold enough to call up Kenny and give him strong words about falsifying supporters. Wade isn't unique either. Many GOP Chairs struggle to stand up to bully office holders. Other people told us that "Kenny had strong words for Wade for even letting Grant run in the first place." In politics, some think it is the county chairs job to make sure only one person runs for each office so that the status quo remains. Others, like me, believe they should want the best Republican in office.

When Grant was thinking about running, he personally called the areas GOP chairs to introduce himself, invite them to a cup of coffee or lunch, and let them be some of the first to know he was considering a run for Congress. Later when Grant made his decision, as a courtesy, he reached out to them again. In some of the county chair races, Grant went out of his way to want to meet with them before their own races were decided. Grant could have easily waited to see who had won and only contact the winner—but he didn't. Many of these same people didn't even bother to return Grant's calls or take him up on his offer to meet for coffee. In fact, when they didn't return Grant's call and they later found out he was running they claimed to be upset. Conveniently forgetting Grant had personally called them—and that was the case with Wade.

"A sitting United States Congressman misleading voters and lying should be a news story," I said over and over to anyone who would listen. I continued to reach out to reporters and one finally bit. When he contacted the two GOP Chairs Marchant listed as supporters on his website, Wade and Diane concocted a bizarre story that I guess they thought people would believe. Diane said she "can't endorse anybody in a contested election, but she does endorse Marchant as the executive director of the National Republican Coalition for Life." She went on to say "I explained this to Grant." None of which was true as our entire office listened to Grant and her conversation on speaker phone.

Wade also changed his story. "I was a Cedar Hill councilman at the time, and he has never listed me as anything but," Emmert says. "So I don't see what the problem is. I endorsed him as a city councilman and I did so because he was very responsive to Cedar Hill. I was happy to endorse him. It's entirely accurate. "How can it be accurate if Wade is the Dallas GOP Chairman and his name is listed on Marchant's website in endorsing him and he claims it was for 2010 election, not 2012, but it's still accurate? It sounded a lot like Bill Clinton with his "definition of is" statement. Then, just to try to make it personal towards me, Wade continues "I guess I'm disappointed his campaign managers chose this path."

Wade called me all night and sent emails demanding conference calls expecting me to take orders from someone that just confirmed he supports our opponent. It didn't make sense for me to spend time with someone who was not on our side or willing to be logical. Wade hadn't been forthright with Grant in the beginning and I thought it appropriate Wade talk directly to Grant. Wade owed Grant as much. It's hard to say how much Wade and Diane's fake endorsements meant to voters or how well they knew them.

But when Congressman Kenny Marchant lied about Congressman Ron Paul endorsing him, well that was entirely different. Tt was a big deal. In the 24th District of Texas, Congressman Paul has strong grassroot activists. There were no doubts those activists were going to turn out to vote for Ron Paul for President. Paul's supporters are known for their loyalty, tenaciousness, and activism. Being that Ron Paul is a long-time Congressman from Texas, he out-performed his national average in the state of Texas. Paul was the second highest vote getter for President in Texas as well as in the 24th District of Texas. It was no secret that in this particular district, the one Grant was running in, the Ron Paul endorsement meant something big. We had to inform the voters that Paul was not supporting Marchant.

Having worked with both Congressman Ron Paul's and Senator Rand Paul's team, I knew how to reach Paul's campaign manager, Jesse, and asked him to get involved. Within minutes, Jesse confirmed to a reporter that Congressman Ron Paul had not endorsed Kenny Marchant in the 2012 primary election.

And while that was good news, Grant's campaign did not have a way to tell all those Republican primary voters that the direct mail pieces Marchant sent were inaccurate. Righting an opponent's wrong costs a lot of money.

Even after the *Dallas Observer* story came out, the Marchant campaign continued to tout Ron Paul's fake endorsement. They did this because they knew what we knew: No one was going to call them out. They had far more to gain by fabricating Paul's endorsement. How could they let Kenny Marchant get away with it? Why would they let him get away with it? What happened to media integrity? "If a sitting member of Congress is willing to lie about endorsements—what else is he willing to lie about?" a veteran reporter asked when I visited with him about my frustrations. He thought it was a story but his boss wasn't interested. More than one reporter told me they were "rooting for us" but that they "just can't get involved in this one."

The lies didn't stop.

Marchant campaign encouraged spies and recruited people to give Grant's campaign illegal contributions. A Marchant staffer submitted his resume to me via email claiming he wanted to work for the Magnolia Group, requesting an interview. What he wanted was to visit the inside of the Magnolia Group office. I played along with the game and suggested we meet in Grapevine and gave him the address. "But that's Grant Stinchfield's campaign office, "the Marchant staffer complained. He went on to tell me he REALLY wanted to meet at my office, the Magnolia office. I didn't budge, so the fake interview never took place. He hid his face when our team showed up at political events.

Marchant supporters/spies/staff spent a lot of gas money driving by, circling our campaign headquarters checking us out. It was easy to spot them because we were in a store-front with ceiling to floor windows and were on the end of the strip center in a low traffic area. There was no doubt in our minds the Marchant campaign had more than enough money to have their staff waste so much time on wondering our whereabouts and "casing" campaign headquarters.

Marchant's tricks never ceased. They thought I would take the bait when they sent some fellas that told us their names were "Kendall" and "Jordan" crashed Grant's golf tournament, just showing up and wanting to play. It's unusual for people to just show up at fundraising events, especially since golf tournaments require pre-planning and assigning teams, handicaps and such. We were happy to have more money for the campaign, but I knew better.

"How'd you hear about the golf tournament?" I asked. "Through the grapevine," a young fella with dark, shaggy hair says. I knew at that moment he and his friends were not supporters. In my dreams, I wished people magically showed up and gave money, but there is simply no such thing. I watched the guy with his dark sunglasses and ball cap pulled tightly over his face grilling Grant after the tournament.

"So, what is your stance on immigration?" before Grant answered he continued "And energy?" Everyone else used their post golf game time to catch up on their emails, voice mails, or just grab a beer. Many re-lived the course, hole by hole. But these two young fellas were not interested in any of that. Instead, they were unusually focused on Grant's views on energy and immigration policy. Nothing else. Real people don't spend time talking about the issues at a golf tournament— even if the person hosting is running for Congress! They enjoy taking a few hours off from work playing a game with friends or meeting new people. In this case, meeting people that wanted to get Grant elected to Congress. That's how I knew these people were on a mission for Congressman Marchant. Everyone else on our team thought I was crazy and a bit paranoid. Admittedly, I was.

"So Grant, would you say you are a moderate?" the stranger asked leaning into Grant. That's it! I had it with these guys. The weird leaning in... I figured the guy had a recording devise or something. Only political hacks and their followers talk and act this way. Or a guy getting a bonus to catch Grant in a "aha" moment. Before I could interject and save Grant, he answered enthusiastically, with no hesitation "No! I am a die-hard conservative." I kept my eyes on the guy. His sunglasses couldn't hide the disappointment on his face.

I jumped into the conversation. "So, what are your immigration and energy views? What would you like to see Grant do when he is in Congress?" I asked him as he got visibly uncomfortable moving from side to side. The Marchant campaign hadn't even prepped their spy. It was obvious this poor fella had no thoughts on the issues he claimed of interest and clearly hadn't anticipated we would ask him for his opinions.

Marchant's fella tried to change the subject and moved on to other attendees, attempting to gather information on Grant's team. What these fellas probably didn't realize, what they thought was a funny joke, was them breaking the law. Campaigns are filled with long hours, tedious work and little sleep. These two fellas gave us an opportunity to have some fun documenting Marchant's dirty tricks. Our video was the highest watched video of the campaign with over 10,000 hits. What did we do? I let Grant go be the investigative reporter and here's the video script from our YouTube video:

Grant begins, "It's no secret that politics is a dirty game. Career politicians will resort to all kinds of tricks to derail a formidable opponent like myself. Kenny Marchant sent out hundreds of thousands of dollars of campaign propaganda, paid for by the taxpayers. Why do you need to pay for it? After all, he's doubled his net worth while in congress. Now, we think he's even resorted to espionage.

You're looking at men who appear to be Stinchfield for Congress supporters, but as you're about to see, looks can be deceiving. They signed up for my Stinchfield for Congress golf tournament, paid their money online, then showed up to play. When we sent out thank you notes, the post office returned the letters, "address unknown." The problem is they used strange names and phony addresses—that is a clear violation of federal election law (FEC). We notified the FEC. While it conducts its own investigation, we thought that we'd do a little investigating of our own.

We could never find any record of "Carter Kendall," but we did track a man listed as "Jordan Sherman" to his mother's house in Frisco." Grant spoke to the neighborhood security guard. "Were you able to get in touch with that Jordan Sherman? He made an illegal contribution to us, and we've got to return it."

Grant, narrating in the video, "The law says it's illegal for us to accept donations from a fake person, so we wanted to return the contributions. Turns out, "Jordan Sherman," is "David Jordan Schirman," with an "i," not an "e."

Grant spoke on phone with Schirman's mother. "What's his cell phone number? I want to get it all worked out. If he's not behind it, we need to know about that." His mother gave us his mobile phone number and Grant called Schirman. He answered, "Hello?"

"Hey, Jordan?" Stinchfield asks.

"Yes," the voice answers. "Hey there, It's Grant Stinchfield. Stinchfield for Congress." Playing it cool, Schirman says, "Hey, how's it going, Grant?" And Grants answers equally as casual, "Hey, I'm doing great man. How are you?" After explaining the situation, Jordan Schirman insisted he was no spy, just a curious participant. Grant, speaking on phone with Schirman, asks "Do you know who put you up to it?" Jordan only answered with a question, "…Um… put me up to what?" Grant answered, matter of fact, "To putting a fake name in, and coming to the tournament." It' a pet peeve of mine when people say "to be honest" because my first reaction is to think have they not been honest to me up to this point? I had that same thought when Jordan tells Grant, "To be perfectly honest, nobody put me up to it. I just don't like filling in my real name and stuff like that. It just makes me a little nervous with all that stuff, and I don't like getting tracked."

"Right," Grant says "Unfortunately we've got a big problem, and now the FEC is involved."

Grant, narrating, says, "We can't say for sure if they are Kenny Marchant spies, but we can tell you that Jordan and Carter are the only two, out of 50 golfers, to attend this golf tournament using bogus information. And adding to the mystery? Jordan also acknowledges that he's best friends with high ranking Kenny Marchant campaign staff member, Chad."

Grant, speaking on phone with Schirman, "I see your friends with Chad Brubaker?"

Jordan, responds nervously, "Yes sir…"

"And so, was he involved in this too?" Grant asks. If I could have seen Jordan, I imagined him swaying back and forth as he answered Grant "…Um…I mean…Uh…He and I have been…um…you know…best friends for a while, I just…I mean, he wasn't involved in any way, shape, or form. Honestly, like I said, Grant, the only thing I'm trying to do here is uh…basically…keep my name protected, 'cause I don't like being tracked, and stuff like that. And with Carter, I didn't know his home address or anything like that, so I didn't put his down. His name is correct, and I'm the one that paid for him.

Grant, narrating on the video says "which actually, is another FEC violation (contributing to a campaign on someone else's behalf.) Later, via text message, I asked Jordan for an on-camera interview to explain his side of the story. His reply via text: "If you ever contact me or my family again, then I will notify the police that you are harassing me."

"How about the Marchant campaign harassing me?" Grant says to the camera. "He continues to spread lies about me, instead of simply agreeing to debate the issues, and he uses fake Facebook profiles to wreak havoc on my Facebook page. It's a desperate game, from a desperate man, that knows he's about to get fired." Grant says.

We reported the incident to the Federal Election Commission (FEC) and because members of Congress regulate the FEC; we knew it wouldn't go far. For a very long time the violation was still "pending." Congressman Marchant took it seriously, hiring one of the most expensive attorneys involved in FEC law. The FEC concluded Congressman Marchant did not break the law. Instead, the law remained with the individuals. Meaning it's all those kids, Jordan and Carter's fault. I bet they didn't know the Marchant team would make them the scape goats when something went wrong.

The FEC might as well not exist because they are beholden to congress. Here's the pathetic part the FEC shared with me. "If the Stinchfield campaign accepted those contributions from 'Kendall' and 'Jordan,' the FEC has the right to charge the Stinchfield campaign with accepting contributions in someone else's name. The burden of proof is on Stinchfield," the FEC representative told me when I explained that those people were planted. No doubt, the Marchant campaign would ensure the FEC come down hard on Grant and his campaign. The double standard is one of many of the tools incumbents have in their tool box that they don't hesitate to use. They have access to more resources. They make the rules. It is not a level playing field.

18 DIRTY TRICKS

The inspiration for one of our controversial commercials "You Deserve the Truth" was from Grant's experience in the news business. The commercial started with Grant talking into the camera and says "I used to bring you the news almost every night, but here is what you didn't know. Too many times, NBC refused to let me tell the stories you needed to here. Was it liberal bias, or simply the fear of losing ad dollars? I believe it was both. But you can rest assured that when I get into Washington, no one will sensor me again. You will hear it all, because you deserve the truth, and that's something career politicians want to avoid. NBC may not approve of this message, but I do."

We thought NBC would pull the spot and we hoped they would. If NBC pulled the spot, we'd get more attention. Some of the NBC staff let Grant know they were "sweating it out" as they debated. Finally, they decided it would get them less attention to just run the spot. The downside was we couldn't afford as many TV spots as we wanted. So, we were playing tricks too. But this one didn't work.

Our other commercial we called "Morning in Washington" and we had Grant to go out to a pig farm to shoot it. In it, he talked of incumbents on a feeding frenzy and of runaway spending and greed. He pledged to expose the fraud and corruption in Washington that governs todays incumbents.

With the presidential election, a highly competitive U.S. Senate seat (to fill Senator Kay Bailey Hutchinson's seat since she retired) and many other open races, we knew we had to push through all the noise by being creative and some day's signs felt more effective than radio and TV. We went up on radio and television early to increase our chances of people hearing our ads before all the political noise began. We continued through Election Day. But when early voting started, Marchant blew us away in ad buys. I wondered if he had purchased every spot on WFIL (during the Rush Limbaugh Show.) Had we not gone up on air, I doubt Marchant would have done radio ads since he had not done so in most of his previous campaigns. But what I couldn't believe is Marchant copied Grant and got away with it. Grant had dedicated his life to exposing waste, fraud and abuse and now, driving to the campaign office, I was listening to a Kenny Marchant radio ad saying how he was an expert on waste, fraud and abuse.

Afterwards two radio hosts came on wondering out loud why so much money was being spent on an open seat in the Texas State Senate "for a job that only pays something like $500 a month" the guy says. I started to call in and then thought better of it. No need to distract myself with such. I wanted to let them know that the job they were wondering about is $7200 a year plus expenses. But the reason people want the job is for the pension. The Texas Legislature's links their pensions to state judges' salary. They do this so people like those radio hosts are under the impression the legislators are making sacrifices by serving. Not so long ago, the Texas legislators boosted their maximum retirement benefit to $125,000 or 100% of a judge's salary, resulting in lifting caps on their own pensions.

Why do I care? Because the State of Texas pays Congressman Kenny Marchant $36k a year pension. That's in addition to the federal pension he'll collect. How can these "businessman" say they aren't enjoying the benefits of being a career government worker? How can they say they are for small government? And how could I be listening to him talk about eliminating waste on the radio now?

This thinking wasn't helping Grant. We needed earned media and we needed a way to get people to start talking about the race. We couldn't think or act like everyone else and expect to win. Most voters didn't know Kenny Marchant refused to be in a room with Grant Stinchfield. Brainstorming, it was Jeff Crilley that said "Let's put a big billboard up saying Kenny Marchant, why won't you debate me?" We brainstormed some more while others were securing billboard quotes. Shortly afterwards the finished product was created. "Why Won't You Debate Me?" …with a shadow of Kenny Marchant and Grant's face. The billboard stood tall, just a few miles from Kenny's house. Fortunately, we got some earned media out of it. As a rule, billboards are not considered a good use of money; but we definitely got $400 worth of headlines, lots of conversations, and new volunteers that were disgusted to learn Congressman Marchant thought he was above being debated.

To this day, I believe if Grant could get in a room side by side with Kenny Marchant, Grant would be in Congress. Not only does Kenny struggle to express himself verbally; he thinks he is above such actions. Debates expose weaknesses. In this case, a debate would expose not only Kenny's lack of legislative accomplishments, but his arrogance. Grant yearned for a debate, was prepared for a debate, and we relished in knowing that Congressman Marchant would have to be held accountable for his actions in government. But it never happened.

"So, who the heck is supporting Kenny Marchant?" someone asked, reflecting on the thousands of homes that were walked. We couldn't believe most of the homeowners we met didn't know Kenny Marchant was their Congressman. I suspect this happens because people just blindly vote as to learn names. The voters we talked to said they were willing to support Grant after asking more about him. Rarely, did we encounter a loyal Kenny supporter. When we did discover one, they were typically continuing their support "out of respect." Hardly did we hear about the good work they thought Congressman Marchant was doing. One long-time precinct chair, Bob, "quietly" agreed it was time for Marchant to go, but he couldn't be the one to make him go as "it wouldn't be right." But Bob did say, "I sure wouldn't mind if your Stinchfield fella won though."

Maybe that's when the Marchant staff recruited others to run against Grant Stinchfield. A whole bunch of groups, organizations, and candidates also ran against Grant. Many organizations, like the Chamber of Commerce and Farm Bureau try to tell voters how to vote, passing out score cards and giving questionnaires. Understandably, voters are busy and they join these organizations that support their views and keep them apprised. The NRA (National Rifle Association) is perhaps the biggest juggernaut of all, but Club for Growth and Eagle Forum may not be known to voters but have many members and influence elections as well. A common thing for them to do is to "grade" Congressmen on their votes.

"How about groups rating Congressman on their actions? Not just their votes?" I asked at one of Grant's cabinet meetings, confusing most. Some argued that votes are important. "Sure, I say, but there are a lot of votes that are simply staged, so they can secure the organizations A-plus rating. They don't think for a minute the bill is going to pass or they are really doing something to solve a problem or change the world." I say to everyone, before adding "they do a heck of a lot of pretend work in Washington!"

"So what are you saying?" one of them asks. "Well, we all know Republicans talk about protecting tax payer money and they all practically vote the right way, but when it actually comes to taxpayers' money do they do just that?" I could tell the room was still confused and needed me to get to the point.

"We all have heard ad nauseam Kenny Marchant's 'conservative voting record', but we've been doing some research and that's not the case." Everyone leaned forward, anxious to hear this juicy new information. "This year, Congressman Marchant ranks number four in the entire Congress as a big spender, when it comes to spending tax payers' monies!" Number three in Republican members! Fiscal conservatives shouldn't be in the top anything; but NUMBER 3?" The room erupts with excitement over this nugget of information.

Grant jumps in. "Kenny's official taxpayer funded car is a Ford Prius. Kenny's financial reports reveal taxpayers pay $800 month for his staff and him to drive around the district. Marchant's district office in Irving costs $6k a month in office rent." Someone asked how we know it and I answer, pointing to Andrew. "Andrew called Congressman Marchant's office to ask what car they drive and they told him a Ford Prius. Andrew looked up how much the taxpayers are paying for the car.

"So, while Congressman Marchant and other incumbents brag about "high marks" from "conservative organizations" they don't tell people those organizations favor incumbents, only grade on votes, and not how actual tax dollars are spent. In other words, Congressmen may introduce bills that never have a snowball's chance of becoming a law but can be perceived as a certain way because of the votes recorded on that bill. Meanwhile, they can screw taxpayer's of out of their money," I say, watching Grant's cabinets' shocked expressions. The room is eerily quiet and I continue to talk.

"No one grades Congressmen on what they actually do with taxpayers' money. Actions don't count when it comes to grades. It's just one more way the system purposefully makes it confusing to voters so it makes uncovering the truth difficult," Grant says. So, a new set of stories were told to voters. Is Congressman Marchant even a fiscal conservative?

Congressman Marchant had an "A" with several groups, like "Texas Alliance for Life. But just because he voted to over-turn Roe vs. Wade and such what was that really doing to further the pro-life efforts? It appeared to me it was just staged-voting. Grant and Kenny didn't differ much on social issues. That's why is was so hard to believe "Texas Alliance for Life" got so involved in this race.

When someone runs for national office (or any office, really) they get inundated with hundreds of campaign pledges, questionnaires, and surveys to fill out. It's understood these groups use that information to share with their members or constituencies the candidates' views on their group's issue. I hate those questionnaires because they are time-consuming and practically impossible to fill them out. They don't allow one to expand on their beliefs. They are not worded in a way to let people know what the candidates think on issues. Their questions are slanted and most of the time one is limited to choosing: a, b, or c or "use 15 words or less to expand on this answer."

I wish we could have taken the Governor Jon Huntsman approach of refusing to let his ideas and opinions be boiled down to multiple choice answers and hard lines in the sand. While originally intended to inform voters, these pledges allow powerful interest groups to control candidates into failed attempts through a "one size fits all" track. These pledges prevent thoughtful discourse on issues. More times than not, the best possible outcome for American citizens is ignored for sake of these groups and their pledges.

Governor Huntsman has suggested that candidates do not take pledges, but take the oath of office. Such thoughtfulness and analytical thinking didn't get Jon Huntsman very far in the Republican primary when he ran for president. That's why we made darn sure Grant filled out every one of those questionnaires and surveys.

I knew all this and pounded into the entire Magnolia team. Too many campaigns had made mistakes I would not tolerate to happen with Grant. The rule was simple—they must all be completed and on time. Everyone had heard me tell stories of how it is common for campaigns to make a mistake because they are so fast-paced, sometimes a questionnaire falls through the cracks and then the groups put the mark of death by putting in bold "candidate refused to answer." Candidate refused to answer is political speak for candidate worships the devil. Totally unacceptable and can cost an election. Seriously.

The team understood what was at stake with these forms. And we knew Grant, as a challenger, was being held to a higher standard. That's why we set up a tracking system that everyone understood and had one person the point of contact—so there would be no mix-ups. Andrew was the ideal person as he is even-keel and has strong organizational skills. There was no confusion. I say this so that what is told next is understood for those normal individuals who are not consumed by these inside political groups that operate under the rouse of "helping to inform voters."

Just days into early voting, an unfair attack came from Texas Alliance for Life when they sent out an expensive direct mail piece "exclusively endorsing" Kenny Marchant. It didn't make sense to me for a group to devote enormous amounts of money and time in our race where both Kenny and Grant would have about the same voting record on their issues. Something was up and I had to find out what was going on.

Our supporters, many who were members of Texas Alliance for Life, thought the mailer claiming Grant would be a baby-killer if he went to Congress was outlandish, but they were very worried the effects it would have on voters. With good reason. A very large constituency that votes in a Republican primary would be outraged by the mailer. I knew this may cost us the election. This mailer would motivate single issue voters in droves. The truth disregarded. Because 501(c4)'s organizations do not have to disclose their donors, no one will ever know who paid for it or how much money was spent on a lie benefiting Congressman Marchant.

Andrew was on top of the situation as much as one can be, as his tracking system revealed that that not only had the survey been submitted, but five days before their deadline. When we contacted Dina, with Texas Alliance for Life, they claimed Grant/we had not submitted their survey. We knew better and re-sent them the information immediately, so they could see for themselves. Their answer was simply "Well, we already printed our materials," More livid than surprised, I despised this group, claiming to "protect life" but in truth, caring more about money and Kenny Marchant than doing the fair thing. Eventually, Dina conceded the ball had been dropped on their end. But Dina knew what I knew. They weren't going to do anything about it. I wanted to the world know that these so-called pro-life people, who say they are filled with compassion, are nothing more than hypocrites. Protecting life? They were protecting Congressman Kenny Marchant.

"Since Grant filled out the questionnaire and turned it in before the deadline would you at least put it up on your website?" Andrew asked Dina. One would think the organization would want the voters to have accurate and informed information to decide. One would think this was an easy yes, but instead Dina hesitated. "Uhh…. I don't think I can do that."

"What do you mean?" Andrew asked, while remaining amazing calm considering we were losing voters by the second. "Grant responded before the deadline and you have the information confirming such. It's not correct to say Grant didn't answer. It's deceiving voters. What do I need do to make this happen?"

"I need to talk to my supervisor," Dina said. They didn't give Andrew the option of visiting with the supervisor, so we were all at Dina's fate as we waited for her to "check-in to the matter." Andrew dedicated the entire day to getting the issue resolved with the best possible outcome given the situation. Finally, when they put Grant's questionnaire answers on their website, Andrew immediately sent out an alert to our supporters, asking them to spread the word. To those working at the polls, we alerted them to pull up the website and direct voters to Grant's completed survey online. But again, this hit piece went out during early voting and it would be tough to recover from it.

It would've been naive to think Texas Alliance for Life would print anything or contact their members by phone or email. We asked, already knowing the answer would be a no. Far too many people never got to learn that Grant's position or that he filled out the organization's survey. The damage was done. Despite our best efforts to at least let the voters have all the materials and information to make their own personal decision, we knew that we had been sabotaged.

Texas Alliance for Life, wasn't the only one that sabotaged Grant. Candidates did too.

There were two hotly contested Texas state Representative races that overlapped the district Grant was running in for U.S. House of Representatives.

The Texas State Race for District 115 had five people running. It was not unusual for the candidates for HD-115 and the campaigns for CD-24 to be working the same polls. While many people remained polite, many didn't bother with niceties as spending 12 hours sweating at a polling location can bring out the worst in people. Our volunteers and the Magnolia team shared these crazy stories late at night or during the early mornings hours when we got a glimpse of each other before starting or ending our day's assignments.

Most candidates in Texas' District 115 race told us "they were staying neutral" in the 24th District of Texas, a pretty typical answer. It came across to our team that most of these state candidates wanted the endorsement of Congressman Kenny Marchant though. But they still didn't want to risk alienating Grant's supporters. After all, it was Grant who had continued winning straw poll after straw poll. Grant surprised people when he, not Kenny Marchant, received the coveted endorsement of the *Fort Worth Star Telegram*. Some candidates' solution was to play both sides, knowing every vote counted, to make it to the run-off election.

District 115 candidate Andy Olivo didn't play both sides. A retired US Army Reserve Colonel and former Carrollton city council wanted to continue to serve his country in the Texas legislature. When people asked who he was voting on the congressional race, he didn't try to argue the point if Marchant was a good congressman or not and instead said, "Maybe Kenny Marchant is a good Congressman, but regardless he's been in office too long. We're overdue for fresh new leadership." While Olivo had an impressive resume, I knew the system would eat him alive without a professional team to guide him through the political swamp.

Bennett Radcliff wasn't afraid to tell supporters he was with Congressman Marchant though. They shared the same consultant. We were grilling hotdogs at the polling place and Radcliff's young daughters told us they were hungry. Of course, we shared a hotdog with them but their daddy's face turned red as he scolded his girls. Will and I shared laughs over such silliness. No one thought Radcliff's children didn't want their daddy to win because they ate a hotdog from Grant supporters.

In contrast to Olivo and Radcliff, candidate Matt Rinaldi, claimed he was neutral when he actively campaigned for Marchant. When people arrived at the polls to vote who were obvious Grant people, Rinaldi gave them the impression he was for us. He did the same thing when he saw people approaching that were Kenny supporters. I guess he thought we were blind. "Ultimately, I am holding out hope for a Kenny Marchant endorsement," Matt told me, "but I like Grant." I couldn't afford him "liking Grant." Rinaldi insisted on working against us by passing out score cards from the Heritage Alliance, a conservative non-profit organization that is a 501c (4).

A 501c (4) means the organization can participate in elections but cannot make it their primary focus and they do not have to disclose their donors. Of course, most organizations know in this political environment it is the wild west of campaign finance and it appears just about anything goes. While the law says a 501c (4) cannot come out and directly say "vote for this person–don't vote for this one," they can issue score cards and voter's guides that make it obvious to voter's who they think should win. And this is exactly what Heritage Alliance does–issue voter's guides and score card that look very official from a voter's perspective.

Matt Rinaldi received an "A" rating from them and understandably wanted to share with voters his good grade by handing out flyers at the polls. Matt's campaign also made the decision to include the 24th District of Texas race, where Heritage gave Kenny Marchant an "A" and Grant Stinchfield a "C." Grant's and Kenny's answers were not that much different so we didn't understand the gap in grades as the "quiz" was multiple choice and only had a few non-multiple choice questions that only allowed answers of less than 15 words. It was hard to distinguish oneself given such limited criteria.

We wanted voters to judge for themselves and posted both Marchant and Stinchfield's answers side by side. Voters could also go to Heritage's website to see as well, where Heritage acknowledged they "give more weight to an incumbent in office." That still didn't answer our question why Rinaldi's campaign was getting involved in Grant's race. We, of course, preferred Rinaldi and his team concern themselves with only their race. They claimed that they hadn't even thought about the ramifications to Grant or how it may come across that they were campaigning for Kenny, but I didn't believe they were that foolish.

Not only did we see it as inappropriate, we clearly saw their flyers as the Rinaldi campaign spending funds on behalf of Kenny Marchant. It should be reported as required by law as an in-kind contribution to Marchant's campaign. Ignoring us and the law, their campaign continued to spend monies on Marchant's behalf. Rinaldi's campaign manager explained to me how "there are too much costs involved for us to print more hand-outs." I responded quickly. "We will gladly pay to have them re-printed or contribute to the campaign so the flyers may be re-printed without Grant's race included." The campaign manager wasn't prepared for my answer and said nothing. I repeated myself, but it was clear no words would come out of his.

Since Rinaldi was not at the polls, I approached his wife, Corley. "I don't have any influence on him" she told me. "You would have to talk to Matt." Corley said. "Grant has a call into him, but since you're here I wanted to visit with you about a solution. Surely you can see where we are coming from?" I ask. "We want you and your team to focus on your race. Passing out the Heritage scorecard with Grant's race is not necessary. And I thought you could visit with Matt about it…"

"Oh, I have no influence on him," Corley coyly and repeatedly told me. "I find that hard to believe," I said. "Really, I don't," Corley said again smiling. Not enjoying being lied to or being called stupid, I simply said in a sarcastic tone "Really? You don't have any influence over the person you sleep with?" She said nothing. I walked away. I let Grant know that Rinaldi and his team would continue to hand out to voters the Heritage results, campaigning against him, but still encouraged him to personally follow up with Matt to not let him off the hook.

Dr. Steve Nguyen was also running for the state house seat. He had strong grassroots support and had an enthusiastic group of volunteers waving signs and literally chanting and cheering with pom-poms at the polls for him. Many in the Party were familiar with Dr. Nguyen because he had been a precinct chair and involved for years. He was learning running in a contested Republican primary was quite different than his other Party involvement. Corley whispered to voters and me that "Dr. Nguyen is a Hindu" and "only recently became a Christian and joined a church," implying that God is on their side–the chosen one. I told her found it more interesting how Dr. Nguyen came to the United States as a political refuge and now was a successful optometrist.

I don't know who Dr. Nguyen voted for—Kenny Marchant or Grant Stinchfield. What I do know is Dr. Nguyen was polite, sharing stories of campaigning that we all could relate to. I don't know when in politics treating an opponent of someone that disagrees with you as the anti-Christ became the norm or a sign of weakness.

Up until Election Day, the Rinaldi campaign continued to pass out the Heritage Alliance score cards with Grant's race included. Perhaps if they had focused more on their own race, they would have at least made it to the run-off election. Instead, Dr. Steve Nguyen and Bennett Radcliff were in the run-off election to be the next state representative from Texas House District 115. Two years later, Matt Rinaldi ran again for the seat, only focusing on his race, and won.

19 EVERYTHING HAS AN END, EXCEPT A SAUSAGE HAS TWO

Between the Heritage Score Cards and the Texas Alliance for Life mailers, I knew it no longer mattered that we won every measure up until now. Grant didn't get the *Dallas Morning News* (DMN) endorsement. But that one can go both ways. Sometimes, people consider NOT getting the DMN endorsement as a badge of honor, or at least that's what Congressman Hensarling said for several years before they finally endorsed him one election season.

Working every minute, hoping to stop the crushing tide of Marchant and his allies' devious tactics, I took to the polls. There wasn't much else I could do, all our money was allocated to T.V., robo-calls, e-marketing–you name it. So, while I knew I couldn't over-turn all the dark money, I still wanted to make a miracle happen away from the computer.

Working the polls is important, exhausting, and entertaining. I joined our crew on the front lines, where polls were open from 7am to 7pm. The only way I got see my Will was if he joined me on the campaign trail. So, Will got into the spirit by even hauling a grill to the polling place.

Will cooked hamburgers, hot dogs, bratwursts, and snacks to make the most of the day. We hung our Stinchfield sign from our pop up tent and brought out our big feather signs to waive and advertise with as well. We happily shared our food, snacks, and shade with fellow campaigns.

Volunteering for Marchant's campaign, three high school siblings, spent long days at the polling place on weekends. We watched the day before as they suffered in the heat with no pop up tent or anything to shield them from the suffocating Texas sun. Worried about them dehydrating, Will and I offered them some water that they eagerly and happily said "thank you" to. Later, when the popsicle cart came by I asked for a watermelon one, hoping it would be just the thing to cool me off.

Will purchased the popsicles while I continued talking to voters. While paying, he looked at the kids and asked "Do you want a popsicle too?" They looked at each other, hesitated. It was obvious to Will and I they wanted some too. One of the siblings broke the silence, finally speaking up with a very loud and enthusiastic "YES!" He thanked Will profusely. So profusely, we were worried about them and their need for hydration as all wore bright pink faces.

Visiting over popsicles, Will learned that the kids were in middle school, not high school, not volunteers either as they were being paid. Their parents must have been as worried as Will and I we were because the next day, they made several trips to check on their children throughout the day and brought water out to them several times as well. Sunscreen was delivered on a different trip. On another, they appeared to be just hanging out and supervising them. I asked Will "What do you think they are doing? Why would the parents spend so much time just watching their children wave Marchant signs in this hot weather?" Will gave me a look like he couldn't believe I had to ask the question and said "You saw how the Marchant campaign treated those kids. What parents wouldn't be out here making sure they didn't get any more sunburnt and thirsty than they got yesterday?" I nod, "Good point."

It was about this time the parents came up to us. "Thank you two so much for taking care of our kids. Thank you!" As they continued thanking Will and I, I couldn't help but be a little surprised. Most Marchant supporters were not polite to us. In fact, they were visceral at times. Finally, with Will's encouragement I got the nerve to ask if they would support Grant and I was floored by their response. "We'd like to support Grant but cannot vote. We're Canadian." Marchant's campaign couldn't even find volunteers or hire people from the U.S.

Will's smile got bigger as I looked at him realizing he had already learned this from the parents earlier. "Would you like a "Stinchfield bracelet?" Will asks holding out a rubber-looking wrist band, like the ones people wear for causes. The girl happily accepts. The mother then asked "Do you have enough that I may have some for the whole family?" Will and I gave her a handful of Stinchfield bracelets. While we knew the Canadian family couldn't vote for Grant, we found humor in the Marchant "volunteers" wearing Grant Stinchfield paraphernalia. The frowny faces of the Marchant staff a few tents from us confirmed they didn't approve of our actions, but it was clear to Will and I the parents didn't approve of them.

The Marchant campaign never stopped being bullies or using their power to get ahead, whether it legal or not. They sent a Carrollton city employee, the city whose mayor is named Marchant, to tell Will and I to "cease and decease" at the polling site. "I apologize, but you cannot have your signs in the ground or touching the ground. You must hold them at all times," the city employee told us.

I am convinced the Marchant campaign hated that Grant's signs were larger than theirs. That's about what this campaign had turned into. Despite the absurdly of it all, we agreed to their terms and were even told "you may let them rest on your foot and you will be complying," the lady whispered. This must have not been the answer the Marchant campaign was looking for as they were upset we were still waiving our Stinchfield signs.

This poor unlucky city employee came out to the polling site again. This time telling us "I was instructed to come out to address "peoples' complaints," even if it meant leaving the baby shower I was at," she says dressed in a multi-colored sari. "Again, I am sorry. But this is very important to the city. It turns out you are not allowed to rest the large signs on your feet but must hold them in the air at all times. Since that would be a hardship, you probably don't want to use these signs. Maybe?" she says meekly as Will and I both feel sorry for this lady and share with her how sorry we are she is a pawn for Mayor Matthew Marchant. His Daddy must have been proud. But we waived the signs even more as this was all simply too entertaining.

The nice lady who was a city employee came out twice, but that was not the end of the city's involvement that day Sunday. The police were also then sent out. I was talking to an elderly couple when the Carrollton police approached the Stinchfield tent. Not wanting to end my conversation with potential voters until I heard a positive response, I glanced at the police approaching "We're on-site to let you know that grills are not to be used city property," they told Will.

"I've never heard of such a law. You can't grill on city property?" Will asked, seeking clarification. The policeman responded sympathetically "We didn't even know there was such a law either," he says, the other policeman nodding. "But we got a call just now telling us about it." Will and I understood. We didn't want to make the police or any other city worker should work anymore than necessarily. Or worse, take them away from solving crime because the Marchant's were willing to use their powers to thwart Grant's campaign presence at the polls. The police noticeable appreciated we were polite. It was obvious they weren't sure what to expect. We shook hands and they left.

But Will and I got carried away with politeness and hadn't noticed the grills throughout the polling area, which was on a city library and park grounds. We wished for the police to come back so we could ask them about those grills. "I wonder what those nice police officers would say then?" I asked Will. Although both of us hated to put the police in such a position, we weren't about to tolerate bullies. Worked up, I called the city of Carrollton and confirmed with a woman with my name, Leslie, that there was no such law. Upon having confirmation from the city, Will fired the grill back up and we secretly looked forward to the police returning. But atlas, I suspect the police decided their time was better spent fighting crime as we didn't see them again.

Kelsey meanwhile had her own issues to deal with while working the polls. While she didn't have city employees and policemen approach her at the cities of Irving, Grapevine, and Hurst, she had her plenty of challenges to face. Kensley, who attended the first town hall and heckled Grant managed to plant himself wherever Kelsey was. He led the efforts with other Marchant volunteers and staff shouting over Kelsey whenever she tried to talking to voters. Other times they would get on the phone and call for additional people to join the Marchant group to intimidate and outnumber her.

Each morning of early voting, Kelsey would put up Stinchfield signs in the early hours of dawn, to replace the stolen ones from the previous night. Worse, she would find her newly put out signs "covered up" by Marchant signs. Despite her efforts, she was not successful in explaining everyone had a right to have a sign displayed at the polling places. Kelsey got creative and parked her car up front at the parking lot of a polling place, but that only lasted a day. The next morning, Kelsey discovered Kensley and a large fat woman with a Marchant sign, parked their cars and others overnight to prevent Kelsey from having a parking space upfront. And while none of this was significant, it simply added to the pettiness and irritability one can experience during a campaign. Kelsey had been involved in a few campaigns before, but they were nothing like this one. At times, their mean-minded antics caught her off guard. How could it not? These were grown adults treating another adult like they were in a middle school competition. What Kelsey might be surprised to learn is that after the election, Kensley asked Grant to endorse him for a race for city council. Worse, Grant did it. I, on the other hand, hadn't forgiven Kensley for all the grief he caused "sweet little Kelsey" as many of our supporters referred to her.

Grant's message was being drowned out by more than 15 slick mail pieces sent out by the Marchant campaign alone, boasting of his "conservative" record and ratings from "conservative organizations." Other organizations, groups, and candidates piled on too. Mysterious letters were conveniently mailed to "Four R voters" spreading lies about Grant. Voters didn't get to hear both stories as it was too expensive for us to compete.

We lost. By a lot.

Losing caused a pain so raw in me that I had no idea how to react. It didn't matter though because there was no time to grieve. I had a job to do. As I was about to call Grant to make sure he talked to me before making an appearance to his supporters, I saw his SUV pulling up under to the valet stand at Via Real, the neighborhood grill where we chose to gather to watch the results with Grant's supporters.

Still dressed in my Stinchfield t-shirt and now grimy jeans, I met Grant as he was opening the door, relieved he'd found some time to shower, change, and pick up his parents. At a loss for words, but vowing not to let him enter the restaurant without me telling him of the catastrophic results, I blurted out softly. "We didn't do it. We lost." I was proud there was no moisture in my eyes, but a lump formed in my throat as I made eye contact with Grant. Before I could apologize or say anything more, Grant jumped in "Leslie, I am sorry. I let you down."

"No, Grant. I let you down…" I interrupted, but didn't say anything else. For a brief moment, we shared a great sorrow. We gave all that we had to this shared cause-one few could understand. It was our secret, but only for a second.

Supporters came out to greet Grant and pulled us away. They were happy. Discussing the early results and remaining naively optimistic. They didn't understand what Grant and I already knew—no matter the numbers, the gap was too large too close. The media sometimes only releases certain precincts and such, but the Secretary of State's website already showed the results. It would take most of our supporters a few hours to fully comprehend we'd lost, despite me, as delicately as possible saying to them "there's no path to victory."

Before I shared with them the bad news, I made it point to talk to our team first—Andrew, Kelsey, Matt, David, Ben, Amy, and everyone. Other volunteers too. I realized others on our team couldn't be there, interns who had dedicated semesters and such, like Stuart. I knew they would take it hard too. As I surveyed the room, I realized our group was sun-burnt from working the polls and phones the entire Election Day. They could not hide their exhaustion any longer. I was so proud of the job they had done, but despite by genuine appreciation and admiration, they only had tears, shock, disbelief, and denial for responses to the news I told them.

I tried my best to console everyone but nothing worked. "There was nothing you could have done that we didn't do." I said and proceeded with such repetitive statements for hours saying it over and over to our supporters. I desperately yearned to go home, crawl in bed, or even a hot bath, wish for victory, and a year of my life back. Give everyone a year too as Andrew and Kelsey's were troopers. Matt had taken his precious days off from training for the Olympics to work on Grant's race. And now, he had to return to training with this defeat. Because of me.

While I talked to our team, volunteers and supporters, I delegated the task of telling Grant's parents to him. Grant wouldn't have had it any other way, but I dreaded it for him. Particularly Grant telling his Dad, also named Grant, who worked so hard to get Grant elected and was a sounding board to Grant during the campaign. Grant Sr. made Get Out the Vote calls throughout the campaign, put pressure on family and friends to donate, and came to town for the final push. I also chose not to be the person to tell Matt's Dad, Dennis, who had made the trip down so Matt didn't have to drive back to Utah by himself. It was the first time I had met him in person, even though he too had contributed and got involved in the campaign. While I thought this spoke volumes of so many team members' parents at Grant's election night event, it's one of the few times I was relieved none of them were my parents.

Everyone made crazy sacrifices that seemed pointless at this moment. The sacrifices alone could fill a book. There were so many things that went right. Our strong grassroots organization, committed people dedicated to Grant winning, decent fundraising, legends supporting him...I could go on, but it doesn't matter. We lost. The best person doesn't always win. I knew this, but didn't want to accept it.

20 RED, BLUE, IT'S ALL THE SAME

Staying in my bathrobe, I caught up on all the other races as I literally didn't bother to check out how everyone else running for office did the night before. I finally went out for pancakes and coffee, by myself. I hoped to figure out what the meaning of my life was….and figure out how I could I keep doing what I was doing.

Shocked, I learned Taj Clayton, a striking man who has one of those life's that they make movies out of: modest growing up…amazing athlete…. goes to Harvard, meets Barack Obama…later serves on his finance team, all while working as an attorney and managing to be super-involved in giving back to his community and family. He lost worse than Grant. I just knew he would win and be the next Congressman from South Dallas. I had been following this race because it gave me hope that I may be able to still believe in the process. From a far, it felt like the Democrats' version of our race with Grant.

Taj Clayton challenged long-time incumbent, Congresswoman Eddie Bernice Johnson, in the Democrat primary. Clayton raised serious money and I caught myself envious of all his earned media. Clearly the *Dallas Morning News* went out of their way to help Clayton, not even pretending to be unbiased. I didn't blame them. For years, Congresswoman Eddie Bernice Johnson, EBJ as some call her, was my Congresswoman, being that my home and office were in the 30th district of Texas. Over the years, I've watched her become bolder and believed she thought she was unbeatable. Phone calls to her office don't get returned and the mail she sent out many times had the wrong information in it.

Under the ruse of encouraging minority development, Congresswoman Johnson's trust has a quarter of the *Hudson News* business and a little less of the Pappas restaurants at the airport. It's no secret she also owns large percent at Dallas's Love Field *Hudson News* as well. The *DMN* impressed me for standing up to her, giving her a hard time for refusing to answer reporters' questions, ignoring her constituents, and the mishandling of the Congressional Black Caucus Foundation scholarship funds, that she made into her own slush fund.

It was discovered Congresswoman Johnson awarded 23 scholarships to two of her grandsons, two great nephews, and the children of her top aid. All the scholarship recipients were ineligible under anti-nepotisms and residency rules. After the news came out, Congresswoman Johnson later repaid the foundation. So why would all the Democrat members of Congress endorse her over her opponent, Taj Clayton?

Stranger still to me, was how none of Congresswoman Johnsons' Republican colleagues said a word. They were remarkable quiet. There is all this talk about visceral political environments and Republicans and Democrats can't get along, but not one person in the Texas delegation–even the Republicans–said a word. The public and me are being told Republican and Democrats hate each other, but not one Republican went after the lone Democrat in North Texas. They go after each other for all kinds of nonsense, but not this. When one of the biggest party bosses——Congressman Pete Sessions, who chairs the National Republican Congressional Committee Chairman (NRCC) whose job is to be partisan, maintain, and increase the Republican majority didn't speak up all I could ask is "why?" Was everyone in on this together? What the heck happened on this race?

For me, the race between Congresswoman Johnson and Taj Clayton was eerily similar to Congressman Marchant and Grant Stinchfield's. They were parallel story lines. One being a safe Democrat seat and the other being a safe Republican seat–meaning the primary races decided these elections. Both Congresswoman Johnson and Congressman Marchant are long-time bureaucrats, serving in Texas Legislature first, so they both receive a Texas pension and a federal one they're accruing. (I already knew Congressman Marchant's Texas pension is $36k year, but I looked up and saw Congresswoman Johnson's is almost the same at 35k a year).

Each of the Party's leadership chose to stay with the status quo despite having a promising, younger, energetic candidate that would bring more people to the Party and the process. It's common in primaries to accuse an opponent of not being part of the Party but a member of the opposing Party. (So, Democrat incumbents claim their opponents are Republicans in disguise and Republican incumbents claim their opponents are Democrats.)

Working from the same playbook, the incumbents in Texas 24 and 30 did just that. The incumbent, Johnson, called Taj Clayton a Republican. As you might imagine telling Democrat voters that someone running in their Democrat primary is a Republican…well it's scandalous. It's also something people can easily understand as opposed to a more complicated issue. The Marchant campaign called Grant a "Kennedy," a subtler way of calling him a Democrat. But while Grant could address the issue and over-come their attacks, Taj was never able to convinces voters otherwise. He had been tattooed "tea party Taj" by the Johnson campaign.

In the days after the election, and still too upset and exhausted for sleep, I spent a lot of time by myself. I re-watched the documentary *Street Fighter*. It tells the story of the Cory Booker's campaign against long-time incumbent Sharpe James for Mayor of Newark. A real David vs. Goliath story–except Goliath won in this one. To anyone living outside of Newark the election results seemed impossible to believe as the bad guy won. As I watched the movie, knowing what happened already, I still couldn't believe Booker lost. He deserved to win. The good guy deserved to win. Grant deserved to win.

There is no other way to say it, but Sharpe James was a crook. He relished the power of the incumbency. He created his own slush fund, had dirty cops in his pocket, and anyone else that would take his money. Yet all James could say about Booker is to tell voters he's a Republican. Emotional over everything, in this race, I think "who cares?" wouldn't they prefer a Republican to a known Democrat crook? I know better, but I get just as worked up about watching this campaign play out because it's a train wreck. It's so wrong. Booker and his team practically do everything right and he loses. I find some sick comfort in this.

Cory Booker didn't give up though. He ran again. And that time he won.

People were already talking about Grant running again. Grant was talking about Grant running again. I just didn't know. Regardless, I would go on vacation first I thought. But here is the real sickening part about when Booker ran again. He won—but not because he took down the incumbent. James made a last-minute decision to not run and "focus on his state senate responsibilities." (Sharpe James held simultaneously both the position of Mayor of Newark and a New Jersey State Senate seat.) Then, it took several more years for justice to prevail. Finally, Sharpe James was sentenced to jail! And of course, Cory Booker is now a rising star in the Democrat Party and is now a United States Senator. I still can't decide if I hate that documentary or love that documentary. What does it mean about voters and the election process? Would Grant's only hope for victory, if he ran again, would be if Kenny Marchant pulled out of the race?

"Taj is the Cory Booker of the 30th District of Texas!" I say to myself out loud.

They both faced backlash from their own Party. Most the Democrat elected officials stood by and endorsed Congresswoman Johnson over Clayton. I am pretty sure most voters may not realize an incumbent securing other incumbents endorsement is not some big cue but simply an act of self-preservation. The

Dallas Democrat County Chair supported incumbent Johnson, despite clearly having a questionable reputation because that's what most county chairs do—support the current office holders.

County chairs aren't prepared to stand up to elected officials, even if it means a potential better one because the incumbents make sure of it. That's why Dallas GOP Chair, Wade Emmert supported Congressman Marchant. Why Dallas Democrat Chair Darlene Ewing supported Congresswoman Johnson. Congressmen remind them who sends the Party funds. They pay for protection. Voters probably don't know that those Congressmen use their campaign fund to make these donations. Which means, it's someone else's money.

Like the county chairs, most of the Democrat precinct chairs also decided that they were not concerned with Johnson's disappointing actions either and supported her against Clayton. I grew up with my Daddy talking about old bulls needed to be culled for a strong herd, so I found it disappointing neither party culled their old bulls. It seemed obvious the Parties desperately need new blood.

President Barack Obama mysteriously chose to get involved in this congressional race—but not for his fellow Harvard grad, member of his national finance team, Taj Clayton. Obama went against him to endorse Congresswoman Johnson! In disbelief, I thought, if it crushes me I can't begin to think how profoundly it would affect Taj Clayton. Why did President Obama get involved in this race, supporting the lawmaker who had broken the law numerous times? It didn't make sense to me. It couldn't have made sense to Taj Clayton.

So, why did I care so much about the Democrat primary for the 30th district of Texas? I needed to figure out a way to keep going. Who would I even want as a client? I wanted to see the best person in office and for them to win. I believed most Americans did too. If it's not the Party of your preference, I believe people still want the best person of the opposing Party. So that's why I called Taj Clayton on a whim, disregarding that I am called a Republican and he's called a Democrat.

There was already talk of him running again, I had watched *Street Fighter*, and had spent quite a bit of time determining the meaning of the political world and vowed to save it. To save me! Democrats and all! My enthusiasm spilled over, getting carried away, already creating a campaign before hardly introducing myself to the person I decided I wanted to represent.

"You should have won. You were the better candidate. I just wanted to call and personally let you know I appreciate your running." Being all gooey and patriotic and meaning every word, I continue. "I hate that you didn't win." I wasn't ready to accept a world where Party means more than country, where labels mattered most.

"Who are you again?" Taj asked. "Leslie Sorrell. I am in politics and own the Magnolia Group. I followed your race some. I just thought if someone hadn't told you, I would. You should have won."

"Thank you." Taj said quietly. I suspect I was the first call like this he had taken from a stranger, so I continue to give him my take. "You were fighting inertia. I don't believe for a second that the voters of district 30 want a crook in office like Eddie Bernice Johnson. It's the system, not you." And then, I ask him out. "I would like to go to lunch and visit more about your race."

Taj agreed and I was all smiles. We setup a time for the following week at a restaurant convenient to his law office. I was back to my old self...I felt good again, energized and then before I could even plan what I would wear Taj called me back. I recognized the number as I had called it minutes earlier. This was not good a good sign.

"Oh, no! He's calling to cancel. He's going to cancel our lunch." I say dreading hearing the bad news. "He googled me, I bet!" I took the call. "This is Leslie." I say as I close my eyes. Taj crushes my make-believe image of him. "I didn't realize who you are. I am a Democrat and I am not sure why you would want to meet with me..." I hope I can win him back. "Because I want the best person representing me and it's not EBJ! A Republican cannot win in that district. You know that. It's a safe Democrat seat, so I want to see you win."

"I appreciate that. I don't even know what I am going to do, but Johnson called me 'tea party Taj' on the campaign trail. I can't be seen with a Republican or it might come back to me on the trail." I wanted to tell him he could just brush it off and say he's my attorney, or meeting about business, or that we could simply meet in his office as opposed to lunch but I knew it was pointless. He had already made his decision.

We said good-bye and had hardly said hello. I wanted to get the inside scoop on his race to see just how bad it was and if it was as much like Grant's as it appeared to be. I knew he was still toying with the idea of another run since he was so concerned about being seen with me. It would play too perfectly with Johnson's past attacks. I understood. Sort of. I mean, here I was getting involved in a job no one asked me to do.

How did we get to where leaders in our community cannot be seen with people from the "other side" or it will be ammunition used against them? Why can't two people sit down and talk? How did we get to where a simple photo of two people together can represent something more than just a photo?

How many members of Congress, like Johnson and Marchant, can choose to not do their job, have the luxury of not worrying about being fired, or be replaced? And what was I going to do with my life now that my plan on helping Taj Clayton was out. I mean, I couldn't go back to working with people I now believed were whores for financial gain.

While Grant recovered from the election with golf and guys' trips, a vacation with his Dad, and pouring himself back into his Kwik Kar business, I didn't have any of that. When the world seemed to getting back to normal, I wasn't. I was still upset I lead an amazing team to slaughter. I've been told "time heals all wounds" but I pretty much roll my eyes when I hear that. I was once told "Time doesn't heal love. Love heals love." I wondered what heals failure and loss?

I could not come up with a solution on how Grant could beat Kenny. I don't like having questions without answers. But until I came up with one, I wasn't going to meet with Grant. What would I say if he asked me to do it again? And I felt confident Grant would ask because everyone I saw and spoke with practically begged me to encourage Grant to run again. Grant Stinchfield made Kenny Marchant a better Congressman the moment he announced. But the moment Grant lost, Marchant reverted to his old ways of doing nothing.

I hated the arrogance of it all but couldn't stand the thought of the ensuing slaughter as nothing in the system had changed that would make anything come out differently. I couldn't come up with anything that we could do on our end to get to a win in the next cycle. Overwhelmed by now knowing the system is rigged in such a way, I still didn't see how there was a path to victory for Grant. I had to face that our primary system with two Parties does not produce the best person for each Party as intended, but the worst. I felt like Eve, eating the apple, seeing a world I didn't want to see. I had been banished by the establishment but was still sticking around. For now,

I didn't know why I was upset at members of Congress operating too close to the edge of right and wrong. Sometimes, I was so much like them I hated myself for it. That's how I felt when I ended up agreeing to work for a Ted Cruz Super PAC. My heart wasn't in it but I saw an opportunity and took it. I not only didn't like Ted Cruz, I thought he was an arrogant jerk.

The first time I met him was with a group of "affluent young professional" that outsiders would perhaps call spoiled and arrogant. They called themselves Mav PAC. Like so many groups they started out united and did amazing things but quickly became bureaucratic in their ways. Originally, they were united in their candidates. But now, this group operated like the union team bosses. The leaders making the decisions they thought best for the group, even though the group is funding them. I had always thought Republicans were anti-union but this groups actions reminded me of *Animal Farm* when the pigs revised their rules to "some pigs are better than others." I can say all this because to help Mitt Romney, I joined this group and paid $3,000. I had other Romney supporters join too.

At this level, I was supposed to "receive invitations to all events" and "get to vote." But when it was clear I was not supporting the Party bosses' favorite—Rudy Giuliani—I would be black balled. At that meeting, Ted Cruz announced that there was no time for voting, officers would decide, and get back to the group later. No one ever got back to me. I never received one email, one update, or even anyone asking me for more money. They knew I would not get in line. I was disgusted. And now, disgusted at myself that several years later I jumped on the band wagon of a Ted Cruz Super PAC for his U.S Senate race in Texas. I didn't even want to vote for him. I knew I'd hit rock bottom.

I needed to find a project, a good one. Fortunately, George Seay told me about his. Seay, grandson of legendary Republican Governor Bill Clements and successful businessman, impressed me with his ability to raise money effortlessly while still having his pulse on the messiness of campaigns.... pulling teeth to fill phone banks and recruit walkers. From my view, Seay appeared to have a comfortable life he could live out eating bon-bons and having fruity drinks on a yacht, but instead, choose to painstakingly devote countless hours to candidates and causes he believed in. He "gets it" as we say in politics. I am in awe with his unwavering optimism. It's what I like best about him. He doesn't act all Machiavellian but just goes for it.

"Our system of government was meant to be shaped by everyday citizens serving their community and then returning to private life, to live with the laws they passed!" Seay tells me, as I have heard him say many times before. He knows I am in violent agreement but continues anyway. "Instead, in Texas and in Washington D.C. our government is controlled by career politicians. No longer citizen servants, they are controlled by lobbyists and the campaign money lobbyists give them. They are out of touch with the real world." I can hardly contain my desire to stand up, clap, and shout "hooray!" but I remain professional and continue listening.

Seay started Texans for Term Limits, a grassroots organization focused on implementing term limits in Texas. We knew term limits weren't sexy but I thought this was something I could get behind and get excited about. This could be a game-changer. While I didn't share with Seay my falling off the wagon and working on behalf of Cruz, I was frank in letting him know how desperately I needed a project I could believe in and make a positive difference in the world.

Seay spent a lot of time, energy, and money on this worthy project even though he knew the challenges ahead. At first glance, our task appeared simple. Eighty-seven percent of Texans waned term limits. For voters to get term limits on the ballot, a bill would have to get introduced and passed in both the Texas House and Senate. Seay found a Representative and a Senator to introduce the bill.

Seay's plan was to start simple with realistic and achievable goals. He knew better than to think the Texas Legislature could pass limits on themselves. Instead, his plan was to limit the time Texas' statewide office holders could serve in office. Baby steps. Start in Texas, be successful, take it to Washington. Surely, we could make this work.

But I couldn't get one darn person to care. I was beginning to feel like quite the failure. How could I not get people to see this is exactly what we needed? Everyone I talked to, for the most part, agreed with the premise. Just not enough to give money or even put pressure on their elected official to vote for it. No one wanted to invest anything. They prefer someone else take care of it for them.

Occasionally, I ran into an extremist that wanted to lecture me on our Founding Fathers. While I was prepared to engage them, I knew I would never get their support. It wouldn't have helped matters to share with them that term limits were highly discussed by the Founding Fathers. It's my understanding they decided not to go with term limits because they couldn't imagine anyone would want to be a career politician. They all found politics to be something they should do for their country, but found it disgusting.

Seay did so much behind the scenes that I will never fully know about. I do know he assembled a great team of both hired guns and grassroots support that would've impressed just about anyone. His timing appeared to be right too. The Texas Senate passed it, but a rogue group in the House abandoned conservative principles for the sake of self-service. The bill failed. Term limits died. Another death to mourn.

I can only conclude the legislator killed term limits because they have ambitions of serving a long time and holding higher office. They don't want to have to get off the government-funded pension. These Republicans who preach about government welfare don't mind if they are the ones on the receiving end. Seay knew that term limits prevent entrenched politicians. But elected officials know that if they duck their heads, say the same things, the public will stop caring. When will Americans be ready to care enough to stick it out? And what will happen if the George Seays of the world give up?

That's it! I had my answer for Grant!

The George Seays of the world I believe, have more power and ability to impact policy and good government from outside the halls of Congress. Grant had been presented with an opportunity to host a one-night a week radio shows and this was his moment. It didn't take long for him to move to the five-days a week drive time. And who wants to be a Congressman these days? Their disapproval rating continues to breaks new records of historic all-time lows. I thought Grant could still accomplish his goal of exposing Washington.

But what would I do?

Grant and I knew he wouldn't run again and he told people as much. Everyone believed us except the Marchant team. Why else were they still keep tabs on Grant and me? Grant did have an ever-increasing growing audience and he still stayed involved. I guess that's why Brian, Congressman Marchant's chief of staff, wanted to know why Grant was at a political event with another member of Congress and Rush Limbaugh's producer, James Golden aka "Bo Snerdley."

Annoyed that Congressman Marchant and his team concerning themselves with Grant after all this time. I answered politely, "Tonight's hosts, the Colonetta's, supported Grant and his campaign. Several of Grant's supporters were attending and Grant contributed as well." I answered his question, now it was my turn. "So, who cares about this?" I ask again. "Marchant's chief caught wind of Grant's presence," he said, making sure not to use Brian's name. Congressman Marchant was still bullying others, including members of Congress and businessmen.

One of our clients, Congressman Tim Griffin, came to Texas a few times a year and we'd help him raise money. He's about Grant and my age and I wasn't ready to put him in the "bad" column yet as what I knew, I liked. Congressman Griffin even gave us a personal referral that resulted in us working with the Jim and Joe Ricketts's foundation, Opportunity Education, an organization that came out of Joe's frustration with the political process.

Joe Ricketts spent time and energy on his PAC Ending Spending whose focus was educating Americans about wasteful and excessive spending in Washington. They wanted to change the way Washington operates. After Obama won re-election, Joe Ricketts decided to focus his efforts with his brother, Jim, on "educating children around the world" by bringing in resources and a quality education for teachers and students in resource-poor areas. That sounded much better to me these days!

Being paranoid, Andrew and I were surprised Congressman Griffin hadn't been scared off by Marchant, especially since he serves on the House Ways & Means Committee with him. Congressman Griffin let Andrew know he was returning to Dallas for fundraising. Andrew immediately made reservations at one of the Congressman's favorite places, Sevy's, a local neighborhood grill. "Do you think Congressman Marchant even knows?" Andrew asks me. "I don't know how he couldn't," I say.

As Andrew and I got to talking, we created a scenario where we imagined the Marchant team just didn't realize we worked with Congressman Griffin. Or he would have tracked him down or called him like the other clients of ours he knew about. When Congressman Griffin called back to "postpone indefinitely" his Dallas trip, we imagined that Griffin casually mentioned to Marchant about looking forward to coming to Texas…. but we will never know.

I expected as much and was surprised to get Congressman Griffin's call in the first place given Congressman Marchant's determination to bully our clients. I think this time it really bothered Andrew. I completely understood. Congressman Griffin came to Dallas very shortly after Andrew started working at the Magnolia Group. It may have even been his first day. Andrew seeing a young, energetic Congressman that came across well and down-to-earth, excited not only Andrew but all three of our interns that attended and worked the event.

Their impression upon meeting Congressman Tim Griffin was nothing short of impressive. He made it to Congress, secured a seat on the powerful ways & Means committee–all of which meant he was doing something right. How could he not make a great first impression? He came across smart, took a Southwest flight with no staff, and stayed at his cousin's home–not exactly the actions of a stuffy, ruling-class politician. He spoke enthusiastically about how the Republican Party needed to be nimbler and increase youth outreach. "Give me a call!" Congressman Griffin told the room as he held up his cell and proceeded to give out the number. "I intend to keep a pulse on the world outside the beltway," Griffin told the packed room. Andrew looked forward to his new roles at Magnolia Group in a big part because of what Congressman Tim Griffin said that day.

Someone out there still did not believe Grant wasn't going to run. The Republican primary voters in the 24th district of Texas received an odd letter almost 18 months AFTER Grant ran and lost. The letter was from Texans for Life, a non-profit dedicated to "protecting innocent human life." Like the mysterious mailers that arrived during the heat of the campaign, this one wasn't much different in that it subtly attacked Grant and would be our word against theirs. Being a 501(c)3 charitable entity, they are not legally allowed to engage in political activity.

"Interesting that it was addressed to the tea party at MY home address. The legal address is a business in Irving and our donations address is our banker's home address in Bedford," said an activist and Grant supporter. This was insider code for the letter was mailed to the address where they were registered to vote.

On page two of their mailer, there was a color photo of Grant and his family at a Veteran's Day Parade, standing next to Texas Democrat State Senator Wendy Davis. The caption read: "Conservative" talk show host Grant

Stinchfield with abortion activist Wendy Davis." Underneath the photo of Grant, in his NRA hat with son, Wyatt, waiving the American flag, it said "photo courtesy of Grant Stinchfield photo album." There was no Grant Stinchfield photo album.

Joe Lafko, a marine who volunteered on Grant's campaign, remembers taking the photo and said to me "Senator Davis asked for a photo just before the parade began. So, I snapped it." None of us have any idea to how or where Texans for Life located the photo. But it was taken with Senator Davis's camera by a Stinchfield volunteer and not from the non-existent "Stinchfield photo album" as stated.

The photo was taken long before Senator Davis's notorious filibuster on abortion in pink tennis shoes. But that is not what the mailer wanted anyone to think. Grant told people as much as said something to the effect of "Veteran's Day should not be a red or blue day, but a day for all American's to come together and be grateful for the way in which they have served our country."

So maybe Taj Clayton knew his opponent better than I knew Grant's. Just like Taj Clayton was afraid a mysterious photo of me would somehow appear in Congresswoman Johnson's mailers, here it was happening to Grant, years later. And Grant wasn't even running!

"Why would a non-profit, like Texans for Life, spend time and money attacking you?" I asked Grant. (Grant is pro-life.) He didn't know either, but he wanted to get to the bottom of it. By the end of the day he spoke to Texans for Life Executive Director, Kyleen Wright. She assured Grant that her organization didn't mail the piece despite the photo being included behind a letter on Texan for Life letterhead. She even told Grant she would be happy to come on his radio show the following week to set the record straight. "You're kidding me?" I ask Grant. "I mean, she could have said a lot of things, but there is no wiggle room in that answer. She flat out denied it? Who is she saying would send out information about her organization? That doesn't even make sense." I say with a raised voice.

"I hear yah. But I want her to come on the show. I welcome the truth. I was surprised myself, but glad she is coming on." I couldn't believe she would go on his show. It would be too good to be true. But of course, Kyleen Wright was a no show. She never took any more of Grant's calls.

But what if Grant was running? A voter who received this mailer, with the Davis/Stinchfield photo and all Marchant's previous mailers probably lost somewhere the fact that Grant Stinchfield is pro-life. Since so many voters are "one-issue" voters, attacking on prolife/prochoice is an easy punch shot. It's one Congressman Marchant always wanted to take. (Congressman Marchant had no desire to talk about fiscal issues.)

How many people support these groups with their hard-earned money, with anticipation that the money will be used to counter those who do not share their same views? What would they think?

The whole thing got me worked up, but it shouldn't have. Technically, I am still "in politics" but my days were spent preparing to leave the country, not save it. Will and I decided to retire to Belize several years earlier when we purchased some land there. We were ready to go. I told people, much to their disbelief, I was getting out of politics.

"You've been in the swamp for so long. I am relieved you're getting out of it" said Steve, a friend of mine. "It's a poisonous business" he continued. As we ate lunch, I wondered why he never mentioned this to me before. Probably because I wouldn't have listened. Others asked "how can you just leave?"

"Leave what?" I responded, thinking there was nothing to miss. Over a cup of coffee, a lobbyist I worked with quite a bit over the years asked "So, you're just taking your toys and not going to play in the sand box anymore?" I smiled, as that's exactly the type of thing I would expect him to say. I thought about it and responded "Well, if we were playing in a sandbox, maybe you could look at it that way. In reality, we've been hanging out in a toxic waste site and I am getting out before I am poisoned." He laughed. "Fair enough, true enough."

Then one day I received a call like, pretty much like all of them I get. "I read about your company and talked to some people I know and they had good things to say about you and the Magnolia Group. I am contacting you because I am thinking about running for Congress against an incumbent and…"

"Don't do it!" I chime in cutting him off. The fella gives an awkward laugh. I am guessing he thinks I am making a joke. I wasn't. He tells me the dynamics of the race as if they are unique to his race alone or as if I have never heard these lines before. It's almost always the same. They could be almost any challenger running against any incumbent.

The guy says, "I am not sure if you know this Congressman, but he's been in for decades, a lot of people out here are frustrated and ready for new blood. He just hasn't done anything. And I would like to visit with you more about running."

"Don't run for Congress against an incumbent. It's not a fair fight. You won't win. You will end up spending a lot of time, energy, and money only to be disappointed." Before I told him that he would probably have more of an impact as an outsider or in some other capacity he is anxious to share what a great candidate he will be and his willingness to work hard. He's just like that boy that keeps asking you out and doesn't understand you're not going to say "yes."

"Look, I have some good supporters and people lined up to help me. I have a strong business background and have served my country and done several tours."

"All that's good, but it's not enough." I say already googling him, seeing that he is too young, too "poor", and already exaggerated the amount of money he raised. The more push back I gave him, the more committed he is to changing my mind "I think you will be impressed as a lot of people think I will make a pretty good candidate. I'll give him a run. He hasn't even had a serious challenger since his first election."

This fella thinks he is surprising me, telling me something I haven't heard before. "And you just may. But it's not about you." I tell him harshly, giving him the cold hard facts. Because of course, he thinks it's about him. He offers me quite a bit of money. I quickly think I could just take the money, not worry about this loser, and go to Belize. While I continue to debate the merits of such a stunt, I explain the primary world to him.

"Only about 6% of the population votes in primaries and they have been voting for that guy for Congress for decades. They are trained to vote for him- not you. You're fighting inertia."

"Well, he doesn't have as much money as most incumbents," he tells me. But it's still more than this fella has. "He doesn't have to. Once his fellow members of Congress get word he has drawn an opponent they will each chip in a thousand bucks from their campaign. Make no mistake, they will do it. It costs them nothing because that thousand dollars came from someone else. The incumbent immediately is flushed with cash—-about $200k just from his fellow Republican Congressmen." I say all this and continue not letting him speak.

"That will buy him some time while he gets the PACs lined up to give. And I don't care what people have told you; you won't get any PAC money. So, the Congressman will have more money than you with the PACs and other members of Congress. On top of that, the Congressman will get personal contributions from some of his loyal and faithful supporters. None of this is even counting the taxpayer dollars the Congressman has at his disposal that he can use for mass conference calls and mailers, mobile office hours, newspaper, and social media ads to supposedly keep his constituents informed when in reality he is campaigning—all which will drown out any messages you may think can reach people."

I may have gone too far, but I know this guy is gonna lose. I know he may put more of his own money in than he can afford. After all these years, I simply know these things. I figure I've crushed his sprits, but saved him hundreds of thousands of dollars and other misery. Instead, he surprised me when he said "So, you're saying I shouldn't run?"

I smile, ready to walk away. I say one more time "Don't run!"

ABOUT THE AUTHOR

Leslie Sorrell was born and raised in Hopkinsville, Kentucky. A recovering political junkie, she lives in a small fishing village in Belize, but still maintains a home in Columbus, Mississippi. When not writing, she runs a bed and breakfast on the beach with her husband. They have dreams of opening a creamery where they will make fresh cheese and ice cream. Sorrell won the Writers' League of Texas 2015 "Best Manuscript" contest for memoir.

ACKNOWLEDGEMENTS

The Magnolia Group team. We were in the trenches together with clients I believed in and the ones I wanted to believe in.

Thank you to the friends, family, and colleagues that experienced the adrenaline highs and anxiety-filled political world with me, even though you didn't ask for that experience. I am forever grateful.

The late Philip Mullins. We simply got each other. Thank you to all the Mullins and Moore families. To the strong women in my life—my Aunts—who inspired and nurtured greatness. My parents. Mom, for decades of telling me "I can," encouraging me to not squander the talents given to me, and most of all for demonstrating the excitement of risk. To Will, when I told you my plan, you were excited and cheered me on. A true-life partner, sticking by me, even when you were under fire. And maybe even sick and tired of it all.

I shared my first words not with a family member, best girlfriend, or even my Will, but instead to a hard-nosed, hold nothing back editor, Steve Mundy. I went to him because I knew he'd deliver the cold hard truth and that's what I was seeking. I am out of the swamp in part because of his encouragement and feedback.

The Writers' League of Texas (WLT) for introducing me to a community of writers and for honoring me in winning their manuscript contest for memoir. Donna Johnson strongly encouraged me to read my work out loud to a large group of strangers at the WLT's writers' retreat in Marfa. Afterwards, audience members approached me and asked questions that re-affirmed my belief the public wants access to the behind the scenes dealings in Washington D. C. Christine Wicker shared her advice and insights over numerous meetings, phone calls, and emails. Donna and Christine's generosity was overwhelming! Over and over I received the feedback I needed from those I respected to keep going when I entertained otherwise.

Terry Whalen, some whom call agent, but I call ambassador, for believing in my story.

A free eBook edition is available with the purchase of this book.

To claim your free eBook edition:

1. Download the Shelfie app.
2. Write your name in upper case in the box.
3. Use the Shelfie app to submit a photo.
4. Download your eBook to any device.

Shelfie

A **free** eBook edition is available
with the purchase of this print book.

CLEARLY PRINT YOUR NAME ABOVE IN UPPER CASE

Instructions to claim your free eBook edition:
1. Download the Shelfie app for Android or iOS
2. Write your name in **UPPER CASE** above
3. Use the Shelfie app to submit a photo
4. Download your eBook to any device

Print & Digital Together Forever.

Snap a photo

Free eBook

Read anywhere